P9-CDX-234

HODGES UNIVERSITY
LIBRARY - NAPLES

Understanding Keynes' General Theory

Understanding Keynes' General Theory

Brendan Sheehan

Leeds Metropolitan University, UK

© Brendan Sheehan 2009

All rights reserved. No reproduction, copy or transmission of this publication may be made without written permission.

No portion of this publication may be reproduced, copied or transmitted save with written permission or in accordance with the provisions of the Copyright, Designs and Patents Act 1988, or under the terms of any licence permitting limited copying issued by the Copyright Licensing Agency, Saffron House, 6-10 Kirby Street, London EC1N 8TS.

Any person who does any unauthorized act in relation to this publication may be liable to criminal prosecution and civil claims for damages.

The author has asserted his right to be identified as the author of this work in accordance with the Copyright, Designs and Patents Act 1988.

First published 2009 by
PALGRAVE MACMILLAN

Palgrave Macmillan in the UK is an imprint of Macmillan Publishers Limited, registered in England, company number 785998, of Houndmills, Basingstoke, Hampshire RG21 6XS.

Palgrave Macmillan in the US is a division of St Martin's Press LLC, 175 Fifth Avenue, New York, NY 10010.

Palgrave Macmillan is the global academic imprint of the above companies and has companies and representatives throughout the world.

Palgrave® and Macmillan® are registered trademarks in the United States, the United Kingdom, Europe and other countries.

ISBN-13: 978-0-230-22013-3 hardback
ISBN-10: 0-230-22013-4 hardback

This book is printed on paper suitable for recycling and made from fully managed and sustained forest sources. Logging, pulping and manufacturing processes are expected to conform to the environmental regulations of the country of origin.

A catalogue record for this book is available from the British Library.

Library of Congress Cataloging-in-Publication Data
Sheehan, Brendan, 1957–
   Understanding Keynes' General Theory / by Brendan Sheehan.
      p.   cm.
   Includes index.
   ISBN 978-0-230-22013-3
   1. Keynesian economics.   I. Title.
   HB99.7.S475 2009
   330.15'6—dc22   2008037791

10   9   8   7   6   5   4   3   2   1
18   17   16   15   14   13   12   11   10   09

Printed and bound in Great Britain by
CPI Antony Rowe, Chippenham and Eastbourne

*To Jane
and my parents with love*

Contents

List of Tables and Diagrams

Tables

Diagrams

Preface

I hope that you find this book interesting and rewarding. But most of all I hope that it encourages you to read the *General Theory* itself. Keynes' book is audacious, flawed, profound, revolutionary and conservative. It has the ability to both move the spirit and stimulate the mind. If there is one book every economist should read it is the *General Theory of Employment Interest and Money*. But to get the most from the experience, read this book first.

The first time I read the *General Theory* was in the summer vacation between my first and second year studies. With youthful precocity I thought my knowledge of macroeconomics would allow me to read the book about which I had read so much. How wrong I was. To say the least the book was challenging and at points just plain confusing. Yet I persisted buoyed by finding the occasional telling phrase or pointed argument that kept me engaged. During the rest of my undergraduate degree I was lucky enough to be required to read various chapters again and the material in the book began to become more familiar to me. By the time of my postgraduate degree I had become confident enough to write an extended essay on the monetary connections between the *Treatise on Money* and the *General Theory*. Becoming capable to read and thoroughly engage with the material in the *General Theory* was a long torturous journey. It struck me that what the new novice reader of Keynes needed was a primer for the *General Theory* – a book to help them read *the* book. This is what I have set out to do in this publication.

It has taken me a lot longer than I originally envisaged. I started writing during the Easter vacation in 1988. It has undergone any number of revisions and improvements over the intervening period. Earlier drafts were used as teaching materials on which I have received valuable comments from students past for which I am most grateful. Moreover I am also grateful to fellow academics who have been kind enough to have read and provided insightful comments on earlier drafts. These include Geoff Harcourt, John King, Malcolm Sawyer, Vicky Chick and Paul Downward. I am also grateful to two past colleagues who have encouraged me to persist with the project – Karl Petrick and John Sutherland. I must also thank Steve Dalton who has listened with patience and debated various arguments I proposed. Finally I thank my wife Jane for her perpetual support. Of course all errors and omissions are entirely my responsibility.

Extracts from Keynes, J.M., *The General Theory of Employment Interest and Money*, 2007, Palgrave Macmillan, reproduced with permission of Palgrave Macmillan.

Extracts from Keynes, J.M., *The General Theory and After Part II Defence and Development*, Collected Writings of J.M. Keynes Volume XIV, 1973, Macmillan, reproduced with permission of Palgrave Macmillan.

The extract from Samuelson, P., Lord Keynes and the General Theory, *Econometrica*, 1946, reproduced with permission of the Econometric Society.

Brendan Sheehan
June 2008

1

A Primer for the General Theory

[The General Theory] is a badly written book, poorly organised... It is not well suited for classroom use. It is arrogant, bad-tempered, polemical, and not overly-generous in its acknowledgements... In it the Keynesian system stands out indistinctly, as if the author were hardly aware of its existence or cognisant of its properties... When it is finally mastered, we find its analysis to be obvious and at the same time new. In short, it is a work of genius.

(Samuelson, 1946, p. 190)

a) Why should you read this book?

John Maynard Keynes was the greatest economist of the twentieth century. Keynes' best-known book, the pinnacle of his intellectual achievements, was the *General Theory of Employment Interest and Money*. In the third quarter of the twentieth century the book was particularly influential in changing the way economists and policy-makers thought about macroeconomic issues, although not always in the way Keynes intended.

Yet a growing body of Post-Keynesian scholarship argues that the *General Theory* is an audacious book that is neither fully understood nor properly appreciated by modern economists. This new scholarship claims that Keynes' central theoretical and policy insights have been systematically removed from mainstream "Keynesianism". Indeed mainstream Keynesianism is actually founded on the work of Hicks and Pigou, not Keynes. Put succinctly far from Keynes' new theory replacing orthodox thinking, the orthodoxy successfully *strangled* Keynes' ideas at birth. Consequently Keynes' hope of revolutionising the way we think about economic problems failed, much to the disadvantage of economics (Chick, 1983; Amadeo, 1989; Lawlor, 2006; Hayes, 2006; Tily, 2007).

Of course such bold scholarship needs to be checked and assessed against the record of Keynes' writings and those of his interpreters. This however throws up a serious problem for the inquisitive person who wants to read the *General Theory*. It is a notoriously difficult book to understand easily or quickly, if at all. It is written by an exceptionally intelligent economist with little regard for the need to popularise its contents. The quotation from Samuelson at the start of the chapter ably sums up the problem.

That said in the late 1940s and early 1950s there were a number of attempts to popularise Keynes in a more accessible manner, especially for the American audience (Klein, 1947; Dillard, 1950; Hansen, 1953). There is much of value in these texts, but all are *very selective* in what they offer as Keynes' theory, entirely discarding the parts that do not aid easy exposition. Each seeks to make broadly Keynesian ideas popular rather than developing an understanding of the *General Theory* itself.[1]

The distinct aim of this book is to help those who want to tackle the *General Theory*. It is essentially a *primer* for the *General Theory* – which unlike the literature on Marx is absent for Keynes. This book provides all the essential background detail – the key definitions, equations, numerical examples and diagrams – that Keynes left out of the *General Theory*, but which the reader new to the topic will require to properly appreciate a work of genius. Put succinctly you read this book in order to read the *General Theory*.

The method applied in this primer is that of reconstructing Keynes' analysis – from now on referred to as the General Theory model – *in its own terms*. Such a reconstruction must first explain all aspects of an economist's work; it cannot be overly selective in what it includes or excludes. It must face up to the difficult parts of the theory as well as the easier sections. Moreover it should explain an individual's work using the economist's *own* definitions, concepts and models, even though they may have been replaced or redefined in subsequent popular interpretations of the author. It must piece together the sometimes disparate books and articles into an integrated whole and restate the original purpose of the economist. The aim is to clarify and explain, in greater detail where appropriate, whilst retaining the essential vision of the original works.[2]

As a beginner's guide this primer makes a conscious effort to ensure Keynes' ideas are accessible to a wide audience. It carefully guides the uninitiated reader through the complete General Theory model; it provides an explanation of each key category, especially those usually ignored by other writers (e.g. wage units, supplementary costs, aggregate supply price etc.) to ensure they are properly understood. Moreover a variety of methods are used to communicate the key ideas, so that each reader can find their own route to understanding. First and foremost the book outlines all the arguments in *narrative* form. In addition the explanations are supplemented by quotations from the *General Theory* and related works, especially when the arguments advanced run counter to the prevailing view of Keynes. Where appropriate the narrative arguments are supplemented through the use of *spreadsheets* with numerical examples to illustrate the point. Often the spreadsheets are transformed into *diagrammatic representations* to depict the numerical examples. Finally at the end of most chapters *causal maps* are outlined to portray the development of the General Theory model throughout the book. All this will prepare the interested reader to take on the greater challenge of reading the *General Theory* itself, and then the work of the Post-Keynesian scholars mentioned earlier and the wider Keynesian literature.

The reconstruction of Keynes' work requires the integration of a wide range of academic material produced by Keynes. The first and foremost source is the *General Theory* itself. All aspects of the book are examined, including a number of chapters that have received insufficient attention by the followers of Keynes. The two volumes of the *Treatise on Money* are invaluable in clarifying important definitions and concepts subsequently used in the *General Theory*. Moreover the *Treatise* provides some insights into Keynes' rejection of the classical theory of money and prices. The *Collected Writings of Keynes Volume XIV* provides material on Keynes' defence and development of the General Theory model after it had been published. This volume also has two articles – "The General Theory: Fundamental Concepts and Ideas" and "Alternative Theories of the Rate of Interest" – that are of the utmost importance. Keynes' *Essays in Persuasion* is of great use for appreciating his policy recommendations for the great interwar problems and the conduct of the Second World War. Whilst the *Collected Writings of Keynes Volumes XXV and XXVII* are pertinent because they include many of Keynes' Treasury reports and papers that outline the new public policies he proposes for application in the post-Second World War period. Finally, the *Tract on Monetary Reform* and the *Treatise on Probability* are mentioned where appropriate to supplement the arguments advanced. All these key texts must be properly considered to achieve a rounded view of Keynes' *General Theory*.

b) Outline of the book

A constant theme of this book is the contrast between the special case classical analysis and the more generally applicable General Theory model. This requires that the classical theory be set out, inevitably through the prism of Keynes. Hence Chapter 2 outlines the classical theories of interest and employment and money and prices. The theory of interest and employment focuses on Say's law, the loanable funds market (incorporating the calculus of probability) and the aggregated labour market analysis. The theory of money and prices relates to both the Cambridge and Fisher equations. An appendix contains Keynes' critique of the classical theory of money and prices from the *Treatise on Money*. In this chapter the special case assumptions that underpin both the theories of interest and employment and money and prices are carefully identified. Once the special case character of the classical theory is appreciated it is easy to understand Keynes' departure from the classical approach.

Chapter 3 carefully explains concepts such as the aggregate demand price, the aggregate supply price, the aggregate demand function and the aggregate supply function. It concludes with a proper specification of aggregate effective demand, derived by assuming short-term expectations are correct. Aggregate effective demand is the key overarching concept of the General Theory model as it determines the equilibrium volume of employment. By the end of the chapter distinctive aggregate demand–supply diagrams are derived, which are applied throughout the rest of the book. The chapter has two appendices. The first explains some important Post-Keynesian criticisms of Keynes' specification of effective demand and how it might be improved. The second reviews the Post-Keynesian discussion about the need to incorporate incorrect short-term expectations into the General Theory model.

The central part of the General Theory model is contained in Chapters 4 through 8. Chapters 4 and 5 take the reader through Keynes' analysis of consumption and the multiplier. Chapter 4 explains in detail the derivation of Keynes' consumption function and what causes it to shift and swivel. It applies Keynes' working assumption that the marginal propensity to consume is declining, which although not essential to the General Theory model is important for understanding the *General Theory* itself. It then explains Keynes' concepts of the investment and employment multipliers; these are distinctive as they only explain *changes* in aggregate income and employment, respectively. Finally the chapter considers the role of saving as a dependent variable in the

General Theory model. The *negative* relationship between saving and the rate of interest in the General Theory model is contrasted with the *positive* relationship in the special case circumstances of the classical analysis. An appendix to this chapter makes comments about how Keynes' treatment of the propensity to consume might be improved.

Chapter 5 then relates the analysis of consumption to the derivation of the aggregate demand price and the determination of effective demand and employment. It works through various spreadsheets of numerical examples and illustrative diagrams. This chapter also examines Keynes' idea of the Paradox of Thrift, which is founded on his rejection of Say's law. An appendix to this chapter examines the relationship between Keynes' ideas and those of the under-consumptionists.

Keynes' analysis of the inducement to invest is covered in Chapters 6, 7 and 8. Chapter 6, though short, is the pivotal chapter as it explains Keynes' concept of the state of long-term expectation. The latter is based on the conventional method of calculation which is contrasted with the classical hypothesis of a calculable future. In the General Theory model short-period changes in the state of long-term expectation is the principal reason for economic fluctuations.

Chapter 7 begins by defining both the stock of capital and aggregate investment (i.e. additions to the capital stock) that are outlined in the *Treatise* and applied in the *General Theory*. In the General Theory model the inducement to invest is determined by the interaction of the marginal efficiency of capital and the long-term money rate of interest. The chapter explains in some detail Keynes' treatment of the marginal efficiency of capital and the liquidity preference theory of the rate of interest. It sets out how changes in investment spending result from shifts in the marginal efficiency schedule, or changes in the rate of interest (*or both*), primarily caused by short-period changes in the state of long-term expectation. Finally the chapter outlines how Keynes' treatment of investment requires the rejection of both Say's law and the loanable funds market. Chapter 7 includes two appendices. The first examines various Post-Keynesian criticisms of Keynes' treatment of the marginal efficiency of capital. The second considers why the *money* rate of interest is the most significant *own* rate of interest.

Chapter 8 systematically examines the impact of fluctuations in the inducement to invest on effective demand and employment, showing how adverse or beneficial changes in the marginal efficiency and the rate of interest reinforce one another to change investment spending. The role of the finance motive in facilitating capital accumulation is highlighted. This chapter also includes spreadsheets of numerical examples, illustrative diagrams and causal maps to outline how fluctuations in the rate of investment spending impact on employment. The investment multiplier is applied to further illustrate the analysis.

The next major section of book – Chapters 9 and 10 – deals with money wages, real wages and prices, all of which are influenced by aggregate effective demand. Chapter 9 deals with issues raised in the famous *Chapter 19* of the *General Theory*. *Chapter 19* is often read, but usually misunderstood, as it is interpreted through an orthodox prism. Once the reader has put aside the aggregated labour market, the "difficulties" with the chapter disappear. Chapter 9 of this book contextualises the analysis by reminding the reader of Keynes' contribution to the policy debates about wage cutting in the 1920s and 1930s. It then systematically explains Keynes' investigation of the influences on effective demand and employment resulting from a generalised money wage cut. Once again numerical examples and diagrams are utilised to reinforce the arguments advanced. It concludes that in the General Theory model the consequences of money wage cuts are ambiguous; employment can rise (the special classical case) or fall (the more generally applicable case). Finally the chapter returns to the Gold Standard debate of the 1920s to show how the General Theory model establishes criteria by which to choose between a flexible wage policy and a flexible monetary policy.

Chapter 10 provides a generalised examination of the response of money wages, prices (inflation) and real wages to changes in effective demand. Moreover it demonstrates how the General Theory model brings together the theories of value and prices, and why this acts as a springboard for Keynes' generalised analysis of prices and inflation. The important distinction that Keynes makes between semi-inflation and true inflation is utilised in this chapter. The chapter goes on to explain Keynes' treatment of the real wage rate as a *dependent* variable, just like the volume of employment. This causation is one of the less-appreciated parts of the General Theory model, but it is a necessary corollary of Keynes' rejection of the classical aggregated labour market noted above. The chapter examines a seeming paradox of the *General Theory* that whilst Keynes *rejects* the classical labour market analysis he *accepts* the classical labour market assertion that a rise in employment occurs as real wages fall – which is known as the *first classical postulate*. This paradox has probably confused followers of Keynes more than anything else, but its solution is quite straightforward. The chapter also revisits Keynes' rejection of the key element of the classical labour market analysis – the *second classical postulate*. Finally the interwar debate between Keynes and

Pigou about the role of real wages in any stimulation of employment is examined.

Chapter 11 brings together a range of themes with respect to the treatment of employment and unemployment mentioned in earlier chapters. First the chapter focuses directly on the relationship between aggregate effective demand and employment, through the *employment function*. Secondly, the concept of the elasticity of employment is outlined and explained. The analysis of the elasticity of employment allows a refinement to be made to the simple conclusion of earlier chapters that a change in employment depends solely on a change in the level of effective demand. This also allows the analysis of the investment and employment multipliers to be enhanced. Moreover by utilising the employment function the chapter outlines a definition of full employment used by Keynes which is not reliant on either of the two classical postulates. Finally the chapter considers the possibility of an economy in *equilibrium* with demand-deficient unemployment, perhaps Keynes' most contentious idea. The employment function is used once again, this time to illustrate the concept of the unemployment equilibrium.

In Chapters 9 and 10 reference is made to the policy implications of Keynes' analysis. However, Chapter 12 provides a more thorough examination of the public policy implications of the General Theory model. The *raison d'être* for Keynes' policy recommendations is the desire to protect the capitalist order whilst correcting its most obvious defects. In the context of the General Theory model the chapter considers Keynes' recommendations for how to cure an economic depression; how to maximise wartime production without inflation, whilst effectively financing the war effort; and how to prevent economic instability and promote long-term prosperity. In peacetime conditions the *leitmotiv* of Keynes' proposals is the call for an expansionary rather than a contractionist cure for economic ills. Hence Keynes proposes permanently low interest rates coordinated with active fiscal policy built around a state-led programme of socialised investment. Moreover domestic expansionary policies of nations should be combined with a new trading and payments system to buttress the pursuit of global full employment. Finally the chapter examines Keynes' musings on the longer term implications of his policies for a future reformed capitalist system, with specific reference to the inequality of incomes and wealth and the future survival of the rentier class. There is a short appendix to the chapter on Keynes' practical definition of full employment developed in the 1940s, which provides an interesting contrast with the theoretical definitions contained in the rest of the book.

Chapter 13 sets out a short overview of the Keynes versus the classic debate – both the theoretical underpinnings and the policy differences. It seeks to encapsulate the analysis contained in the earlier chapters. It then examines the emergence of mainstream Keynesianism. It demonstrates how mainstream Keynesianism, in departing from the *General Theory* and incorporating microeconomic foundations, has sought to smother Keynes' key ideas and replace them with ones more palatable to economic orthodoxy. Yet the chapter offers hope with the emergence of what it calls authentic Keynesianism.

As previously mentioned at the end of a number of chapters appendices are included. The purpose of some appendices is to offer clarification on technical points – this is true of the appendices at the end of Chapters 11 and 12 and the second appendix to Chapter 7. The other appendices provide a critical perspective: both Keynes' criticisms of the classics and Post-Keynesian criticisms of Keynes' analysis. These appendices usually make suggestions for future theoretical developments. Given that the book is aimed at readers new to Keynes, who might easily be put off by material requiring specialised knowledge, it is clear that such material is best included in appendices. This means the new reader is able to concentrate on mastering the General Theory model in each chapter free from excessive complications. Once the reader has mastered it, and perhaps read the *General Theory* itself, he/she can return to the appendices and begin to master the criticisms and the improvements offered by Post-Keynesian writers. As a by-product of such activity this will also open up a much wider Post-Keynesian literature to the interested reader.

2
Classical Macroeconomic Theory: The Special Case

a) Introduction

It might be thought strange that a book setting out to understand the General Theory model starts by examining the classical theory, but there are good reasons for this. In the *General Theory* Keynes constantly makes reference to the classical theory pointing out its errors and showing how the General Theory model takes a fresh and distinctive approach to analysing a macroeconomy.[1] This should not be a surprise for Keynes was trained as a classical economist having a foremost follower of Ricardo, Alfred Marshall, as a teacher.[2] Indeed Keynes for a time was a leading classical economist, making noteworthy contributions to monetary theory in the 1920s.[3] Keynes took time to free himself from the chains of his classical background. In part the *General Theory* is a cathartic exercise for Keynes as he finally breaks the classical umbilical cord.

Another reason to examine the classical model is that in the *General Theory* Keynes constantly refers to this analysis as a "special case", applicable to a broadly unchanging economy operating at full employment. Mainstream Keynesians, starting with Hicks, claim that Keynes' theory is actually a special (but perhaps more practically useful) or short run case of the classical analysis. This chapter seeks to redress the balance. It outlines Keynes' "take" on the classical macroeconomic analysis and clarifies why he views it as applicable only in special circumstances.

Classical macroeconomics is something of an analytical backwater. It is almost a by-product of other parts of the classical analysis. In some areas where Keynes seeks to set out its foundations he discovers it has rarely been systematically written down. According to Keynes classical macroeconomics relates to two broad areas: the analysis of interest and employment and the theory(ies) of money and prices.

Section (b) considers the classical theory of interest and employment by focusing on the loanable funds theory of the rate of interest and the aggregated labour market theory of employment. Section (c) examines the classical theory of money and prices, concentrating on two quantity equations – the Cambridge and Fisher equations. Section (d) highlights the special character of the classical theories and compares it with the general applicability of the General Theory model. Finally Section (e) uses a causal map to outline the classical school analysis and its special case characteristics.

b) The classical theory of interest and employment

The classical theory of interest and employment is made up of two frameworks – the loanable funds market and the aggregated labour market. The loanable funds market, and especially Say's law, provides the classical school with a theory of aggregate demand. Supply creates its own demand, savings fund investment and the loanable funds market guarantees the system effectively self-adjusts to any economic shocks. But aggregate demand does not play a role in determining employment. Classical economists upgrade the analysis of Smith and Ricardo to include an aggregated labour market. On this economy-wide market the equilibrium volume of employment is determined by the forces of aggregate labour demand and aggregate labour supply responding to real wage rates. In this section both these foundations are considered in more detail and in the process their special case assumptions are highlighted.

Classical loanable funds market

In the classical model saving is a key moving force of the economic system. From Smith onwards the classicals view individual and community parsimony as a means to individual and national wealth. Individuals and nations that are prodigal, and spend rather than save, set themselves on the road to ruin (Smith, 1976). Ideologically this is attractive to the educated elite as it places affluent households that save, the wealth-holding rentier class, in the central role of facilitating wealth creation. But in the classical model what of the reverse of saving – that is consumption and investment? How are they to be analysed? Moreover how can the classicals be certain that the levels of aggregate spending on consumption and investment are always sufficient to maintain full employment? To solve this perplexing problem the classical school relies on Say's law.

> From the time of Say and Ricardo the classical economists have taught that supply creates its own demand; – meaning by this in some significant, but not clearly defined, sense that the whole of the costs of production must necessarily be spent in the aggregate, directly or indirectly, on purchasing the product.
>
> As a corollary of the same doctrine, it has been supposed that any individual act of abstaining from consumption [i.e. saving] necessarily leads to, and amounts to the same thing as, causing the labour and commodities thus released from supplying consumption to be invested in the production of capital wealth.
>
> (Keynes, 2007, pp. 18–19; abridged quote)

Therefore, the classical analysis supposes that an individual adds to the total demand for goods and services as much by saving as he/she does by purchasing consumer products, incredible as this may seem to the layperson. The classical model therefore *assumes* that what is saved is available to fund investment in new capital equipment; in terms of causation, saving is cause and investment effect. With such a "law" the total demand for goods and services can never be deficient, unless there are short-term errors in entrepreneurial expectations of demand. If saving rises then investment spending will increase by an amount just sufficient to counteract the decline in consumption spending. If saving declines, the fall in investment spending will just match the increase in consumption expenditure. With Say's law supply creates its own demand, and changes in aggregate supply are always matched by equivalent responses in aggregate demand. A deficiency of effective demand cannot logically occur; and if experience proves differently, then experience must be wrong.

This is as far as Smith and Ricardo take classical economics. Subsequent followers of Ricardo build upon these insights to develop a loanable funds market; this market ensures that *a price mechanism*, the rate of interest, exists to equalise investment spending and money saving. As Keynes explains:

> It is fairly clear, however, that [the classical] tradition has regarded the rate of interest as the factor which brings the demand for investment and the willingness to save into equilibrium with one another ... so the rate of interest necessarily comes to rest under the play of market

forces at the point where the amount of investment at that rate of interest is equal to the amount of saving at that rate.

(Keynes, 2007, p. 175)

The analysis underpinning this classical loanable funds market can be set out as follows. The investment demand schedule is defined for a *given state of expectation* about the profitability of investment projects. As the rate of interest declines additional investment spending becomes more attractive to businesses and *vice versa*. Although the classical theory is less than explicit about why this is the case it can be argued that, using the net present value method, a lower rate of interest increases the net present value of a given investment project, making firms more willing to embark on the new capital projects. The reverse is true when the rate of interest increases. The investment demand schedule is therefore downward sloping.

As for the formation of profit expectations on investment projects the classical school is strangely silent. For Keynes the classical investment demand schedule is derived on the assumption that only the yield on a capital asset in the present financial year is of importance. Any mention by the classical school of entrepreneurs estimating the prospective yield of a capital asset over its whole life is not emphasised. The classical school has a special case theory of the future which assumes that decision-makers have sufficient knowledge of the future consequences of present actions to be able to derive mathematically precise calculations of future yields and risks on investments. This *calculus of probability* allows the classical school to accept the *hypothesis of a calculable future* and apply it to their analysis of wealth accumulation in a stationary state. This approach should not be surprising given that the classical school is "dealing with a system in which the amount of the factors employed [is] given and the other relevant facts [are] known more or less for certain" (Keynes, 1973a, p. 112). In this special case the classical analysis of wealth accumulation avoids concerns about uncertainty and the precariousness of knowledge of the far future. Moreover the calculus of probability provides an *inter-temporal link* between the present and the future in the classical model, by arguing that the future is much like the present and that the consequences of any future changes are easily assessed.[4]

In terms of the supply of savings schedule, it is important to understand why the classicals claim it to be upward sloping. Crucial to the classical analysis is the special case assumption that the level of aggregate income is constant. With income given they argue that the rate of interest influences the *inter-temporal* decision of households between consumption today and consumption in the future. If the rate of interest falls this makes saving a less attractive option and encourages greater consumption out of a given level of aggregate income. Conversely if the rate of interest increases, saving offers greater returns and the volume of consumption declines out of a given income.

The classical loanable funds analysis is illustrated in Diagram 2.1. On the vertical axis is the rate of interest (r), on the horizontal axis are loanable funds (LF) available. The I_d curve represents the investment demand schedule which is negatively related to the rate of interest. The S_s curve represents the amounts saved by a community out of a given aggregate income which is positively related to the interest rate. Another way of explaining the S_s curve is that it shows the influence of the rate of interest on the propensity to save out of a given income. Where the two curves intersect the equilibrium rate of interest is determined – r^* in Diagram 2.1. According to the classical school the rate of interest r^* is optimal, in the sense that it is best suited to the social advantage and compatible with full employment. This can be referred to as the full employment rate of interest, or the *natural rate* towards which actual interest rates gravitate.

The classical analysis also suggests that fluid rates of interest equilibrate changing desires to save. Indeed in this model two variables change the position of a supply of saving schedule; they are a change in aggregate income and a change in the propensity to save out of a given income level. How does the loanable funds market respond to such

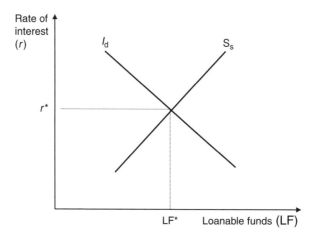

Diagram 2.1 The classical loanable funds market

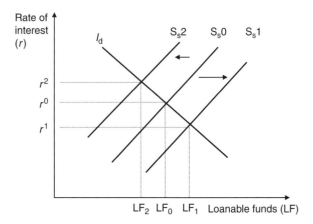

Diagram 2.2   Changes in the propensity to save

changes? Consider Diagram 2.2 which shows changes in the propensity to save out of a given income. Suppose the loanable funds market is initially in equilibrium with investment demand schedule I_d and supply of saving schedule S_s0, at interest rate r^0.

Allow an increased propensity to save by the community at every rate of interest and the saving schedule shifts from S_s0 to S_s1. At the initial interest rate there is an excess supply of savings forcing a fall in the interest rate to r^1. The lower interest rate stimulates greater investment demand until it equals the additional aggregate saving. The equilibrium volume of loanable funds increases to LF_1. The composition of aggregate demand changes with more investment spending and less consumption, but aggregate income remains constant. In this context classical economists argue that the solution to a lack of investment in an economy is for a community to conduct a *thrift drive*. Keynes' concept of the Paradox of Thrift (see Chapter 5) *cannot exist* within this analytical framework.

Conversely say the propensity to save by the community decreases at every rate of interest. The saving schedule shifts from S_s0 to S_s2. This raises the equilibrium interest rate to r^2 and investment demand is reduced until it equals the lower aggregate saving. The equilibrium volume of loanable funds falls to LF_2 whilst aggregate income is unchanged. The extra consumption expenditure generated by the lower propensity to save does not stimulate an increased level of aggregate income as it is fully compensated for by a decline in investment spending. Put another way the composition of a given volume of aggregate demand shifts away from investment towards more consumption.

The loanable funds market acts as an inter-temporal connection between decisions made today and those in the future. The saving schedule is underpinned by the decisions of households about consumption today versus consumption tomorrow with the rate of interest playing a crucial determining role. Moreover the investment schedule is founded upon today's decisions by firms to invest in capital equipment to meet future consumption demand which is also strongly influenced by the rate of interest. The rate of interest is the price mechanism that coordinates the economic present and future.

Say's law, the calculus of probability and the loanable funds market provide the classical school, however flawed and inadequate, with a theory of aggregate demand. As Keynes notes this theory is not explicit, being derived from other parts of the classical schema, but it is a theory nonetheless. It justifies Ricardo's argument against Malthus in their early nineteenth-century debate that deficient effective demand cannot be a persistent problem. Supply creates its own demand and the loanable funds market guarantees the macroeconomic system adjusts to any shocks. Aggregate saving may rise or fall, but the compensating changes in aggregate consumption and investment spending ensures that aggregate income is unchanged. In the classical analysis, therefore, aggregate demand and income can be taken as given. But if aggregate demand and income do not play a role in determining aggregate employment in the classical world, what does?

The classical aggregated labour market

The early classical school, of Smith and Ricardo, treated real wages as a given in an economy and set at the subsistence level (Eatwell and Milgate, 1983). Later classicals upgrade this analysis of wage determination in an economy through the introduction of an aggregated labour market. On this economy-wide market the equilibrium real (or money) wage rate is determined by the forces of aggregate labour demand and supply, as is the equilibrium volume of aggregate employment. Using Pigou's treatment of the aggregated labour market as an exemplar, Keynes argues that the classical determination of aggregate employment is based on two fundamental postulates (or conditions):

1. The real wage is equal to the marginal product of the last unit of labour employed.
2. The utility of the real wage is equal to the marginal disutility of the last unit of labour employed.

The first postulate provides the aggregated labour demand schedule for the economy by making the special case assumption that aggregate demand for output is given. The reasoning of the classicals, though rarely made explicit, seems to be as follows. That each firm in every industry demands workers until the marginal product of the last worker just equals the real wage rate paid to the last worker; and that as the marginal product of each additional worker declines, due to the law of diminishing productivity, each firm in every industry will only demand more workers if the real wage rate is lowered. In this way the classical school derives a downward sloping labour demand curve for an industry. When they transfer the argument to the economy as a whole they simply assume that what is true for each firm and industry must also be true for the macroeconomy. Essentially the classics summate the labour demand curves for each industry, where it is legitimate to assume that aggregate demand for output is given, in order to derive an aggregated labour demand schedule for the economy as a whole. They do not seem to fully appreciate that in moving from a microeconomic to a macroeconomic frame of reference it is no longer legitimate to assume that the level of aggregate demand for output is fixed, or that if they do so it reduces the general applicability of the analysis.

The second postulate provides the schedule of aggregated labour supply. In the classical analysis each worker experiences disutility from giving up leisure and offering labour services. By contrast the worker receives compensation for this disutility in terms of the purchasing power of the real wage rate. As more workers supply labour services the disutility of employment for the last worker increases; this analysis applies equally to labour supply for every industry and for the economy as a whole. In order to induce workers to supply more labour, the real wage rate offered has to increase.

All this can be represented on an aggregated labour market (see Diagram 2.3). The real wage rate (W/P) is on the vertical axis and units of employment (N) are on the horizontal axis. The N_d schedule represents aggregate labour demand at each real wage, and the N_s schedule shows the aggregate supply of labour at each real wage.

Where the two curves intersect the equilibrium real wage and the equilibrium volume of aggregate employment are determined – $W/P*$ and N_*, respectively. At this point "the utility of the marginal product balances the disutility of the marginal employment" (Keynes, 2007, p. 6). The volume of employment N_* is also compatible with what Keynes refers to as full employment. According to Keynes this is an accurate exposition of the Pigouvian aggregated labour market theory, although it must be recognised that there is some doubt about whether

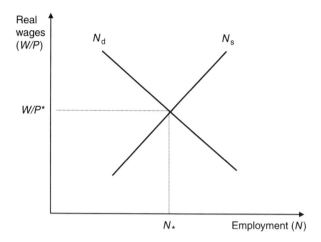

Diagram 2.3   The classical aggregated labour market

Keynes dealt entirely fairly with Pigouvian economic theory (Ambrosi, 2003).

The two postulates together suggest that the equilibrium volume of aggregate employment is determined primarily by the level of *real wage rates*. The classics, however, are indifferent as to whether their argument is expressed in terms of either *money wage rates* or *real wage rates*. With the general price-level being determined by the quantity theory of money (see Section (c)), the classical analysis supposes that any reduction (increase) in money wage rates is equivalent to a reduction (increase) in real wage rates. It should also be noted that the price-level which workers are supposed to take into account when deciding how much labour to supply is not the general price-level, but the money price of what Pigou describes as *wage goods*. That is the range of goods normally purchased by wage and salary earners, the prices of which determine the utility associated with a money wage. Wage goods can be viewed as reasonably close to what, in modern parlance, are termed consumer products.

The second postulate is crucial to the classical approach because it reveals what types of unemployment the classics seek to explain. According to Keynes the second postulate is only compatible with *frictional* and *voluntary* unemployment. Within the frictional category Keynes claims the classical school has in mind:

> unemployment due to a temporary want of balance between the relative quantities of specialised resources as a result of miscalculation

or intermittent demand; or to time-lags consequent on unforeseen changes; or to the fact that the change-over from one employment to another cannot be effected without a certain delay, so that there will always exist in a non-static society a proportion of resources unemployed "between jobs".

(Keynes, 2007, p. 6)

In the voluntary category the classical school, according to Keynes, includes:

unemployment due to the refusal or inability of a unit of labour, as a result of legislation or social practices or of combination for collective bargaining or of slow response to change or mere human obstinacy, to accept a reward corresponding to the value of the product attributable to its marginal product.

(Keynes, 2007, p. 6)

It is interesting that included in the voluntary category is both the refusal of workers collectively to accept wage cuts, thereby causing wage rigidity, and the inability of a group of workers to respond quickly to change, also, potentially, causing real wages to be too high. What is of equal importance to realise is that in Keynes' mind both classical categories of unemployment are consistent with the full employment position. So in the classical model unemployment can coexist with full employment, yet the causes of the unemployment are due to *supply-side* difficulties, such as slow responses, obstinacy, miscalculations and time lags and so on, not a deficiency of aggregate effective demand.

It may help the reader's understanding of the classical school's approach if the aggregated labour market analysis is illustrated in a slightly different way (see Diagram 2.4). Once again on the vertical axis is the real wage (W/P), and on the horizontal axis is employment (N). In this diagram there are two aggregate labour supply curves. N_s1 represents a *perfect world* situation; there is perfect information of job opportunities, a perfect match of job opportunities and skills, no trade unions, no restrictive government intervention, no time lags or miscalculations. The N_s^* curve represents the *real world* labour supply curve taking into account lack of job information, mismatches of skills available and job opportunities, trade union restrictions, government legislation, time lags and miscalculations. In other words N_s^* has imbedded in it all the imperfections outlined in Keynes' definitions of frictional and voluntary

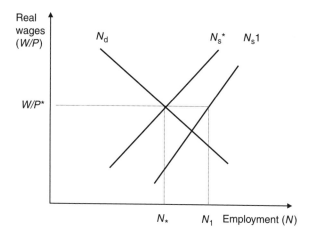

Diagram 2.4 The aggregated labour market – an alternative version

unemployment noted above. Imperfections reduce labour supply at each real wage rate, hence N_s^* always lies to the *left* of the $N_s 1$.

In this classical world market forces grind out an equilibrium position where labour demand equals *real world* labour supply. At real wage rate W/P^* the equilibrium level of employment – or full employment – is N_*. There is unemployment equal to $N_1 - N_*$. The horizontal distance between the two labour supply curves represents the aggregate of frictional and voluntary unemployment's combined. Although neither the classics nor Keynes uses this diagram it is a fair representation of the classical position. Indeed this representation clearly shows the classical antecedents of Milton Friedman's reference to the *natural rate* of unemployment. In terms of Diagram 2.4 the natural rate of unemployment equals to $(N_1 - N_*)/N_1$.

If an economic shock disturbs the full employment equilibrium the classical school relies on fluid money wage rates to resolve the problem. Consider a disturbance that changes prices or conditions governing the wage bargain that results in the money wage rate being above the equilibrium level (see Diagram 2.5). On the vertical axis is the general level of money wages (W), and on the horizontal axis are units of employment (N). The N_d schedule represents the aggregate labour demand curve with respect to money wages, and N_s is the real world aggregate labour supply curve with respect to money wages (consistent with schedule N_s^* in Diagram 2.4). The economic disturbance causes the general level of money wage to be at W^1 consistent with aggregate employment N_1 (determined by the demand side of the market).

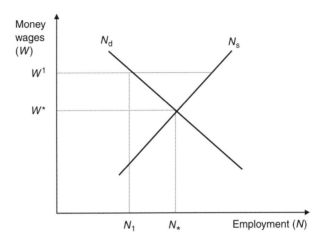

Diagram 2.5   The aggregated labour market – money wages

The classical solution to an excess aggregate supply of labour is that the general level of money wages should fall to W^* – the equilibrium level consistent with full employment N_*. The excess supply of labour is eliminated and a new equilibrium position established. The reverse holds if the general level of money wages is below the equilibrium rate. Money wages tend to increase in order to remove the excess aggregate demand for labour. If money wages are not flexible then the economy cannot adjust to the new equilibrium position. This is most likely when wages must fall to remove an excess supply of labour and the result is persistent unemployment. It is in this context that Keynes writes:

> the classical theory has been accustomed to rest the supposedly self-adjusting character of the economic system on an assumed fluidity of money wages; and, where there is rigidity, to lay on this rigidity the blame of maladjustment.

> (Keynes, 2007, p. 257)

In the classical analysis flexible money wages guarantee the maintenance of full employment or strong market forces pushing the economy towards that point. Unemployment in the classical model is caused by supply-side difficulties and rigid money wages. There is no mention of unemployment due to a lack of effective demand, although there can be temporary problems of demand, for example, caused by the trade cycle. But demand-deficient unemployment cannot permanently exist for supply always creates its own demand. Lay people may complain about the lack of demand during a recession, but the classics know better. What seems to the untrained eye as unemployment due to a lack of demand is actually due to a lack of fluid money wages. The solution lies not in increasing total demand but in making money wages more fluid, in a downward direction – the *contractionist cure*. This is why the classical school persists in offering generalised wage cuts as a solution to the global mass unemployment experienced during the Great Depression of the 1930s (see Chapter 9).

c) The classical theory of money and prices

As part of its monetary theory the classical school has two quantity theories – the Cambridge and Fisher (or Yale) approaches – emanating from either side of the Atlantic. Both theories have a basic quantity equation and each equation has two objectives. First, both are designed to determine the purchasing power of money – the *quaesitum* of the classics; second both examine how the price-level responds to changes in the money supply. Another often overlooked fact is that in the 1920s Keynes makes an important contribution to the theoretical development of the Cambridge equation. This section outlines both of the quantity equations and their special case assumptions.

Before outlining the two equations it will be useful to consider Keynes' treatment of money as this will help us appreciate Keynes' contribution to the Cambridge quantity equation (and the monetary component of the General Theory model). He first sets this out in the *Treatise on Money* (Keynes, 1971a, b) where he makes an important distinction between notes and coins and *bank money* (money held in bank deposit form). According to Keynes bank money is the most important means of exchange with notes and coins playing a minor role. Therefore Keynes' treatment of money is conducted, for the most part, in terms of bank money.

Keynes accepts the classical assertion that money is held for three main purposes:

1. as a means of exchange for personal transactions;
2. as a means of exchange for business transactions; and
3. as a "store of value".

He then examines how, from the standpoint of a depositor, bank money fulfils these purposes. First there is the individual or household that holds money to cover the interval between receiving personal income and spending it in various ways determined by personal preferences. Bank money held for this purpose Keynes calls *income deposits*. In the same way a business unable to perfectly coordinate income and expenditure will be required to hold cash balances which Keynes terms *business deposits*. Income and business deposits when aggregated together Keynes calls *cash deposits* used in order to facilitate exchange with ease and convenience. But there is a third purpose for money, that of an asset held as a store of value.

> But a bank deposit may also be held, not for the purposes of making payments but as a means of employing savings i.e., as an investment .... We shall call deposits of this type *saving deposits*. It is the criterion of a savings deposit that it is not required for the purpose of current payments and could, without inconvenience, be dispensed with if, for any reason, some other form of investment were to seem to the depositor to be preferable. ... [Therefore a] savings deposit also corresponds to what used to be called in theories of money, which were stated with primary reference to a commodity money, the use of money as a "Store of Value".
>
> (Keynes, 1971a, pp. 31–32; abridged quotation;
> Keynes' emphasis)

It is to this third purpose of money that Keynes pays much attention. It plays a crucial role in Keynes' many criticisms of the classical treatment of money and prices when he still could be counted as a (somewhat heretical) member of the classical school in the 1920s and early 1930s (see the appendix at the end of this chapter). But money's role as a store of value – in savings deposits – subsequently plays a crucial role in the monetary section of Keynes' General Theory model.[5]

The classical quantity equations

According to the classical school the purpose of the quantity equations is to determine the purchasing power of money. That is "the power of money" to buy a specific bundle of *consumer* products; therefore the price-level which the quantity equations seek to explain relates to this specific bundle of consumption goods. This general consumption price-level Keynes refers to as the *consumption standard*. In the *Treatise* Keynes reviews the two major classical quantity equations – the Cambridge and Fisher equations.

The Cambridge equation

This equation starts from the contention that a community holds a stable portion of its real income in a money form. The argument is first put forward by Marshall that the community holds some proportion of income as cash for the convenient and smooth conduct of transactions. The key classical contention is that the proportion of cash held is a stable function of income; if real income increases (decreases) then cash holdings rise (fall) in a stable and predictable manner. Pigou refines Marshall's approach into the Cambridge equation; he is more explicit about the reasons why the community holds cash outlining the *transactionary and precautionary motives* to hold money (concepts that Keynes subsequently uses and develops). The transactionary motive covers the use of money as a means of exchange; the precautionary motive explains money held as a store of value. Once again Pigou argues that the total demand for money is a stable proportion of real resources, which he measures in terms of wheat, and this allows an equation to be developed that determines the price-level for wheat. But in using wheat Keynes argues that Pigou shirks rather than solves the problem of determining the consumption standard.

Keynes amends the Pigou equation in the *Tract on Monetary Reform* (Keynes, 1971c) where he develops the *real balances* equation. This is a refinement of the original Cambridge approach and in modern textbooks it is referred to as the Cambridge equation. According to Keynes the real balances equation emerges from the idea that

> what a holder of money requires is a quantity of real balances which bears the appropriate relationship to the quantity of *real transactions* upon which he employs his balances. Consequently, if this appropriate relationship remains *unchanged*, the quantity of *cash* balances which he will need will be equal to the quantity of *real* balances as determined by the above "appropriate relationship", multiplied by the price-level corresponding to the prices applicable to the various real transactions against which cash balances are held.
>
> (Keynes, 1971a, p. 199; my emphasis)

Real transactions relate to the purchase of *consumption products* only. Therefore the real money balances held by the public can be measured in terms of *consumption units* – in other words in terms of a bundle of consumption goods normally purchased by the public. Keynes' equation highlights the price-level of consumption goods in general (rather than the price of wheat), which can be taken to represent the purchasing power of money. Hence Keynes proposes the following equation:

$$n = p \cdot k$$

where n is the total quantity of cash held by the community, p the price of a consumption unit and k the number of consumption units which the public require to hold in cash. Implicit in this analysis is the special case assumption that the level of real income (YR) is given, thereby defining the number of consumption units the community requires to hold.

This Cambridge equation provides an explanation of why a change in the money supply causes a proportional change in the price-level of consumption units. Suppose the monetary authority increases the money supply whilst the level of real income remains unchanged; the public's actual holding of cash balances are now greater than the level of real balances they wish to hold. Individuals use these surplus balances in an attempt to purchase additional consumption products, but with output given, only the price-level of such items can increase. This process continues until the value of nominal cash balances is again equated with the desired level of real balances. Moreover, assuming that k is constant, the increase in the price-level is fully proportionate to the increase in the money supply. The reverse holds true when the money supply is lowered. Interestingly in the *Treatise* Keynes returns to this real balances equation and outlines a number of deficiencies. This is not the proper place to consider these issues, though they do form part of the appendix to this chapter.

The Fisher equation

The other formulation of the Quantity Theory of Money, developed at Yale University by Irving Fisher, remains today by far the most popular method of exposition. According to Keynes the Fisher equation starts "neither from the flow of income against consumption goods, nor from real balances, nor from the proportion of resources held in cash, but from the total volume of cash transactions" (Keynes, 1971a, p. 209). From this starting point Fisher outlines his famous equation:

$$M \cdot V = P^* \cdot T$$

In this equation M is the volume of cash outstanding, V the average number of times that a unit of cash is used in transactions, P^* the price-level of *all articles traded* that is consumer products, investment goods, shares and so on, and T the number of units of articles traded (or what Fisher calls the volume of trade). Notice that in this model all money is held solely for the purposes of facilitating exchange and there is no role for money as a store of value.

Actually the supply of money (M) multiplied by the speed with which it circulates around the economy (V) must equal the volume of transactions conducted (T) times the price-level of all articles traded (P^*). If, for example, MV is less than P^*T, then households and firms have insufficient money to pay for goods and services they have agreed to purchase, and the volume of transactions conducted declines. If MV is greater than P^*T, households and firms have excess money holdings which they use to buy more goods and services, causing the price of articles and the volume of transactions to rise.

Irving Fisher turns a truism into a theory by making three assumptions. First, he claims that the volume of transactions is constant, determined by the real forces of supply and demand on each individual market. Second, he assumes that the technology of the banking system is unchanging, so that the velocity of circulation is constant, at least in the short run. Third, he assumes that a rise (fall) in the money supply *causes* an increase (decrease) in the general price-level, and not the other way around. Once Fisher's assumptions are applied, an increase (decrease) in the supply of money causes an *equi-proportionate* rise (fall) in the price-level of articles traded. When the money supply increases by say 10 per cent then, with the values of V and T given, the price-level rises by 10 per cent as well. If the money supply falls by 10 per cent, on the same basis, the price-level declines by an equal percentage.[6] In the *Treatise* Keynes reconsiders the Fisher equation and its significant limitations; the most important being the failure to consider a role for money as a store of value. But once again this is beyond the remit of this chapter though it does form part of the appendix.

In the efforts to derive the purchasing power of money both the Cambridge and Fisher versions of the quantity theory do not mention the determination of the price of a single commodity (i.e. the Marshallian theory of value). It is as if there is an analytical dichotomy in the classical analysis between the microeconomic determination of the price of a single commodity through the laws of supply and demand (i.e. Marshall's scissors) and the macroeconomic derivation of the general price-level. Keynes caustically notes that when the classical school analyses:

> the theory of value, they have been accustomed to teach that prices are governed by the conditions of supply and demand; and, in particular, changes in marginal costs and the elasticity of short-period supply have played a prominent part. But when they pass to volume II, or more often in a separate treatise, to the theory of money and prices, we hear no more of these homely but intelligible concepts.
>
> (Keynes, 2007, p. 292)

This is a result of the methodology of the classical school. The price of a single commodity is determined by one set of forces, the general price-level by another separate set of forces, and the two analytical frameworks are never brought into close connection. It is a position with which Keynes feels uneasy, and he rectifies it in the General Theory model. Using the concept of aggregate effective demand Keynes attempts to bring back the analytical connection between the theories of value and prices as part of a broader general theory (see Chapter 10).

d) Keynes versus the classics revisited

In the *General Theory* Keynes makes continual reference to classical macroeconomics as a special case, one that applies in certain limiting circumstances, to which he adds his more generally applicable theory. Mainstream Keynesianism sees the distinction between Keynes and the classics in a very different way; Keynes' theory is viewed as a special case of the classical (or neo-classical) model, applicable in the short run, when price expectations have not fully anticipated an unexpected shock, but giving way to the classical case in the long run. *This book takes a very different view. Its aim is to appreciate why Keynes claims the classical model is a special case of his more generally applicable theory.*

In the analysis above it is transparent that classical macroeconomic theory is created by bolting together different conceptual analyses. Each separate component of the model – the loanable funds market, the aggregated labour market and the quantity theory – is derived independently of the other, using the *cet. par.* assumption. This only works when special case assumptions are made. Hence the loanable funds theory assumes aggregate income is constant; the aggregated labour market model assumes that aggregate demand and the general price-level are given; the quantity theory of money assumes that the level of real income (or volume of transactions) is given; and the quantity theory assumes that the general price-level is determined separately from the value of any single commodity. These characteristics, plus the calculus of probability, make the classical theory a special case dealing with a broadly unchanging economy operating at the full employment position. With the inclusion of Say's law the classical theory becomes by default a macroeconomic analysis. By accepting this law the issue of how aggregate demand and income is determined is side-stepped, as supply creates its own demand. With the demand side of the model specified, however inadequately, the classical model focuses on supply side and monetary issues.

Keynes applies a very different method in his analysis. Most importantly he rules out assuming that aggregate effective demand and income are given, indeed his theory is designed to explain the values of these aggregates. He starts by rejecting Say's law. Once this is put aside Keynes needs an analysis of aggregate demand. He develops theories to explain both aggregate consumption expenditure and aggregate investment spending; he also relates these two aggregates together through the multiplier effect. He applies a practical theory – the conventional method of calculation – to explain how decision-makers cope with the precariousness of knowledge of the future. The rate of interest is treated as a monetary phenomenon, specified by the demand and supply of money. The rate of interest, through its influence on aggregate investment spending, connects together the monetary and non-monetary sectors of the economy. Keynes then combines an aggregate demand function with an aggregate supply price concept to define *the key overarching concept of his generalised theory – the level of aggregate effective demand.*

Effective demand is the unifying concept that brings all the disparate elements of his theory together. The level of aggregate effective demand determines the volumes of aggregate income and employment. Changes in effective demand, usually caused by fluctuating investment spending (amplified by the multiplier effect), generate changes in total employment. Persistent mass unemployment exists in a capitalist economy if effective demand is not sufficient to generate full employment. A reduction in money wages can influence the level of aggregate employment, but only in so far as it changes the level of effective demand, and the impact on employment need not be beneficial. Effective demand also influences the general level of prices (and the prices of wage goods). Apart from the limiting case of a fully employed economy, increases in effective demand pull up the price-level and vice versa, but the change in prices is not proportional to the variation in nominal effective demand. Finally, through its influence on general prices, the level of effective demand helps to specify the real wage rate in an economy. In this sense real wages are as much a dependent variable in the General Theory model as the volume of employment.

Keynes' approach is not constrained by special case assumptions; the model applies to all cases: slump or boom, mass unemployment or full employment, price deflation or price inflation. This is why Keynes' theory is generally applicable and the classical model is not. In the rest of this book these contentions will be fleshed out considerably, and the contrast between the classical and General Theory models will be constantly highlighted.

e) Causal maps of the classical theory

To further illustrate the classical theory of interest and employment it can be expressed as a causal map. The classical model has a number of crucial independent variables. They are labour demand with respect to money wages (N_d), labour supply with respect to money wages (N_s), the supply of saving with respect to the rate of interest (S_s) and investment demand with respect to the rate of interest (I_d). The hypothesis of a calculable future ensures that investment demand is relatively stable at any point in time. Furthermore, the general price-level (P) is determined by the quantity theory of money.

Additionally the classical model requires two special assumptions to determine the rate of interest (r) and the volume of employment (N). First, aggregate labour demand as a function of the money wage is specified assuming the nominal level of aggregate effective demand (AED) is given, though clearly the argument is never expressed in these terms; second, the supply of saving as a function of the rate of interest is specified assuming the nominal level of aggregate income (Y) is constant. Assuming that short-term expectations are correct, the levels of AED and Y are equal.

With nominal effective demand given, N_d and N_s specify the money wage rate (W). With the price-level set by the quantity theory, the money wage rate determines the equilibrium real wage rate (w); hence workers can decide the level of real wages by bargaining for money wages. With aggregate income given, S_s and I_d define the equilibrium rate of interest (r). In turn r specifies the level of aggregate saving (S) by a community. Say's law ensures that the volume of S determines the funds available for investment spending (I) and consumption expenditure (C).

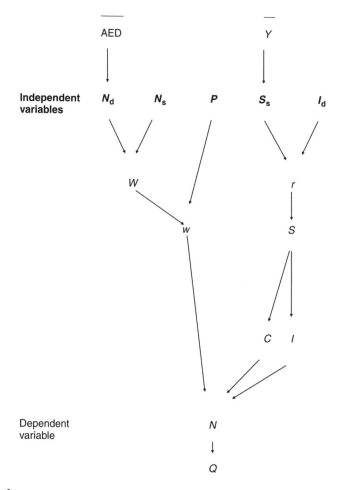

Map 1

In equilibrium the volume of *C* and *I* combined equal the level of nominal effective demand and aggregate income previously assumed to exist.

In a competitive economy with fluid money wages, and assuming AED equals *Y*, the level of real wages determines the equilibrium volumes of employment and output (*Q*); the volume of employment, given the special assumptions, is consistent with a full employment equilibrium position. The model does not deny the existence of an economy with unemployment; it is merely limited to cases of frictional and voluntary unemployment.

The Cambridge real balances equation has three key independent variables: the demand for money function (k), the level of real income (YR) and quantity of cash held by the community (n). Moreover, the value of k is a stable function of the level of real income (YR). The sole

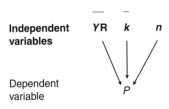

Independent variables $\overline{YR}$ $\overline{k}$ n

Dependent variable P

Map 2

independent variable is the price-level. A rise (fall) in the money supply, assuming YR and k are given, causes an equi-proportional rise (fall) in the price-level.

Using the Fisher equation, the independent variables are the velocity of circulation (V), the volume of trade (T) and the supply of money (M_s). The values of both V and T are treated as being stable and determined by real forces that is the forces of supply and demand on individual markets and banking technology. The dependent variable is the price-level for all articles traded (P^*).

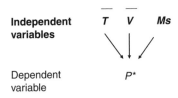

Independent variables $\overline{T}$ $\overline{V}$ Ms

Dependent variable P^*

Map 3

Once again, a rise (fall) in the money supply, assuming V and T are constant, causes an equi-proportional rise (fall) in the price-level for all articles. Note, in both the Cambridge and Fisher equations the only active independent variable is the money supply, and the only dependent variable is the price-level.

f) Summary

Say's law and the calculus of probability underpin the loanable funds market and provide the classical school with a theory of aggregate demand. Supply creates its own demand and aggregate saving funds investment spending. The loanable funds market guarantees the macroeconomic system adjusted to shocks. Saving may rise or fall, but the compensating changes in consumption and investment spending ensures that aggregate income is unchanged.

In the classical analysis the volume of employment is determined in an aggregated labour market. Keynes argues that the classical approach to the labour market is based on two fundamental postulates (or conditions). The two postulates together suggest that the equilibrium volume of aggregate employment primarily depends on the level of *real wage rates*. The second postulate is crucial as it reveals that the classical theory only explains *frictional* and *voluntary* unemployment. In Keynes' mind both categories of unemployment are consistent with the full employment position. So classical unemployment can coexist with full employment, but the causes of the unemployment are due to supply-side difficulties not a deficiency of effective demand.

According to the classical school the purpose of the quantity theory of money is to determine the purchasing power of money, that is the consumption standard. The classical school does not have a unified quantity theory, but has a British and American version – represented by the Cambridge and Fisher equations, respectively. Keynes makes an important contribution to the theoretical development of the Cambridge equation whilst still a classical economist in the 1920s. Both quantity equations predict that changes in the money supply cause equi-proportionate changes in the price-levels. And both quantity equations determine the general price-level independently of the classical theory of value.

The classical theory deals with a special case of a broadly unchanging economy operating at full employment. Say's law allows the component parts of the classical analysis to be transformed into a macroeconomic theory. With this law the levels of aggregate demand and income are determined by supply-side forces; the concept of aggregate effective demand is irrelevant. Keynes' General Theory model is not constrained by special case assumptions; its key overarching concept is the level of effective demand. The model can be generally applied to analyse differing circumstances: slump or boom, mass unemployment or full employment, price deflation or price inflation. This means that Keynes' theory is generally applicable whilst the classical model is not.

Appendix
Keynes' Critique of the Classical Quantity Theories of Money and Prices

This appendix will develop some specific criticisms of the quantity equations – both the Cambridge and Fisher versions – that Keynes sets out in the *Treatise on Money*. These criticisms strike at the heart of the classical theory of money and prices. Keynes shows how the classical analysis fails to coherently explain both the consumption standard and the relationship between money and prices. Keynes' criticisms are powerful and effective, and yet have received surprising little attention by mainstream Keynesians.

The purchasing power of money

The price-level which is the *quaesitum* of classical enquiry is the consumption standard. In terms of the Cambridge approach, the Pigou equation is inappropriate for this task as it only determines the price-level of wheat. Keynes' real balances equation in the *Tract* seems to provide a more reasonable measurement. In the *Treatise* Keynes accepts that his real balances approach is also flawed with respect to determining a consumption standard. For the equation implies that cash deposits are only held to facilitate current consumption. In reality cash deposits can be used for a great many business and personal purposes. Keynes notes, for example, that the financial sector conducts large volumes of transactions completely unrelated to the consumption standard.

If this is the case measuring real balances in consumption units is inappropriate. The unit of measurement needs to be more heterodox; it should take account of the many business transactions (e.g. purchasing capital goods, raw materials, stocks and shares, etc.) to which real balances are applied – in other words the business deposits noted in

Chapter 2. The problem with this is that the price-level relating to such a heterodox unit is not the consumption standard.

Consequently the Cambridge equation does not measure the purchasing power of money, yet the latter is the ultimate objective of classical enquiry. It is obvious that the price-level which the Fisher equation explains is not the purchasing power of money either. The Fisher equation relates to all articles traded, not just those products which are available for consumption. Therefore the Fisher equation suffers from the same fundamental flaw as the Cambridge analysis; that is a failure to identify the *quaesitum* of classical enquiry.

The "velocity" of circulation and monetary forces

The Fisher equation asserts that a stock of money circulates around an economy at a certain velocity in a given period of time. According to Keynes, however, this concept of velocity is only unambiguous when money is used to facilitate exchange. As soon as money is used as a "hoard" (i.e. as a store of value) the concept of velocity is stultified; for, by definition, money which is hoarded has a velocity of zero. Keynes complains that the Fisher concept of velocity is not a "true" velocity at all, but is a composite of two "true" velocities – namely the velocities of cash and savings deposits (the latter being zero). Given the composite nature of the velocity of circulation it becomes obvious to Keynes that Fisher's claim that the value of V depends solely on real forces is wrong. If it is accepted that money is held as a store of value then Keynes argues the value of V can fluctuate due to changes in purely *monetary* forces.

This might occur if, with a given supply of bank money, the relative proportions of saving deposits and cash deposits held by the public change. If there is a relative increase in the proportion of saving deposits held by the public this causes a superficial reduction in the value of V, even though the velocity of cash deposits remains steady. Conversely a decrease in the relative proportion of saving deposits held by the public causes the velocity of money to seemingly increase, even with a constant cash deposit velocity.

To show this clearly consider the following numerical example; please note this is a stock not a flow example. To begin with suppose an economy with the following characteristics:

Units of Money (M) $\quad\quad = 100$
Units of Cash Deposits ($M1$) $\;= 90$
Units of Saving Deposits ($M2$) $= 10$

Velocity of Cash Deposits ($V1$) $= 2$
Velocity of Saving Deposits ($V2$) $= 0$
Price-level for all articles traded (P^*) $= 1$
Volume of Transactions (T) $= 180$

A relationship between active cash deposits and the price-level can be derived in the following way.

$$M1 \cdot V1 = P^* \cdot T$$
$$(90)\,(2) = (1)\,(180)$$

Combining cash and saving deposits together allows the overall velocity of circulation (V) to be derived. In this case the value of V is 1.8 – that is:

$$M \cdot V = P^* \cdot T$$
$$(100)\,(1.8) = (1) \cdot (180)$$

The value of V is clearly a composite of the two true velocities $V1 = 2$ and $V2 = 0$ (i.e. $(2)\,(0.9) + (0)\,(0.1) = 1.8$). Suppose that the proportions of cash and saving deposits held by the public change so that:

$$M1 = 60$$
$$M2 = 40$$

If the values for $V1$ and T remain the same it follows that the price-level must fall to a lower level that is:

$$M1 \cdot V1 = P \cdot T$$
$$(60) \cdot (2) = (0.66) \cdot (180)$$

It follows that the overall velocity of money (V) must fall to 1.2 (i.e. $(2)\,(0.6) + (0)\,(0.4)$), if the truism $M V \equiv P T$ holds. Hence:

$$MV = PT$$
$$(100)\,(1.2) = (0.66)\,(180)$$

This means that in the Fisher equation the overall velocity (V) can vary purely due to changes in monetary conditions; that is a relative change in the demands for cash and saving deposits by a community. This demonstrates that Fisher's assumption that V is determined solely by real forces cannot hold if a community is able to change the amount of money it holds as a store of value. Furthermore, if the velocities of income deposits and business deposits differ (as is likely) this further complicates the position, as changing the proportions of such deposits held by the public causes further variations in the value of the overall velocity.

Finally note how in this numerical example the price-level changes without any change in the overall money supply. The Fisher equation is obviously seriously flawed once the role of money as a store of value is taken into account. For if the overall value of the velocity fluctuates due to monetary forces, the equation can no longer say anything unambiguous about the effect on the price-level of a change in the quantity of money. Consequently the Fisher equation fails to offer a consistent answer to the second major objective of classical monetary enquiry.

3
Aggregate Effective Demand

a) Introduction

In the *General Theory* Keynes finally breaks with Say's law.[1] In its place he outlines a theory of what determines aggregate income, output and employment in which the central unifying concept of aggregate effective demand plays the leading role. *Effective demand is the single most important idea in Keynes' General Theory model.* It is essential that the reader has a proper appreciation of this category of analysis.[2]

This chapter sets out the principle of aggregate effective demand as first described by Keynes. The reader should not be put off by some of the unusual terminology applied by Keynes. The terminology is unusual because it has not been used by followers of Keynes and does not appear in modern textbooks. Moreover Keynes' mode of expression can seem difficult and laboured at times, but one must appreciate that he is undertaking the difficult task of setting out an entirely new theory for the first time. But once the initial shock dissipates, the reader will realise the model itself is quite straightforward. This chapter is a primer for the next five chapters of this book. Once the reader has completed Chapters 4–8, he/she will find it useful to return to this chapter before progressing further through the book.

This chapter begins by examining Keynes' specification of units of measurement for aggregate values in his theory and his definition of aggregate income and aggregate net income – Section (b). This is all helpful for an accurate derivation of the aggregate supply function – Section (c). Section (d) considers the reasoning underpinning the aggregate demand function. These concepts are combined in Section (e) to define aggregate effective demand. This section also considers the relationship between effective demand and income and specifies the determinants of effective demand. Finally, Section (f) outlines a basic causal map of Keynes' model.

b) Units of measurement and key definitions

One reason that new readers find the *General Theory* a difficult book to understand is a lack of appreciation of the units of measurement Keynes uses in his analysis. A beginner's guide to the *General Theory* must therefore rectify this situation. In macroeconomics once a theory moves beyond the simplicities of a one-commodity economy the issue of how to measure aggregates must be addressed. All the great economists have had to define a measuring rod for dealing with aggregate volumes in a consistent manner; hence Smith's labour command theory of value and Ricardo's and Marx's focus on the labour theory of value. Keynes is no different in terms of the need to address the issue, but the distinct problem he faces is to develop a general theory of employment.

Keynes resolves the issue in the General Theory model by measuring aggregates in three ways: in *nominal money terms, in labour units (or "quantities of employment") and in wage units.* A quantity of nominal money value, for example, aggregate consumption is £750 billion, is a relatively straightforward and homogeneous measurement. However measurement by labour units and wage units (which are two sides of the same coin) requires further explanation. To measure quantities of employment Keynes requires an unambiguous and homogeneous measurement of units of labour, yet clearly there are very different forms and classifications of paid work. To get around this problem Keynes uses the device of assuming that:

> the quantity of employment can be sufficiently defined for our purpose by taking an *hour's employment of ordinary labour as our unit* and weighting an hour's employment of special labour in proportion to its remuneration; i.e. an hour of special labour remunerated at double ordinary rates will count as two units.
>
> (Keynes, 2007, p. 41; my emphasis)

This provides a unit measurement which can be varied in a consistent way to take account of different grades and payments for labour. A second problem with identifying a homogeneous labour unit is that it is usual to assume that as more labour units are applied to a given capital stock the law of diminishing productivity will set in, and the last worker employed will become progressively less productive. This means that each unit of labour is not equally productive, undermining its assumed homogeneous character. To overcome this Keynes uses the device of assuming that as output increases additional units of labour are regarded as *homogeneous and equally productive* (i.e. each labour unit has the same average and marginal physical productivity), whilst the capital equipment is assumed to become less productive as it experiences the law of diminishing productivity.

> We subsume, so to speak, the non-homogeneity of equally remunerated labour units in the equipment, which we regard as less and less adapted to employ the available labour units as output increases, instead of regarding the available labour units as less and less adapted to use a homogeneous capital equipment.
>
> (Keynes, 2007, p. 42)

Regarding all labour units as equally productive is an important assumption which underpins Keynes' derivation of the aggregate supply function – see Section (c). Moreover in Keynes' analysis employment is always measured in labour units not in terms of actual jobs. Therefore, throughout this book when reference is made to *employment* or *units of employment* this is just another way of expressing the volume of *labour units*.

Having defined a homogenous labour unit, Keynes goes onto to identify the concept of a wage unit. He explains that "the money-wage of a labour unit we shall call the wage unit. Thus, if E is the wages (and salaries) bill, $W[U]$ the wage unit, and N the quantity of employment, $E = N \cdot W[U]$" (Keynes, 2007, p. 41). The wage unit (WU) is the other crucial unit of measurement in the General Theory model as Keynes uses it to measure the *real* levels of aggregates such as aggregate consumption, aggregate investment and aggregate income (i.e. that is to deflate the money values of these aggregates). This may be shown in terms of a simple example. Suppose an economy with the following characteristics set out in Table 3.1.

Table 3.1 The wage unit measurement

	Year 1	Year 2
Aggregate income – in money terms (Y)	£10 million	£15 million
Money wages per labour unit	£10	£12
Aggregate income – in wage units (Yw)	1,000,000	1,250,000

In money terms national income seems to have risen by 50 per cent over the 2-year period, but what is the change in real income, that is income measured in wage units? Suppose that in period 1 the wage unit is £10 and that it rises to £12 in period 2. If the nominal income levels are measured in wage units, real income in year 1 is 1,000,000 wage units, and in year 2 is 1,250,000 wage units. That is income in year 2 has increased by 25 per cent in real terms and 50 per cent in nominal terms. The wage unit measurement will be constantly used in the following chapters and it is of the utmost importance to properly understand the concept.

In the General Theory model Keynes provides a precise definition of aggregate income within a specific time period. A rigorous definition of aggregate income helps Keynes to properly specify an aggregate supply function; the aggregate supply function in turn contributes to Keynes' definition of aggregate effective demand, see Section (e). Given the importance of aggregate income it is surprising that Keynes' treatment of the topic is insufficiently appreciated in the mainstream Keynesian literature. This is an unsatisfactory position which must be rectified.

Keynes' definition of total income is derived from the perspective of an entrepreneur. "Entrepreneur" is the short-hand term Keynes uses to describe any enterprise, corporation or institution that employs workers with the purpose of making profits. In a time period an entrepreneur's revenue (A) comes from either the sale of goods to consumers or from the sale of capital equipment to other entrepreneurs. At the end of the period the entrepreneur has a stock of capital equipment which includes inventories of raw materials, unfinished and final goods (G). From this must be subtracted purchases of capital equipment from other entrepreneurs during the time period ($A1$). Hence in terms of an equation an entrepreneur's income is equal to $A + G - A1$. Some portion of this income, however, will be generated by capital equipment installed before the time period. Therefore to identify the entrepreneur's income derived from activities in a specific time period, it is necessary to make an appropriate *deduction* from the value of his capital stock at the end of the period.

There are two elements of this deduction. The first relates to a change in the value of capital equipment which is due to the *voluntary* decisions of entrepreneurs seeking to produce output in order to maximise profits, which Keynes refers to as *user cost* (U). User cost measures the sacrifice involved in using the equipment rather than *leaving it idle*. In other words user cost is equal to the *excess* of the estimated value of capital equipment if it had not been used to produce output over the actual value of the equipment at the end of the production period. This user cost is then added to the factor cost of the entrepreneur to calculate the *prime cost* of producing output. Hence the income for an entrepreneur within a specific time period is equal to "the excess of the value of his finished output sold during the period over his prime cost" (Keynes, 2007, p. 53). Entrepreneurial income is therefore equal to gross profit which the entrepreneur seeks to maximise. Having specified the income of a single entrepreneur Keynes then notes that "since the income of the rest of the community is equal to the entrepreneur's factor cost, *aggregate income* is equal to $[\sum (A - U)]$" (Keynes, 2007, p. 54; my emphasis). This means that in the General Theory model aggregate income is defined net of aggregate user cost.

The second deduction Keynes identifies which needs to be taken into account is *supplementary cost* (*V*) which allows Keynes to define *aggregate net income*. Supplementary cost covers the *involuntary* loss (or gain) of value of an entrepreneur's capital equipment due to "a change in market values, wastage by obsolescence or the mere passage of time, or destruction by catastrophe such as war or earthquake" (Keynes, 2007, p. 56). Although for entrepreneurs this cost is involuntary, and beyond their control, it is an expected (or at least not an unexpected) cost to be incurred. It is reasonable, therefore, to deduct *V* from aggregate income to determine aggregate *net* income. In the General Theory model aggregate net income is equal to $\sum (A - U - V)$; that is aggregate income net of supplementary costs. Aggregate net income is an important concept because it influences the consumption decisions of entrepreneurs – it is as if *V* is deducted from gross profit, *after which* entrepreneurs decide what they are free to spend on consumer products. This is a subject taken up again in Chapter 4.

c) The aggregate supply price and function

To properly understand Keynes' concept of aggregate effective demand it is of the utmost importance to clarify two concepts: first the *aggregate supply price* and second the *aggregate supply function* defined net of aggregate user costs. Moreover it is important to be clear about what Keynes means by the phrase the *proceeds of employment,* which underpins his definition of the aggregate supply function. Keynes begins by noting that in the short period:

> In a given state of technique, resources and costs, the employment of a given volume of labour by an entrepreneur involves him in two

kinds of expense: first of all the amounts which he pays out to factors of production (exclusive of other entrepreneurs) for their current services, which we shall call *factor cost* of the employment in question; and secondly, the amounts which he pays out to other entrepreneurs for what he has to purchase from them together with the sacrifice which he incurs by employing the equipment instead of leaving it idle [i.e. user cost] ... The excess of value of the resulting output over the sum of its factor cost and its user cost is the profit or, as we shall call it, the *income* of the entrepreneur.

(Keynes, 2007, p. 23; Keynes' emphasis)

In Section (b) it was shown that the factor cost of entrepreneurs is the income to the other factors of production and aggregate income is defined net of user cost. Hence, aggregate income is the sum of factor costs plus the profits of entrepreneurs. From this Keynes defines the *proceeds of employment* as being the aggregate income generated from the production and sale of the output of a given amount of employment. With this in mind, the aggregate supply price of output is defined by Keynes in the following manner:

[T]he aggregate supply price *of the output* of a given amount of employment is the *expectation of proceeds* which will *just make it* worth the while of the entrepreneurs to give that employment.

(Keynes, 2007, p. 24; my emphasis)

Let us clarify Keynes' reasoning here. Taking as given the degree of competition, the techniques of production, the quality and quantity of available equipment, the skills of available labour and systems of organisational supervision, for each level of employment there will be a corresponding output as a whole. Moreover associated with each level of output entrepreneurs have an expectation of revenue from the sale of that output that is just sufficient to persuade them to keep the level of employment steady, assuming a given scale of wage costs.[3] From this Keynes formally defines an *aggregate supply function* in nominal terms.

Let Z be the aggregate supply price of the output from employing N men, the relationship between Z and N being written $Z = \phi(N)$, which can be called the aggregate supply function.

(Keynes, 2007, p. 25)

In this case Z is the *nominal* aggregate supply price and N signifies the number of labour units. The aggregate supply function specifies the expected revenue for each level of aggregate output that *just induces* entrepreneurs to keep the corresponding volume of aggregate employment steady. Keynes does not formally give a name to the ϕ function; however, for ease of exposition, in what follows it will be referred to as the *aggregate supply relationship*.

Alternatively the nominal aggregate supply function can be expressed in a way that specifically identifies the role of labour costs in entrepreneurs' decisions about employment – see Equation 1.

$$Z = WU \times \phi(N) \tag{1}$$

where Z is the aggregate supply price in nominal terms, WU is the wage unit, N is the employment of labour units and ϕ is the aggregate supply relationship. From Equation 1 it is possible to define an aggregate supply function in real terms. Hence, dividing both sides of the equation by the wage unit (WU) Equation 2 is derived:

$$Z_w = \phi(N) \tag{2}$$

where Z_w is the real aggregate supply price, N represents labour units and ϕ is the aggregate supply relationship.[4]

A key question is what is the value of the aggregate supply relationship, ϕ? Keynes does not address this issue directly, but it needs to be discussed.[5] To answer this it is helpful to begin by making some simplifying assumptions. Suppose the supply curve of each entrepreneur is independent of employment in other industries; wage costs are the only factor cost considered; and there is a given distribution of total output between the consumption and investment good industries (Chick, 1983; Keynes, 2007).[6] It is also reasonable to suppose that underlying the aggregate supply function there must be an aggregate production function which relates total employment to total output – see Equation 3.[7]

$$Q = f(K, N) \tag{3}$$

In this equation N represents labour units, K is the given stock of capital equipment and Q is the total output. This production function, however, must have the distinctive characteristic that any tendency for diminishing productivity to set in as output increases is attributed *to the increasing inefficiency of the capital stock*. This means that the productivity of labour units (both average and marginal) remains the same as output increases.

In terms of the expected revenue generated by the sale of output associated with a level of employment, suppose that the price of a product in any industry ($P\#$) is equal to:

$$P\# = WU\#/Q1\# \tag{4}$$

where $WU\#$ is the wage unit facing each entrepreneur and $Q1\#$ is the constant marginal physical product of a labour unit. If the supply curve of each entrepreneur is independent so that they can be summed together, what is true for one entrepreneur is true for all. Hence Equation 4 can be expressed in an aggregated form – see Equation 5:

$$P^e = WU/Q1 \tag{5}$$

In this equation WU is the wage unit for the whole economy, $Q1$ the marginal physical product of all labour units and P^e the expected price of a composite unit of total output.

Suppose the value of the nominal aggregate supply price (Z) for each level of labour units (N) is equal to P^e multiplied by total output (Q) associated with each level of N. It is then possible to develop a precise relationship between Z and N in the following manner. First, multiply both sides of Equation 5 by total output (Q). This gives Equation 6:

$$Z = P^e Q = (WU/Q1)Q \tag{6}$$

Second, note that the total output is equal to the average product of labour units (Q/N) multiplied by the number of labour units employed – see Equation 7.

$$Q = (Q/N) \times N \tag{7}$$

Substituting Equation 7 into Equation 6 allows the value of ϕ to be defined – see Equation 8.

$$Z = \frac{WU \times (Q/N) \cdot N}{Q1} \tag{8}$$

With the nominal aggregate supply function expressed as $Z = WU \cdot \phi(N)$, Equation 8 suggests that the value of ϕ must be equal to $(Q/N)/Q1$, that is the average productivity of a unit of labour divided by the marginal productivity of the last unit of labour. And because Keynes assumes that every unit of labour is equally productive [i.e. $(Q/N) = (Q1)$] it follows that the aggregate supply relationship (ϕ) must equal unity. The value of ϕ is also unity in the case of the real aggregate supply function – see Equation 2.

Having specified the value of the aggregate supply relationship, precise relationships between Z and N and Z_w and N can be derived – using spreadsheets and diagrams. Consider Table 3.2 with columns representing the nominal aggregate supply price (Z) in terms of £millions; the wage unit (WU) in terms of £'s per labour unit; the real aggregate supply price (Z_w) in terms of millions of wage units; and the volume of labour units (N) in terms of millions of labour units. Suppose initially that the wage unit is £10.

Considering a range of employment levels it can be seen that the nominal aggregate supply function is linear, with a slope equal to the money wage per labour unit. The real aggregate supply curve is also linear and its slope is equal to unity. Suppose that the wage unit falls to £5 per labour unit; the relationship between Z and N and Z_w and N is represented in Table 3.3.

The nominal aggregate supply curve is still linear, with a less steep slope equal to the now lower wage per labour unit. Interestingly, the

Table 3.2   The aggregate supply functions – wage unit £10

N (millions)	WU (£)	Z (£millions)	Z_w (millions)
0	10	0	0
1	10	10	1
2	10	20	2
3	10	30	3
4	10	40	4
5	10	50	5

Table 3.3   The aggregate supply functions – wage unit £5

N (millions)	WU (£)	Z (£millions)	Z_w (millions)
0	5	0	0
1	5	5	1
2	5	10	2
3	5	15	3
4	5	20	4
5	5	25	5

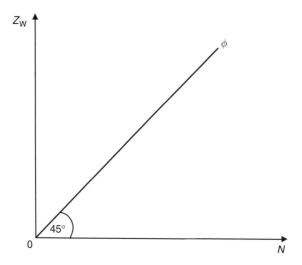

Diagram 3.1 The real aggregate supply function

real aggregate supply relationship remains stable despite the change in the wage unit. In fact the real aggregate supply function remains stable *no matter how the wage unit fluctuates.*[8] The aggregate supply function in real terms is illustrated in Diagram 3.1. On the vertical axis is the real aggregate supply price measured in wage units (Z_w), and on the horizontal axis are quantities of employment measured in labour units (N). This aggregate supply function is stable *no matter how the wage unit fluctuates*; the function is linear with a slope equal to unity.

In other words, in typical Marshallian terms, the slope of the real aggregate supply function shows that entrepreneurs will be just induced to offer employment up to the point where the real expected proceeds of the last labour unit employed is just equal to one wage unit. In this case Keynes asserts that:

$$\Delta N = \Delta Z_w = \Delta \phi(N) \tag{9}$$

In this equation Keynes claims that the value of dZ_w/dN is equal to one.

Keynes defines the aggregate supply function in terms of the price of *total* output, yet calculating aggregate output using a consistent and homogeneous measuring rod is a problem fraught with difficulties. This is one reason why Keynes later defines an employment function which is the inverse of the aggregate supply function measured in terms of wage units – see Chapter 11. Keynes uses the employment function rather than the aggregate supply function to convey key aspects of his theory.

d) The aggregate demand function

Next, Keynes introduces the idea of an *aggregate demand function*, which he defines net of aggregate user costs. The concept of the proceeds of employment plays a role in the definition of this function as well. With this in mind Keynes reasons that for each volume of employment there will be a specific *aggregate demand price* (*D*). Each volume of employment will have associated with it a corresponding level of aggregate output and for each specific volume of employment entrepreneurs *actually expect* to receive a level of revenues from the sale of the associated aggregate output. This level of revenues is the aggregate demand price.

This allows Keynes to define a nominal aggregate demand function.

[L]et D be the proceeds which entrepreneurs expect to receive from the employment of N men, the relationship between D and N being written D = F(N), which can be called the aggregate demand function.
(Keynes, 2007, p. 25)

The aggregate demand function specifies, for every level of employment, what proceeds entrepreneurs expect to receive from the sale of each corresponding level of output.

Keynes defines the aggregate demand function in *nominal* terms, but it is also possible to define the function in *real* terms by dividing the nominal aggregate demand price by the wage unit. The reader is warned to be careful about this function because Keynes never explicitly defines it, although it is implicit in much of his analysis. In this case the function becomes:

$$D_w = F_w(N) \tag{10}$$

where D_w is the aggregate demand price measured in wage units and N represents labour units. This function shows the levels of the real aggregate demand price associated with a hypothetical range of employment levels.

The aggregate demand function in real terms is illustrated in Diagram 3.2. The aggregate demand price measured in wage units is represented on the vertical axis, with units of labour on the horizontal axis, and F_w represents the real aggregate demand function. This function is

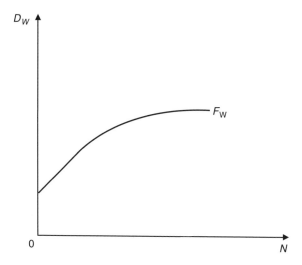

Diagram 3.2   The real aggregate demand function

drawn assuming a stable consumption function and a constant level of expected investment spending at all levels of employment.

Note the unusual shape of the aggregate demand function which is due to the assumptions Keynes makes about the aggregate consumption function – see Chapter 4. Examining the reasoning behind the aggregate demand function is obviously important; indeed, Keynes devotes a great deal of the *General Theory* to an explanation of the propensity to consume and the inducement to invest which define this function. At this point, however, the reader should take the unfamiliar shape of the function as given and wait for a comprehensive examination of the motivations underpinning the functions provided in later chapters.

e) Aggregate effective demand

How then does Keynes calculate aggregate *effective* demand? Quite simply it is determined at the volume of employment where the aggregate demand price is equated to the aggregate supply price that is where the aggregate demand and supply functions intersect. Expressed in another way, aggregate effective demand is derived where the actual *total* expected proceeds from the sale of output produced by a particular volume of employment (D or D_w) equals the expectation of *total* proceeds which just induces entrepreneurs to provide that employment

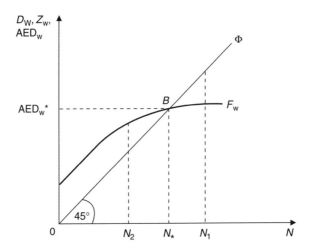

Diagram 3.3   Aggregate effective demand

(Z or Z_w). At this point Keynes claims that entrepreneurs will have no incentive either to increase or reduce the employment of labour units as the expectation of profits is maximised. This claim is the subject of further discussion in Appendix A to this chapter.

The determination of aggregate effective demand, measured in wage units, is illustrated in Diagram 3.3. On the vertical axis there is the real aggregate demand price (D_w), the real aggregate supply price (Z_w) and real aggregate effective demand (AED_w), on the horizontal axis there are units of employment. The aggregate supply function (ϕ) is equal to unity and the aggregate demand curve is represented by the F_w function.

The values of D_w and Z_w are only equated at point B, which defines the real volume of aggregate effective demand (AED_w^*); the latter then determines the *equilibrium* volume of total employment at N_*. If the volume of employment is N_1, the expected proceeds are less than the proceeds which induce entrepreneurs to provide that employment (i.e. Z_w exceeds D_w); entrepreneurs can raise profits by cutting back on jobs, and the volume of employment falls back to N_*. Conversely, if the volume of employment is N_2, aggregate expected proceeds are greater than the level which just induces entrepreneurs to offer that employment (i.e. D_w exceeds Z_w); and, according to Keynes, profitable opportunities exist if entrepreneurs expand employment up towards N_*.

Keynes claims only at employment level N_* is there no incentive for entrepreneurs to either raise or lower the volume of jobs. This analysis clearly shows that, according to Keynes, it is the level of aggregate effective demand (measured in wage units) that determines the equilibrium volume of total employment. There is no recourse to, or need for, an economy-wide market for labour, an aggregated labour market, where the equilibrium volume of aggregate employment is determined by a real wage rate as the classics argue. In the General Theory model the equilibrium level of aggregate employment is determined by the level of effective demand not the rate of real wages.[9] All this can also be expressed in nominal terms but the essence of the argument remains the same. *The level of aggregate effective demand determines the equilibrium volume of aggregate employment.* The seminal importance of this point for a proper appreciation of Keynes' model cannot be overstated.

It is essential to clarify the relationship between aggregate effective demand and aggregate income. Keynes defines aggregate effective demand from the viewpoint of entrepreneurs, as the *expected* result from employing N labour units. Aggregate income, he defines, as the *realised* result from the employment of the same N labour units. If, however, short-term (or current) expectations are fulfilled the volume of effective demand will be identical to the level of income – that is expected and realised results are the same. In the *General Theory* Keynes normally uses the working assumption that the short-term expectations of entrepreneurs about revenues and costs are correct. Another way of expressing this is that in Keynes' model the following conditions hold. That is:

$$D = Z = Y \qquad (11)$$

and

$$D_w = Z_w = Y_w \qquad (12)$$

In these two equations Y is the aggregate income measured in money terms, and Y_w is the aggregate income measured in wage units.

If the short-term expectations of entrepreneurs are wrong, that is if expected and actual results diverge, it is possible for entrepreneurs either to under or overestimate the expected results from employment. This is a disequilibrium position. In this case the level of effective demand diverges from that of aggregate income, which will continue until expected and actual results are realigned. For Keynes the assumption that short-term expectations are fulfilled distinguishes his work from that of his contemporaries such as Hawtrey and Ohlin (Keynes, 1973c).

The analysis of Hawtrey focused on situations where short-term expectation is not correct and entrepreneurs seek to move towards a true equilibrium position by trial and error. This results in entrepreneurs expanding operations when their expectations have been overly pessimistic, and contracting operations when their expectations turn out to be over-optimistic. Keynes criticises Hawtrey for mistaking "this higgling process by which the *equilibrium* position is discovered for the much more fundamental forces which determine what the *equilibrium* position is" (Keynes, 1973c, p. 182; my emphasis). And responding to Ohlin's contribution to the ex ante–ex post debate about saving and investment Keynes claims "I'm far more *classical* than the Swedes, for I am still discussing the conditions of short period *equilibrium*" (ibid., p. 183; my emphasis).

The strength of Keynes' approach of assuming entrepreneur's short-term expectations about revenues and costs are correct is that if aggregate effective demand is an equilibrium concept, then effective demand must determine the *equilibrium* volume of employment. Moreover changes in aggregate effective demand will cause changes in the equilibrium volume of employment. The classical aggregated labour market analysis can be jettisoned, replaced by the analysis of why effective demand and employment fluctuates. There is however no reason why the short-term expectations of entrepreneurs must be correct. Appendix B to this chapter reviews the Post-Keynesian debate about incorporating erroneous short-term expectations into the General Theory model.

Following on from this Keynes addresses two important questions. First, what *fundamental forces* determine the volume of aggregate effective demand (and hence income and total employment)? Secondly, why does the level of aggregate effective demand fluctuate? Assuming a stable aggregate supply relationship, the answer to the first question is that the level of the aggregate demand price (D_w) determines the volume of aggregate effective demand (AED_w). The key determinants of the aggregate demand price are expected aggregate consumption spending measured in wage units (D_w1) and expected aggregate investment spending measured in wage units (D_w2). The following equilibrium condition expressed in real terms applies:

$$AED_w = D_w = D_w1 + D_w2 \qquad (13)$$

This condition can also be expressed in nominal terms, that is:

$$AED = D = D1 + D2 \qquad (14)$$

It follows that the answer to the second question is that changes in consumption expenditure and investment spending are the principal causes of fluctuations in aggregate effective demand and the equilibrium volume of employment. This seemingly simple assertion in fact reveals a decisive difference between Keynes' model and the classical analysis. With Say's law the classicals concentrate on *saving* as the central independent variable, treating investment and consumption spending as dependent variables. Keynes argues, by contrast, that it is the positive decision of individuals to *spend* – either on consumption or investment goods (i.e. the moving forces of the system) which should be the proper focus of attention. The negative act of refraining from spending then becomes a residual in Keynes' model.

> Clearness of mind on this matter is best reached, perhaps, by thinking in terms of decisions to consume…rather than of decisions to save. A decision to consume or not to consume truly lies within the power of the individual; so does a decision to invest or not to invest. The amounts of aggregate income and of aggregate saving are the *results* of the free choices of individuals whether or not to consume and whether or not to invest…In accordance with this principle, the conception of the *propensity to consume* will, in what follows, take the place of the propensity or disposition to save.
>
> (Keynes, 2007, pp. 64–65; my emphasis)

The classical school neglects the propensity to consume and the inducement to invest; the former because it is a residual of decisions to save; the latter because of the doctrine of Say's law, which implies that what a community saves is, by definition, invested. The General Theory model should be thought of as an effort to generalise macroeconomic analysis by introducing an explicit treatment of what determines consumption and investment spending. This generalisation is examined in the next few chapters.

f) A causal map of the General Theory model – The story so far

It is possible to develop a causal map to illustrate the General Theory model which will be amended and updated throughout the rest of this book. Indeed two causal maps may be developed – one expressed in nominal values, the other in real terms measured in wage units. In the nominal map the ultimate independent variables so far are expected aggregate consumption spending (C), expected aggregate investment spending (I) and the wage unit (WU). The other independent variable is the aggregate supply relationship (ϕ), but this remains stable and only plays a passive role in the model.

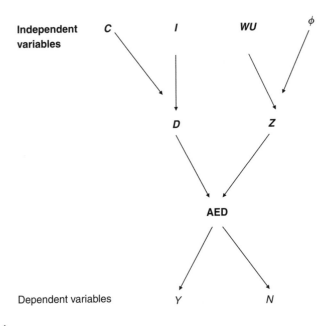

Map 4

Nominal aggregate consumption and investment spending determine the nominal aggregate demand price (D). The wage unit and the aggregate supply relationship specify the nominal aggregate supply price (Z). Where the aggregate demand price and the aggregate supply price are equal aggregate effective demand is determined (AED). The level of aggregate effective demand, in turn, determines the equilibrium values for the two dependent variables – aggregate income (Y) and the total employment of labour units (N).

In real terms the causal map is more straightfoward. It has real consumption expenditure (C_w) and real investment spending (I_w) as the ultimate independent variables; the other independent variable being the stable aggregate supply relationship (ϕ).

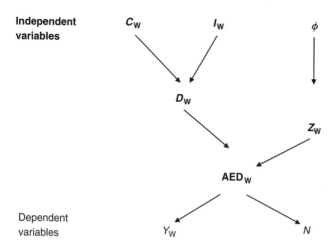

Map 5

The wage unit must be known so that nominal consumption and investment spending can be deflated. The combined total of C_w and I_w determines the real aggregate demand price (D_w). The aggregate supply relationship specifies the real aggregate supply price over a range of employment units (Z_w). Real aggregate effective demand (AED$_w$) is determined where D_w and Z_w are equal; and AED$_w$ defines the equilibrium values for real aggregate income (Y_w) and employment of labour units (N).

g) Summary

For each volume of employment the aggregate supply price specifies the expected proceeds from the sale of the associated output that will *just make it* worthwhile for entrepreneurs to offer that employment. Assuming the average and marginal productivity of labour units are equal, the value of the aggregate supply relationship (ϕ) is equal to unity. Having specified the value of ϕ, precise relationships between Z and N and Z_w and N can be derived. The real aggregate supply function is linear with a slope of unity *no matter how the wage unit fluctuates*.

For each volume of employment the aggregate demand price specifies what proceeds entrepreneurs *actually expect* to receive from the sale of each corresponding level of output. Keynes specifies an aggregate demand function which relates every level of employment to the expected proceeds from each associated level of output. An aggregate demand function can be derived in both nominal and real terms. The aggregate demand function has an unusual shape, which is due to the assumptions Keynes makes about the aggregate consumption function.

The volume of aggregate effective demand is determined by the intersection of the aggregate demand and supply functions. At this point the proceeds which entrepreneurs expect to receive from a volume of employment (D or D_w) equals the aggregate supply price of output (Z or Z_w, respectively). Aggregate effective demand determines an equilibrium volume of employment and the level of income, assuming the short-term expectations of entrepreneurs about revenues and costs are correct. There is no need for an aggregated labour market in the General Theory model.

The fundamental forces determining aggregate effective demand are the expected volumes of consumption expenditure and new investment spending. Consumption and investment are the moving forces in the model. Keynes' model is therefore fundamentally different to that of the classical school. The latter never identifies aggregate effective demand and treats both consumption and investment spending as residuals of saving.

Appendix A
Criticisms of Aggregate Effective Demand

Keynes' treatment of aggregate effective demand is not without its Post-Keynesian critics. One key concern relates to Keynes' specification of the aggregate supply function and especially how it deals with factor costs other than for labour. Another important difficulty with Keynes' aggregate supply function is its idiosyncratic treatment of entrepreneur's profits. Critics have questioned Keynes' claim that entrepreneurs maximise profits when the aggregate demand price and aggregate supply price (as he defines them) are equal.

The aggregate supply function revisited

The character of Keynes' aggregate supply function remains a controversial issue in the Keynesian literature, with many contributors offering varying interpretations on the subject – Patinkin (1982, 1989), Fusfeld (1985, 1989), S. Weintraub (1983), and Brady (1990). Broadly there are three main reasons for the uncertainty over the character of the function. First, some authors have not fully appreciated Keynes' assumptions underlying the homogeneous labour unit; in particular, that diminishing productivity is due to the greater inefficiency of the capital stock. Second, Keynes' acceptance of the first classical postulate has led to the erroneous idea that he also accepts the classical aggregated labour market analysis, and that the real wage rate determines the volume of employment.

Thirdly, and most importantly, critics claim Keynes' treatment of the aggregate supply function is less than comprehensive and contains inconsistencies. It is this latter point that needs to be examined further. The important passage where Keynes explains the gradient of the nominal and real aggregate supply functions is actually included as a footnote in the *General Theory*. The footnote reads as follows:

> let us take $Z_w = \phi(N)$, or alternatively $Z = W[U]\ \phi(N)$ as the aggregate supply function (where $W[U]$ is the wage unit and $W[U]$. $Z_w = Z$). Then, since the proceeds of the marginal product is equal to the marginal factor cost at every point on the aggregate supply curve, we have
>
> $$\Delta N = \Delta A_w - \Delta U_w = \Delta Z_w = \Delta\ \phi(N)$$
>
> that is to say that $\phi'(N) = 1$; provided that *factor cost bears a constant ratio to wage cost*, and that the aggregate supply function for each firm (the number of which is assumed to be constant) is independent of the number of men employed in other industries, so that the terms of the above equation, which hold good for each individual entrepreneur, can be summed for entrepreneurs as a whole.
>
> (Keynes, 2007, footnote pp. 55–56; my emphasis)

Having outlined the slope of the real aggregate supply curve, Keynes turns to the nominal aggregate supply function.

> This means that, if wages are constant *and other factor costs are a constant proportion of the wages-bill*, the aggregate supply function is linear with a slope given by the reciprocal of the money wage [in terms of the Z axis].
>
> (Keynes, 2007, footnote p. 56; my emphasis)

The first problem thrown up by the footnote is the existence of other factor costs – such as rent on land, raw material costs and loan repayments – and the impact on the aggregate supply function. Keynes claims that the nominal aggregate supply function is derived assuming a given wage unit and that "other factor costs are constant per unit of labour employed" (Keynes, 2007, p. 27). If however other factor costs change as employment varies, the slope of the nominal aggregate supply function is *not equal* to the reciprocal of the wage unit in terms of the Z axis (or the wage unit with respect to the N axis). More importantly, the slope of the *real* aggregate supply function is *not equal* to unity if other factor costs are included in the specification of the function.

A simple spreadsheet example can illustrate these points clearly – see Table 3.A1. This table is similar to Table 3.1 in Chapter 3, with the addition of other factor costs per labour unit (OFC); suppose that the wage

Table 3.A1   The aggregate supply functions – including other factor cost

N (millions)	WU £	OFC £	Z (£millions)	Z_w (millions)
0	10	5	0	0
1	10	5	15	1.5
2	10	5	30	3.0
3	10	5	45	4.5
4	10	5	60	6.0
5	10	5	75	7.5

unit is £10 and that other factor costs per labour unit are £5 (i.e. a stable ratio of wages to other factor costs of 1:0.5).

From this it can be seen that the slope of the nominal aggregate supply function is actually equal to the wage and other factor cost per labour unit, whilst the slope of the real aggregate supply curve is equal to the wage and other factor costs per labour unit divided by the wage unit.

What happens if the wage unit changes? With a stable ratio of wage to other factor costs of 1:0.5, if, say, the wage unit falls to £5, this means that the other factor costs per labour unit falls to £2.50. Table 3.A2 outlines the new relationship between Z and N and Z_w and N.

In comparison to the data in Table 3.A1 the slope of the nominal aggregate supply function falls, but it is still equal to the wage and other factor costs per labour unit. The real aggregate supply function however remains stable in response to a change in the wage unit. Interestingly Equations 1 and 2 from Section (c) in Chapter 3 can still be used to represent the aggregate supply functions, but the value of the aggregate supply relationship (ϕ) must be amended to take into account other factor costs.

Table 3.A2   The aggregate supply functions – lower wage unit and other factor cost

N(millions)	WU £	OFC £	Z (£millions)	Z_w (millions)
0	5	2.5	0	0
1	5	2.5	7.5	1.5
2	5	2.5	15.0	3.0
3	5	2.5	22.5	4.5
4	5	2.5	30.0	6.0
5	5	2.5	37.5	7.5

As long as the real aggregate supply function remains stable when the wage unit changes, no great damage is done to Keynes' contention that changes in the real value of the aggregate demand price dictate changes in real effective demand and employment. But if the ratio of wages to other factor costs does *not* remain stable, the real aggregate supply curve will shift in response to a change in the wage unit; and there is no obvious reason why as money wages change the payments to rentiers, that is landlords and bond holders, should change in exact proportion. Ironically it may well be that this does not undermine Keynes' argument that effective demand is liable to fluctuate, but reinforces it.

Profits and effective demand

Another important difficulty with Keynes' aggregate supply function has been identified by a leading mainstream Keynesian. Patinkin (1982) makes the claim that Keynes' treatment of both the aggregate supply function and the concept of effective demand are defective in that they deny the existence of profits. If this is the case it undermines Keynes' claim that entrepreneurs maximise profits at the intersection between the aggregate demand and supply functions.

Quite reasonably Patinkin suggests that a function which purports to show the proceeds (i.e. factor costs plus profits) which just induce entrepreneurs to offer a range of employment levels should include some required profit per labour unit. Keynes does not seem (at least explicitly) to include profits in the aggregate supply price, and some bizarre results follow. Take, for example, Keynes' real aggregate supply function (ϕ) and a given real aggregate demand function (F_w) – see Diagram 3.3. Where the two functions intersect real aggregate effective demand (AED_w^*) is defined, which, in turn, determines the equilibrium volume of employment N_*.

With the value of the aggregate supply relationship (ϕ) equal to unity, the aggregate supply function is represented by a 45° line. It follows that the volume of real effective demand measured in wage units *is equal* to the volume of employment measured in labour units. Furthermore, assuming that short-term expectations are correct, the volume of real effective demand is always equal to real income, that is:

$$AED_w^* = Y_w^* \tag{A1}$$

where $Y_w{}^*$ represents the equilibrium level of aggregate income measured in wage units. If $AED_w{}^*$ (measured in wage units) equals N_* (measured in labour units), it follows that:

$$Y_w{}^* = N_* \qquad (A2)$$

Note that the equilibrium wage and salary bill (E^*) is equal to the equilibrium volume of employment (N_*) multiplied by the wage unit, that is:

$$E^* = WU \times N^* \qquad (A3)$$

If both sides of Equation A2 are multiplied by the wage unit it can be shown that the equilibrium wage and salary bill (E^*) equals aggregate nominal income (Y^*); and, it follows, that the wage and salary bill measured in wage units ($E_w{}^*$) and real income ($Y_w{}^*$) are also equal. Hence:

$$Y^* = E^* \text{ and } Y_w{}^* = E_w{}^* \qquad (A4)$$

This suggests that, when short-term expectations are correct, entrepreneurs receive *zero profits* and rentiers receive *zero income*. Plainly in a capitalist economy this does not make sense.

These deficiencies can be overcome by explicitly introducing profit into the aggregate supply price. The method for introducing profit outlined by Weintraub (1983) will be used in what follows, rather than the approach of Patinkin (1982, pp. 131–132); Patinkin's method involves the dubious use of a Cobb–Douglas production function and the first classical postulate. Weintraub introduces profits into the aggregate supply function by means of a constant mark-up over wage costs (j). Therefore:

$$Z = j \times WU \times N \qquad (A5)$$

$$Z = j \times WU \times \phi(N) \qquad (A6)$$

Equation A5 may be rewritten to make it more compatible with Keynes' specification – see Equation A6, where the aggregate supply relationship (ϕ) has a stable value equal to unity. Although Weintraub does not do this, it is also possible to incorporate other factor costs per labour unit (OFC) into Equation A6 – see Equation A7. In the latter equation j^* can be said to represent the constant mark-up over *all* the factor costs.

Table 3.A3   The aggregate supply functions – including profit per labour unit

N(millions)	WU £	OFC £	PPN £	Z (millions)	Z_w (millions)
0	10	5	3	0	0
1	10	5	3	18	1.8
2	10	5	3	36	3.6
3	10	5	3	54	5.4
4	10	5	3	72	7.2
5	10	5	3	90	9.0

Moreover Equation A7 can be adapted to represent a real aggregate supply function by dividing both sides of the equation by the wage unit. Consequently Equation A8 can be derived:

$$Z = j^*[WU\phi(N) + OFC(N)] \qquad (A7)$$

$$Z_w = j^*[\phi(N) + OFC/WU(N)] \qquad (A8)$$

Table 3.A3 sets out a simple spreadsheet example to illustrate Equation A8. Say the wage unit is £10, other factor costs per labour unit are £5 (the ratio of wage to other factor costs being 1:0.5) and the value of j^* equals 1.2; this means that the profit per labour unit (PPN) is £3. Table 3.A3 considers the relationship between Z and N and Z_w and N in this case.

It can clearly be seen that the slope of the nominal aggregate supply function equals the sum of the wage, other factor costs and profit per labour unit; whilst the slope of the real aggregate supply function equals the wage, other factor costs and profit per labour unit divided by the wage unit. As before, if the wage unit changes and other factor costs and profits per labour unit change proportionately, the real aggregate supply function remains stable. With profit built into the aggregate supply functions a more realistic relationship between effective demand, income and employment can be developed.

This approach has an important advantage: it allows an explicit evaluation of the impact on the aggregate supply function of attempts to change in the distribution of income. For example, if the wage unit is reduced, whilst other factor costs and profits per labour unit remain unchanged, both the nominal and real aggregate supply functions will swivel (upwards and inwards). The overall impact on the value of effective demand then depends on *the relative movements* of the aggregate demand and supply functions.

It is now possible to consider Patinkin's final criticism of Keynes' concept of aggregate effective demand. For Keynes the point where the aggregate demand price and the aggregate supply price are equal defines the volume of employment at which entrepreneurs' expected profits are maximised. This means that at the point of intersection of the aggregate demand price and aggregate supply price entrepreneurs have no incentive to either increase or reduce the volume of labour units employed. Patinkin, however, notes that this cannot be correct. For if:

> the aggregate demand curve....is assumed to be perceived by entrepreneurs as a whole and represent their expected proceeds, then its intersection with the aggregate supply curve [as specified by Keynes]...is not the point at which "entrepreneurs' expectations of profits will be maximised"...Indeed, relative to other attainable points on this aggregate demand function, it is...the point of minimum profits.
>
> (Patinkin, 1982, p. 143)

To see this problem more clearly consider the details in Table 3.A4 below, which has figures for labour units (N), the real aggregate supply price (Z_w) and real aggregate demand price (D_w) at various employment levels. The real aggregate supply function is as specified by Keynes, with the value of ϕ equal to unity. The aggregate demand function is consistent with the character of the consumption function developed in Chapter 4, and a constant level of real investment spending equal to 10 million wage units.

According to Keynes the volume of real effective demand is 30 million wage units (i.e. where $D_w = Z_w$), which specifies the equilibrium volume

Table 3.A4 Aggregate effective demand?

N (millions)	Z_w (millions)	D_w (millions)
0	0	10
5	5	15
10	10	19
15	15	23
20	20	26
25	25	29
30	30	30
35	35	31

of employment at 30 million labour units. As previously noted, at this volume of employment the level of real income (30 million wage units) equals the total wage and salary bill measured in wage units (E_w i.e. E/WU) and no entrepreneurial profit exists. Indeed supposing expected profits are maximised at the point where the difference between D_w and Z_w is the greatest, this suggests profits are maximised anywhere between zero and 5 million labour units.

According to Patinkin this inconsistency in Keynes' argument can be resolved by minor changes in the aggregate demand and supply functions. The aggregate demand function needs to be redefined to represent the *actual aggregate proceeds* at different levels of employment, that is the actual sums of consumption and investment spending that are received by entrepreneurs from the sale of output of a given level of employment. The aggregate supply function is redefined to represent the aggregate supply price that entrepreneurs *expect to prevail* at different levels of employment. In terms of Table 3.A4 above, at an employment level of 5 million labour units, the actual aggregate proceeds (15 million wage units) exceed the *expected* aggregate supply price (5 million wage units) and entrepreneurs have an incentive to expand employment. This process continues until employment reaches 30 million labour units, when actual and expected proceeds are just equal. At this point, according to Patinkin, entrepreneurs have no further incentive to either increase or decrease employment.

Whether Patinkin's relatively minor changes are justifiable, and whether they properly resolve the problem identified, should be a matter for further discussion and debate within the economics profession. Certainly Patinkin's procedure seems to require Keynes' distinction between effective demand (i.e. the expected outcome) and aggregate income (i.e. the actual outcome) to be reviewed. Until more work is done in this area there is a rather unfortunate "black hole" in the General Theory model.

Appendix B
Post-Keynesian Comments on Keynes' Treatment of Short-Term Expectations

A topic that has preoccupied some Post-Keynesian economists is Keynes' treatment of the short-term expectations of entrepreneurs. When short-term expectations of entrepreneurs are correct the expected outcomes in terms of sales revenues and production costs are fulfilled in terms of realised results. Put another way, when short-term expectations are correct entrepreneurs experience neither windfall profits nor windfall losses.

The assumption of correct short-term expectations clearly distinguishes the method of the *General Theory* from that of the *Treatise on Money*. In the *Treatise* it is errors in short-term expectations that explain fluctuations in the volume of employment. This important point requires more elaboration. Amending the language of the *General Theory,* suppose that at a given actual volume of employment the realised sales revenue and the realised costs of production associated with that volume of employment differ from what entrepreneurs expected. There are two possibilities. First is that entrepreneurs enjoy windfall profits, where realised sales revenue is greater and/or realised costs of production are less than expected. Second is the situation where entrepreneurs suffer windfall loses, as realised sales revenue is less and/or costs of production are greater than expected. Windfall profits and losses cause the level of aggregate effective demand (i.e. the expected outcome) to diverge from aggregate income (i.e. the realised result). Inevitably errors in short-term expectations cause entrepreneurs to revise their decisions about the volumes of output produced and employment offered. Windfall profits cause entrepreneurs to upgrade their expectations and increase output and employment, whilst windfall losses do the reverse. This is in essence the approach of the *Treatise*.

Amadeo (1989) charts the development of Keynes' treatment of effective demand from the *Treatise* to the *General Theory*. In doing this he distinguishes between two versions of aggregate effective demand – the *supply* version and the *expenditure* version. The supply version focuses on entrepreneurs' knowledge of costs of production and expectations of demand to determine employment. Short-term expectations can be erroneous in the supply version and employment ultimately depends on decisions made by entrepreneurs. In the early development of effective demand Amadeo suggests that the supply version dominates Keynes' thinking and clearly it is consistent with the analysis of the *Treatise*.

By the time the *General Theory* is published the second dimension of effective demand – the expenditure version – dominates. The expenditure version assumes that short-term expectations are correct in which case expected and actual spending are identical. Hence *actual* consumption expenditure and *actual* fixed investment spending (linked through the multiplier) determine the volume of employment.

Amadeo argues that this shift from the supply version to the expenditure version of effective demand marks a retrograde analytical step in the *General Theory*. For by allowing erroneous short-term expectations the *Treatise* applies a *dynamic method* to examine changes in output and employment in disequilibrium positions. The analysis of how an economy moves *towards* an equilibrium position is the focus of attention. In the *General Theory* by contrast this dynamic method is discarded and replaced by a more conventional *static analysis* of comparative equilibrium positions.

Amadeo though overstates his case and gives insufficient attention to Keynes' main theoretical innovation with respect to expectations. It must be remembered, and indeed Amadeo accepts this point, that many other economists – Marshall, Robertson, Myrdal and Ohlin – and Keynes himself in the *Treatise*, had used mistaken short-term expectations (of various types and causes) to explain fluctuations in output and employment. In the *General Theory* Keynes offers something new to these contributions.

Specifically Keynes wants to explain why an economy moves from say a full employment equilibrium to a involuntary unemployment equilibrium position; hence *the focus is on why an economy moves from one equilibrium to another*, and not how it fluctuates around a given equilibrium position. To take this analytical step Keynes introduces a new type of expectation – *the state of long-term expectation* – into the General Theory model. For Keynes *short-period changes* in the state of long-term expectation is by far the most important cause of an economy moving from one to another equilibrium position. In order then that full attention is directed to long-term expectations in the General Theory model Keynes makes the reasonable simplifying assumption that short-term (or current) entrepreneurial expectations are correct. If this simplifying assumption is not made the purity of Keynes' message on long-term expectations is undoubtedly diluted.

This however should not imply that erroneous short-term expectations cannot be incorporated into the General Theory model. In this sense the Post-Keynesians are right to point out the need to further develop the General Theory model. This can be done quite easily, and if Keynes had not suffered from a debilitating heart attack in 1937 he would probably have done so. In an interesting postscript to the *General Theory* Keynes says he wishes he had treated short-term expectations differently. He claims that if he were to write the book again he would begin by outlining his theory with the assumption that short-term expectations are always fulfilled, and then subsequently relax this assumption to consider what would happen when short-term expectations are disappointed (Keynes, 1973c). Clearly this is an area for further development of the General Theory model.

4
The Propensity to Consume and the Multiplier

a) Introduction

From the time of Smith and Ricardo the classical school tends to view consumption in a negative light, even though it is by far the largest aggregate in total economic activity. From the classical perspective consumption spending is unproductive, acting as a fetter on the amount a community saves and invests, thereby retarding long-term economic growth. Having rejected Say's law Keynes is able to properly appreciate the central role of aggregate consumption expenditure in determining aggregate effective demand and employment. Keynes is the first mainstream economist to treat consumption spending as an ultimate independent variable. For Keynes this represents a pivotal break with the classical frame of reference.

Keynes provides a comprehensive theory to *explain* aggregate consumption expenditure. Central to Keynes' new theory is the concept of the propensity to consume. The propensity to consume is now a quite familiar idea, but at the time Keynes wrote the *General Theory* it struck many as new and interesting, perhaps even threatening. It allows Keynes in *one* simple equation to explain the *largest* aggregate in a macroeconomy – which must count as an act of genius.

Having identified the propensity to consume Keynes makes the small step to detect the marginal propensity to consume and with it the multiplier effect. Familiarity often causes the radical nature of multiplier to be overlooked. With a multiplier effect Keynes can show how changes in investment spending have an amplified influence on effective demand, output and employment. Moreover the multiplier effect proves that aggregate investment and saving are brought into equality by *changes in aggregate income*. If this is the case Keynes rightly points out that the classical loanable funds theory becomes surplus to requirements.

Section (b) sets out Keynes' theory of aggregate consumption. It begins with a precise definition of what constitutes consumption expenditure in a macroeconomy. It then considers the centre-piece of Keynes' theory of aggregate consumption, the fundamental psychological law referred to as the *propensity to consume* out of real income. From this Keynes develops the idea of a *consumption function*. Section (c) considers other factors – subjective, objective and habitual – which influence the value of propensity to consume. Section (d) derives the investment and employment multipliers and considers the strong complementary relationships between consumption and investment once the multiplier is taken into account. Finally the chapter considers the implications of Keynes' analysis for the propensity to save and aggregate saving – Section (e). This section considers the influence of interest rates on saving and demonstrates why the loanable funds theory is superfluous in the General Theory model.

b) A theory of aggregate consumption

To begin with it is important to be clear about what constitutes aggregate consumption expenditure in a macroeconomy. Having provided a definition of aggregate income (Y) made of up of the proceeds resulting from the sale of consumption and investment goods, Keynes has to find a way to distinguish between consumption expenditure and investment spending. Keynes solves this problem by arguing that once it is decided what constitutes the total sales made by one entrepreneur to another (i.e. $\Sigma\ A1$) what is left is by default consumption expenditure (C). Therefore consumption expenditure is defined in a negative way – it is the expenditure which is not made up of sales between entrepreneurs (i.e. $\Sigma A - A1$), where ΣA represents the total sales made during a time period and $\Sigma A1$ the total sales made between entrepreneurs. From this it is also possible to define aggregate saving (S), for it equals aggregate income (Y) minus consumption expenditure. In terms of a set of equations if:

$$Y = \Sigma(A - U)$$
$$\text{and } C = \Sigma(A - A1)$$
$$\text{then } S = \Sigma(A1 - U).$$

Having provided a clear definition of aggregate consumption Keynes provides a theory to determine the level of such spending. The centre-piece of Keynes' theory of aggregate consumption is what he calls a fundamental psychological law – *the propensity to consume*. This law allows him to derive a clear relationship between consumption spending and its dominant determinant, aggregate income measured in wage units.[1] In the short period, taking as given the tastes and habits of consumers and the broad structure of social classes and social interactions, Keynes specifies the concept of the propensity to consume in the following way.

> We will therefore define what we shall call the propensity to consume as the functional relationship χ between Y_w, a given level of income in terms of wage units, and C_w the expenditure on consumption out of that level of income, so that:
>
> $$C_w = \chi(Y_w) \text{ or } C = W[U] . \chi(Y_w)$$
>
> (Keynes 2007, p. 90)

To clarify, C_w denotes aggregate consumption spending deflated by the wage unit, C represents nominal aggregate consumption spending and Y_w refers to aggregate income measured in wage units. Remember that aggregate income is measured net of user cost. In what follows $C_w = \chi(Y_w)$ will be referred to as the real aggregate consumption function; and $C = WU \chi(Y_w)$ will be termed the nominal aggregate consumption function.

Given that aggregate consumption spending constitutes by far the largest single component of the aggregate demand price it is no surprise that Keynes claims that the propensity to consume (χ) is of the utmost importance and "absolutely fundamental to the theory of effective demand" (Keynes, 1973a, p. 120). Yet this psychological law contains within it an implicit assumption that as income levels move upwards a community's consumption spending will ratchet upwards in a deterministic way. Using the terminology of Katona (1960) the implicit assumption is that once the community has the *ability* to spend this will almost automatically create a *willingness* to spend. The distinction between the community's ability and willingness to spend is not something to which macroeconomists give a great deal of attention, but the distinction is further considered in the appendix to this chapter.

Keynes is aware that the consumption function should relate real consumption spending to the volume of labour units (N) – especially if it is to be consistent with the aggregate demand function mentioned in Chapter 3. But for various reasons (to be explored later) Keynes thinks relating consumption to real income has important advantages. The substitution of Y_w for N is possible because Keynes supposes that Y_w can be thought of as uniquely determined by N, in which case Y_w is an accurate and stable proxy for N.[2] This is a subject which is discussed again later in this section.

The part of aggregate consumption spending conducted by entrepreneurs is actually dependent on aggregate net income rather than aggregate income. Specifically entrepreneurs (and indeed public authorities) must deduct supplementary cost from their income before they decide how much to allocate to consumption expenditure. If, however, there is a stable relationship between aggregate income and net aggregate income it is legitimate to say Y_w is the main determinant of C_w. If circumstances are such that the relationship between aggregate income and aggregate net income changes this can then be said to cause of a variation in the propensity to consume. This subject is taken up again in the Section (c).

Keynes has some specific *a priori* views about the value of the propensity to consume which allow him to define the shape of his real aggregate consumption function. He begins by reasoning that a community which is relatively poor will tend to consume *all* of its real income up until some critical point of prosperity. After this point the community will gradually consume a *decreasing* proportion of any additional real income. The consumption function is illustrated in Diagram 4.1, with aggregate consumption measured in wage units (C_w) on the vertical axis and real income (Y_w) on the horizontal axis. Up until some critical

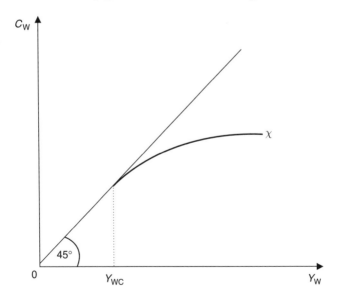

Diagram 4.1 The real consumption function

level of income, Y_{wc}, a community consumes all its available income that is $\chi = 1$. As aggregate income rises above Y_{wc} the community consumes a gradually falling proportion of real income *at the margin* that is the value of $\chi < 1$ and falling. The distinctive character of the consumption function explains the rather unusual shape of the aggregate demand function outlined in Chapter 3.

It is useful to comment on the values of the *marginal* and *average* propensities to consume in Keynes' consumption function. Up to the critical real income level (Y_{wc}) the marginal and average propensities to consume are both unity. After the critical point the values of the marginal and average propensities *both* decline; with the marginal propensity falling faster than the average propensity. Note, in a relatively poor community (experiencing relatively low levels of Y_w) the marginal propensity to consume will be near unity and the average propensity to consume will have a similar value. In comparison, in a wealthy community (experiencing relatively high levels of Y_w) the marginal propensity to consume will be much lower than unity, as too will be the average propensity. This analysis suggests that if a wealthy nation finds itself in equilibrium below full employment, it may find it difficult to alleviate the position. For if:

> the marginal propensity to consume falls off steadily as we approach full employment, it follows that it will become more and more troublesome to secure a further given increase in employment by further increasing investment.
>
> (Keynes, 2007, p. 127)

In part this explains a theme often repeated in the *General Theory*, that if both a relatively rich and a relatively poor nation are experiencing high levels of unemployment, the richer nation may find it more difficult to reach full employment than the poorer state. The possibility that richer nations may suffer more prolonged periods of high unemployment is what Keynes refers to as the "paradox of poverty in the midst of plenty" (Keynes, 2007, p. 30).

After the publication of the *General Theory* various efforts were made to test Keynes' hypotheses of a steadily declining marginal propensity to consume, but with little success. In the light of these failed efforts Keynes drops the rule, claiming for it the status of an *a priori* opinion that is not fundamental to the General Theory model. Subsequent followers of Keynes take his lead, and the declining marginal propensity to consume has been exorcised from the Keynesian literature. The benefits of such an approach are discussed in an appendix to this chapter. But given that the aim of this book is to act as a primer for the *General Theory* it is not permissible to ignore the rule of a declining marginal propensity to consume. Although this rule is not an essential part of Keynes' General Theory model, it is indispensable to fully appreciate the *General Theory* itself. The rule permeates the book, turning up at important parts of the analysis, and it will therefore be applied in the rest of this primer.

As noted earlier the consumption function Keynes outlines can be expressed in terms of labour units rather than real income. It will be useful for the discussion in Section (d) to define Keynes' consumption function in terms of labour units. First, it is important to understand Keynes' assumption that real income (Y_w) is *uniquely* determined by the volume of labour units (N). There is a clear relationship between N and Y_w which is defined by Keynes' real aggregate supply function (see Chapter 3); this suggests that, the equilibrium volume of employment measured in labour units will always equal the volume of real income measured in wage units.[3]

It should be clear then that the consumption function defined in terms of real income:

$$C_w = \chi(Y_w) \tag{1}$$

can also be expressed in terms of labour units as Equation 2:

$$C_w = \chi(N) \tag{2}$$

Indeed the two equations a largely interchangeable. From this it is possible to illustrate the consumption function in terms of labour units – see Diagram 4.2. The properties of this consumption function are the same as the function expressed in terms of real income illustrated in Diagram 4.1. The level of employment N_c is consistent with the critical income level Y_{wc}. Up to N_c the value of χ is unity, after which point the marginal propensity to consume diminishes.

c) Other influences on the propensity to consume

Although real income is the *main* determinant of aggregate consumption spending, it is by no means the sole influence. The other factors affecting aggregate consumption spending can be divided into *subjective*, *objective* and *habitual* influences. Changes in any of these other

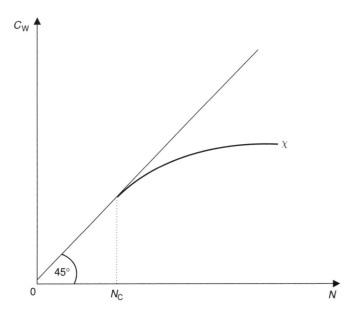

Diagram 4.2   The real consumption function – alternative version

factors will influence the propensity to consume of a community and each requires careful consideration.

Changes in subjective motivations to spend and save

In each society there are subjective motivations to consume (e.g. enjoyment, generosity, extravagance), and to refrain from consumption (e.g. precaution, improvement and avarice). These motivations will depend on the culture, beliefs, history and education of each society. The strengths of the motivations may be different in different societies, for example the strength of motivations to consume in the consumer-orientated USA may diverge from the corresponding motivations in, say, Myanmar. Overall, when the subjective motivations to spend strengthen, the propensity to consume of a community out of any given real income will increase and vice versa. Moreover when the subjective motivations to save strengthen, the propensity to consume will fall and vice versa. This may be represented in Diagram 4.3. Originally, with a given state of subjective motivations, the consumption function is consistent with $\chi 0$. If the subjective motivations to spend strengthen (or to save weaken) the consumption function swivels up to $\chi 1$; and when the motivations to spend weaken (or to save strengthen) it swivels to $\chi 2$.

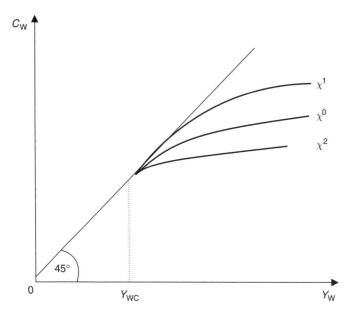

Diagram 4.3 Changes in subjective factors

In the General Theory model Keynes supposes that changes in subjective motives will only occur over long periods of time. When comparing, for example, consumption patterns in different countries over decades it may be an important factor. Actually Keynes thinks it unlikely that this factor will play a pivotal role in explaining short-period fluctuations in the propensity to consume.

Changes in objective factors

Keynes identifies five significant *objective* factors that can influence the value of the propensity to consume for any community. They are windfall changes in capital values, changes in the discount rate, changes in the wage unit and the distribution of income, changes in tax and benefit fiscal policy and changes in the relationship between aggregate income and aggregate net income. Each will be considered in turn.

1. Windfall changes in capital values. Keynes is aware that the proceeds to entrepreneurs are not only influenced by aggregate user and supplementary costs but also changes in the value of capital assets which for entrepreneurs are both *involuntary* and *unexpected*. These changes Keynes refers to as *windfall gains and losses* on the capital account, which because of their capricious character he does not include in his specification of Y_w. Windfall gains (losses) will tend to increase (decrease) consumption spending by entrepreneurs and the wealth-owning classes. These unforeseen variations in the real value of wealth can be said to change the value of the propensity to consume out of aggregate income; a windfall gain (loss) will increase (decrease) the propensity to consume above the critical level. Keynes thinks that this might be an important reason why the propensity to consume fluctuates in the short period, especially when stock markets are volatile.

2. Changes in the rate of discounting. A variation in the rate of discount incorporates both a change in the rate of interest and an expected future change in the price-level. Keynes allows the rate of interest to influence the propensity to consume, and hence the volume of aggregate consumption spending. On balance Keynes accepts that there is a negative relationship between the rate of interest and the propensity to consume. The main reason for this is that interest rate changes have an impact on the value of real wealth held by a community. Hence the propensity to consume is likely to be stronger with a low rate of interest than with a high interest rate. But Keynes is not convinced that the propensity to consume is particularly responsive to *small* changes in the rate of interest, though a notably large change may have a significant influence on consumption.

> There are not many people who will alter their way of living because the rate of interest has fallen from 5 to 4 per cent, if their aggregate income is the same as before ... [Therefore] ... the *short-period influence* of the rate of interest on individual spending out of a given income is secondary and relatively unimportant, except, perhaps, where unusually large changes are in question.
>
> (Keynes, 2007, p. 94; abridged quotation; my emphasis)

3. Changes in the wage unit and the distribution of income. Keynes accepts that poorer sections of the community will have a larger propensity to consume than more prosperous groups.[4] If the wage unit changes this may influence the distribution of income between workers and entrepreneurs, and between entrepreneurs and wealth-holding rentiers. It follows that if the wage unit falls (rises), the distribution of income will skew towards (away from) richer members of the community tending to lower (increase) the values of the propensity to consume above the critical income level. This subject is taken up again in Chapter 9 when examining the impact on employment of changes in the general level of money wages. For simplicity, apart from the distributional issue,

Keynes supposes that a change in the wage unit will have little influence on the propensity to consume because the latter is defined in terms of wage units (see Equation 1), a change in the wage unit will affect C_w and Y_w equally.[5]

4. Changes in Fiscal Policy. Keynes accepts that if taxation changes the distribution of income then it can influence the value of the propensity to consume in the same way as a change in the wage unit. Hence, if income is redistributed from rich to poor (e.g. via changing the tax on unearned income or profits or death duties etc.) the propensity to consume will be higher for real income above the critical level and vice versa. This issue is taken up again in Chapter 12 when examining the public policy implications of Keynes' analysis. Government current expenditure (e.g. on unemployment benefits, road sweeping, park maintenance etc.) which is financed by borrowing (what Keynes refers to as *loan expenditure*) influences the value of the propensity to consume as well. If such loan expenditure increases this will tend to raise the propensity to consume and vice versa.

5. Changes in aggregate income and aggregate net income. As noted earlier the propensity to consume of entrepreneurs depends on the level of aggregate *net* income rather than aggregate income. The difference between the two is supplementary cost (V) – see Chapter 3. Supplementary cost refers to involuntary changes in the value of capital equipment which are nevertheless expected. Entrepreneurs and public authorities can *set aside* an allowance (or financial provision) each year to cover these costs (which is called a sinking fund). If the annual financial provision is spent on the upkeep of the capital stock then effective demand is maintained by this current investment. If, however, entrepreneurs or public authorities increase the annual allowance set aside without increasing the spending on the upkeep of the capital stock a problem arises. For this money set aside is not available for either current investment *or* current consumption expenditure. In other words the allowance for supplementary cost is increased and aggregate net income falls, even though aggregate income remains unchanged. This means that the value of the propensity to consume must decline for levels of real aggregate income above the critical income level. Interestingly Keynes suggests that a fall in aggregate net income relative to aggregate income may have been a factor in the American slump of 1929–1933, due to the actions of entrepreneurs; and in the weak recovery in the mid-1930s in the United Kingdom, due to the actions of the State.

Changes in the propensity to consume due to variations in any of the objective factors above are illustrated in Diagram 4.4. In this diagram

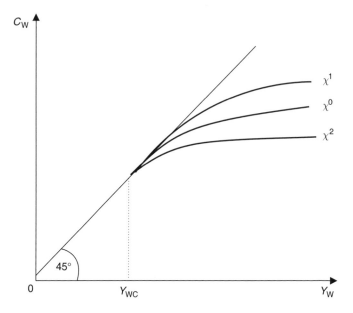

Diagram 4.4   Changes in objective factors

$\chi 0$ represents an initial consumption function before any change in the objective factors. The function will swivel up to say $\chi 1$ if there is a windfall increase in capital values; or a large reduction in the rate of interest; or an increase in the wage unit; or a change in tax which re-distributes income from rich to poor; or an increase in public current spending financed by borrowing.

Conversely the consumption function will swivel down to $\chi 2$ if there is a windfall reduction in capital values; or a large increase in the rate of interest; or a decrease in the wage unit; or a redistributory tax change to the advantage of the rich relative to the poor; or a reduction in public current spending financed by borrowing; or an increase in the difference between aggregate income and aggregate net income

Changes in habitual influences

The last significant factor that can influence the value of the propensity to consume according to Keynes is the *habits of consumers*. Keynes discusses the influence of consumer habits when discussing short-period *changes* in the level of real income. Keynes separates this discussion from his treatment of the more long-lasting psychological propensities (i.e.

the subjective motivations to spend and save) noted above. In the General Theory model changes in aggregate income can cause the value of the propensity to consume to fluctuate because the *habits* of consumers do not instantaneously adjust to the new circumstances.

> For a man's habitual standard of life usually has first claim on his income, and he is apt to save the difference which discovers itself between his actual income and the expense of his habitual standard; or, if he does adjust his expenditure to changes in his income, he will over short periods do so imperfectly. Thus a rising income will be accompanied by increased saving [i.e. a fall in the propensity to consume], and a falling income by decreased saving [i.e. a rise in the propensity to consume], on a greater scale *at first than subsequently*.
>
> (Keynes, 2007, p. 97; my emphasis)

If then the level of real income (Y_w) changes the initial propensity to consume will diverge from the value of what Keynes called the *habitual propensity to consume*. If, however, the change in income is sustained the habits of consumers will eventually adjust fully to the changed objective circumstances, and the propensity to consume will gravitate back towards its habitual value.

Keynes' argument can be illustrated in Diagram 4.5 above. At the original income Y_{w1} the habitual marginal propensity to consume is represented on the χ schedule by point A. Suppose that there is a short-period increase in income to Y_{w2}. The habitual marginal propensity compatible with Y_{w2} is again represented by the χ schedule, this time point B. However, because the consumption patterns of the community do not immediately change fully, the initial marginal propensity is lower and represented by point C. If the aggregate income level Y_{w2} is sustained eventually the consumption habits of the community will adjust fully, and the marginal propensity to consume will rise to point B, its habitual level. The habitual marginal propensity to consume is still lower at Y_{w2} than at Y_{w1}, but it is greater than the initial propensity to consume represented by point C.

All the subjective, objective and habitual factors which influence the propensity to consume defined in terms of real income also influence the propensity to consume defined in terms of labour units. Every shift in the consumption function defined in real income terms can alternatively be expressed as a shift in the consumption function defined in terms of labour units.

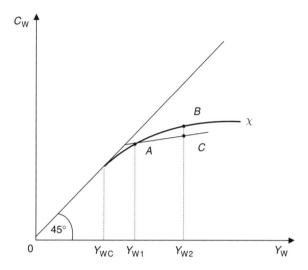

Diagram 4.5   The initial and habitual propensity to consume

Keynes usually assumes that the subjective, objective and habitual influences on the propensity to consume noted above are held constant, *cet. par.* This does not mean he ignores them, it merely allows him to concentrate on the dominant influence on the propensity to consume – the level of real income (and employment). With these other factors given, the propensity to consume is a reasonably stable function. This insight is very important for Keynes. It means that for any given level of real income (and employment), consumption expenditure will form the *stable and predictable* component of the aggregate demand price. Put another way Keynes thinks that consumption spending will *not* usually be the cause of sudden and violent economic disturbances in the short period.

d) The investment and employment multipliers

Keynes' analysis of the propensity to consume allows him to introduce the multiplier effect into the General Theory model. With it Keynes is able to identify the *complementary* and *precise* relationship between the propensity to consume and changes in investment spending on the one hand, and the change in real income and employment on the other. To incorporate the multiplier effect into his framework Keynes first identifies the concept of the *marginal* propensity to consume – that is the change in aggregate consumption for a small change in aggregate real income. In fact Keynes defines *two* multipliers – the *investment multiplier* and the *employment multiplier*.[6] The investment multiplier is derived in the following way. A change in aggregate income (ΔY_w) is equal to the change in expected consumption expenditure (ΔC_w) and the change in expected investment spending (ΔI_w) – see Equation 3.

$$\Delta Y_w = \Delta C_w + \Delta I_w \tag{3}$$

Revising Equation 1 above to consider a change in aggregate consumption spending (ΔC_w) Equation 4 can be derived.

$$\Delta C_w = \chi^* \Delta Y_w \tag{4}$$

where χ^* is the marginal propensity to consume that is dC_w/dY_w. Substituting Equation 4 into Equation 3 allows Equation 5 to be derived. Hence:

$$\Delta Y_w = \chi^* \Delta Y_w + \Delta I_w \tag{5}$$

Reworking Equation 5 to solve for ΔY_w allows the investment multiplier to be developed – see Equations 6 and 7.

$$(1 - \chi^*)\Delta Y_w = \Delta I_w \tag{6}$$

$$\Delta Y_w = \frac{1}{1 - \chi^*} \Delta I_w \tag{7}$$

The value of $1/1 - \chi^*$ is equal to the *investment multiplier* which can be denoted by the symbol *k*. Hence Equation 7 can be rewritten as:

$$\Delta Y_w = (k)(\Delta I_w) \tag{8}$$

The investment multiplier (*k*) shows "that, when there is an increment of aggregate investment, income will increase by an amount which is k times the increment of investment" (Keynes, 2007, p. 115). When the marginal propensity to consume and/or the level of investment spending fluctuate this multiplier defines *by how much* real income will change. Furthermore, Keynes, developing the work of Richard Kahn, outlines an employment multiplier. This concept is obviously related to the investment multiplier, for if investment spending and real income change so too must the employment of labour units. Keynes defines the employment multiplier as "the ratio of the increment of total employment which is associated with a given increment of.... employment in the investment industries" (Keynes, 2007, p. 116). In other words with a change in total employment of labour units denoted by ΔN, the change in employment of labour units in the investment industries (or 'primary' employment) denoted by ΔN_2 and the employment multiplier represented by k_1, the relationship between the change in N and the change in N_2 can be expressed as:

$$\Delta N = k_1(\Delta N_2) \qquad (9)$$

For ease of exposition Keynes assumes that the values of the investment multiplier (k) and the employment multiplier (k_1) are always equal. That said Keynes is aware of the circumstances where the values of the two multipliers will diverge. This occurs when the speed of response of employment in the consumption good sector differs from the employment response in the investment good industries. This subject is discussed again in Chapter 11.

In Section (b) above the *paradox of poverty in the midst of plenty* was mentioned, and with the multiplier analysis *one* source of the paradox can be fleshed out. Remember Keynes applies an *a priori* rule that there is a declining marginal propensity to consume as income rises towards the full employment level. Hence a rich nation (with a large Y_w) will have a lower marginal propensity to consume than a relatively poorer community (with a low Y_w). If this is the case the value of the multiplier associated with a given increase in investment spending will be *lower* in the richer economy than in the poorer country. The consequent rise in aggregate income and employment will also be that much smaller in the richer nation. Therefore unemployment in a richer country may be harder to alleviate than in a poorer country. This is not, however, the whole picture and a further amplification of the paradox is provided in Chapter 7.

Finally note that Keynes does not use the investment multiplier to calculate the relationship between *aggregate* investment and *aggregate* income. Nor does he use the employment multiplier to estimate the association between *total* primary employment and *total* employment. This seems a very strange omission as it is quite easy to do if the marginal propensity to consume is constant at all levels of Y_w. But Keynes applies his *a priori* rule of a declining marginal propensity to consume. Hence his multiplier analysis is restricted to estimating the *change* in aggregate income or aggregate employment for a given *change* in aggregate investment or primary employment, respectively. With a declining marginal propensity to consume calculating the relationship between aggregate investment and aggregate income or primary employment and total employment is possible but rather complicated.

With Say's law the classical school views consumption and investment as *substitutes*; higher consumption spending being associated with lower investment spending and vice versa. In the General Theory model, by contrast, Keynes sees consumption and investment spending as *complementary* activities. Keynes takes this position for at least three reasons.

1. The *greater* the marginal propensity to consume of a community, the *larger* the multiplier value associated with a specific change in the rate of investment spending.[7]
2. The multiplier demonstrates that aggregate income can be increased by higher investment spending, a rise in the marginal propensity to consume *or both combined together*. Indeed aggregate income will grow rapidly when *both* consumption and investment are increasing.
3. Only in the classical *special* case of a fully employed economy will additional investment spending be at the expense of current consumption expenditure. In the more general cases as outlined in the General Theory model additional consumption spending will actually bring forward new investment plans as existing capital equipment reaches its full capacity level more quickly.

e) The propensity to save

The analysis of the propensity to consume has implications for Keynes' attitude towards saving. He argues that once a community has made *positive* decisions about how much to consume, it makes another *negative* decision – the propensity to save. Furthermore, Keynes suggests that because real aggregate income is the dominant influence on consumption it must also be the dominant determinant of the residual saved. Keynes argues that:

> it is also obvious that a higher absolute level of income will tend, as a rule, to widen the gap between income and consumption . . . we take it as a fundamental psychological rule of any modern community that, when its real income is increased, it will not increase its consumption by an equal absolute amount, so that a greater absolute amount must be saved . . .
>
> (Keynes, 2007, p. 97; abridged quotation)

Based on this analysis of consumption a real aggregate saving function may be derived. The equation can be expressed as follows:

$$S_w = \rho Y_w \tag{10}$$

In Equation 10 S_w stands for the volume of aggregate saving measured in wage units and ρ represents the propensity to save. It is important to appreciate that this function determines the level of aggregate saving ex post, as Keynes (1973c) claims an ex ante saving function makes no sense because aggregate saving is a residual (or a dependent variable) in the General Theory model. This ex post savings function is derived from the real consumption function derived above, with the value of $\rho = 1 - \chi$. Therefore up to the critical income level the value of ρ is zero; but after that point the propensity to save rises as the propensity to consume diminishes, whilst maintaining the condition that the sum of the marginal propensities to consume and save always equal unity. An ex post function for nominal aggregate saving function can easily be derived by multiplying both sides of Equation 10 by the wage unit to develop Equation 11:-

$$S = WU. \, \rho(Y_w) \tag{11}$$

In this equation S is nominal aggregate saving and WU is the wage unit and ρ is the propensity to save.

The real savings function is represented in Diagram 4.6. Notice how up to the critical income level (Y_{wc}) the community does not save any income as the propensity to consume equals unity. After this point as the level of real income increases the community saves a *proportionately larger* share of aggregate income, mirroring the declining propensity to

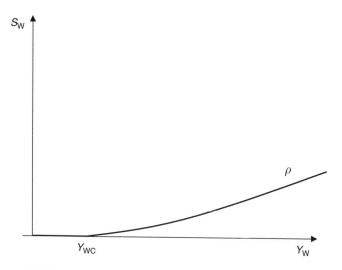

Diagram 4.6   The real aggregate savings function

consume noted above and represented in Diagram 4.1. A similar savings diagram relating real saving to labour units (mirroring Diagram 4.2) can also be derived when needed.

In the General Theory model the level of aggregate saving is determined in a different manner to that suggested by the classical school. According to Keynes proposing that the volume of aggregate saving is positively related to the level of aggregate income marks an essential difference between the General Theory model and the classical analysis. Furthermore, the propensity to save and aggregate saving are clearly *dependent* variables in Keynes' theory. This is the exact opposite of the classical approach where saving is a key independent variable. It is important to be absolutely clear about the role of saving in Keynes' model – for it is very different from the classical perspective. In Keynes' model:

An act of individual saving means – so to speak – a decision not to have dinner today. But it does *not* necessitate a decision to have dinner or to buy a pair of boots a week hence or a year hence, or to consume any specified thing at any specified date. Thus it depresses the business of preparing for today's dinner without stimulating the business of making ready for some future act of consumption.

(Keynes, 2007, p. 210; Keynes' emphasis)

An act of saving does not imply a simple choice between consumption today and consumption tomorrow. Accumulated saving can, of course, fund future consumption spending, but this will be spending on an *unspecified* volume of *undesignated* products at an *indeterminate* time in the future, perhaps (with transfers of wealth between generations) not even by the decision-maker who does the saving in the first place.[8] Hence it is not possible for an entrepreneur to interpret an act of saving today as stimulating a definite act of consumption in the next time period, *and they do not do so*. Therefore for Keynes it is better to think of an act of saving not as being the substitution of present for future consumption, but as the *desire for wealth*, which can potentially be spent on an unspecified consumer product at an unspecified future date. The role of saving as a desire for wealth and its impact on the inducement to invest are subjects taken up again in Chapter 7.

It is now possible to clearly distinguish Keynes' treatment of the influence of changes in the rate of interest on consumption and saving, from that of the classical school. The classics reason that aggregate saving is a *positive* function of the rate of interest. As a corollary of this they presume that the volume of consumption expenditure is *negatively* related to the interest rate. It might be thought that because Keynes argues real income is the dominant influence on the volume of consumption and saving, that neither will be influenced by the rate of interest. Nothing is further from the truth.

> [T]he contention that consumption expenditure is a function of income] does not mean that changes in the rate of interest have only a small influence on the amounts *actually* saved and consumed. Quite the contrary. The influence of changes in the rate of interest on the amount actually saved is of paramount importance, but *is in the opposite direction* to that usually supposed [by the classical school].
>
> (Keynes, 2007, p. 110; Keynes' emphasis)

How does Keynes reach this conclusion? In the General Theory model aggregate investment spending and consumption expenditure *determine* the level of effective demand and income, and, hence, the volume of aggregate saving. Moreover investment spending is negatively related to the rate of interest (see Chapter 7). From this perspective:

> aggregate saving is governed by aggregate investment; a rise in the rate of interest...will diminish investment; hence a rise in the rate of interest must have the effect of reducing incomes to a level where

saving is decreased in the same measure as investment. Since incomes will decrease by a greater absolute amount than investment [due to the investment multiplier], it is, indeed, true that, when the rate of interest rises, the rate of consumption will decrease. But this does not mean that there will be a wider margin for saving. On the contrary saving and spending will *both* decrease.

(Keynes, 2007, pp. 110–111; Keynes' emphasis)

In correspondence with Kaldor after the publication of the *General Theory*, Keynes puts his argument on this point even more explicitly in terms of a fall in the interest rate.

My *normal assumption is that dS/dr is negative*. This is not inconsistent with my admitting that a fall in the rate of interest may increase the propensity to consume, though the effect of changes in the rate of interest on the propensity to consume is not a matter on which I state a definite view. The point is that a reduction in the rate of interest, whether or not it increases the propensity to consume out of a given income, increases the absolute amount of savings owing to its effect on the amount of income through the stimulus of investment...But a state of affairs in which dS/dr is *positive* would, on my argument, be extremely unusual and paradoxical.

(Keynes, 1973g, p. 243; my emphasis).

The association that Keynes identifies between interest rates and saving marks a clear difference between the General Theory model and the classical analysis. To reinforce the point the *negative* relationship between the rate of interest and the aggregate volume of saving in Keynes' model is represented in Diagram 4.7. The rate of interest (r) is on the vertical axis and real aggregate saving (S_w) is on the horizontal axis.

Once the level of income is allowed to vary, the relationship between the volume of saving and the rate of interest is the opposite of that suggested by the classical school in the loanable funds theory of the rate of interest. The General Theory model of consumption and the multiplier also has other implications for the classical loanable funds theory. In Keynes' model it is the level of aggregate *income* which guarantees the equality of aggregate saving and investment. It is aggregate income which is the equilibrating factor, not the rate of interest as the classical school suggests. Keynes' argument that income is the equilibrating factor between saving and investment is reinforced by the multiplier concept. The investment multiplier suggests that changes in investment spending will

Rate of interest (*r*)

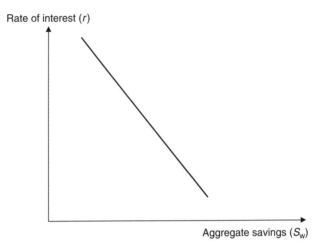

Aggregate savings (*S*_w)

Diagram 4.7   Interest rates and savings – Keynes' view

cause variations in aggregate income that result in an ex post change in aggregate saving that is just equal to the initial change in investment. As a consequence in the General Theory model the classical loanable funds theory is *surplus to requirements*. One of the main limitations of mainstream Keynesianism has been its failure to properly appreciate this point and renounce the loanable funds market.

f) Summary

Keynes analyses the motivations behind aggregate consumption through the propensity to consume. This suggests that real aggregate income is the dominant influence on consumption, although it is also affected by other factors – subjective, objective and habitual. The marginal propensity to consume can be used to derive the multipliers – both for investment and employment. These concepts define precise relationships between the marginal propensity to consume and the *change* in aggregate investment and primary employment on the one hand and the *change* in real income and total employment on the other. Building on the multipliers, Keynes' analysis suggests a number of complimentary relationships exist between consumption and investment spending. Keynes rejects the classical view of a crude conflict between the desires to consume and invest.

The positive decision to consume implies a negative decision to save. Therefore the value of the propensity to consume determines the propensity to save. Just as with consumption, aggregate income is the dominant influence on aggregate saving. The rate of interest influences the volumes of consumption and saving. With consumption the direction of influence is the same as that suggested by the classicals; with aggregate saving the influence is the *opposite* of that outlined by the classics. Keynes' theory of consumption and the multiplier suggests that the classical loanable funds theory of interest is surplus to requirements.

Appendix
Some Comments on Keynes' Treatment of the Propensity to Consume

It can be conjectured that a gradually falling marginal propensity to consume (χ^*) is not an essential part of Keynes' consumption function. It can be removed with little harm to the central thesis that consumption spending is primarily a stable function of the level of real income and that the value of χ^* is less than one. Hence Keynes suggests that:

> [There are reasons which] will lead, as a rule, to a greater proportion of income being saved as income increases. *But whether or not a greater proportion is saved*, we take it as a fundamental psychological rule of any modern community that, when its real income is increased, it will not increase its consumption by an equal absolute amount...
>
> (Keynes, 2007, p. 97; my emphasis)

This argument can be illustrated in Diagram 4.A1 below. For all levels of income above Y_{wc} the consumption function is a straight line, implying a *constant* habitual marginal propensity to consume after the critical income level. If the value of χ^* does not gradually decline Keynes' argument is strengthened by simplification.

One additional simplification is to suppose that the marginal propensity to consume is constant for *all* levels of real income. This means that at levels of income below Y_{wc} the marginal propensity to consume is constant but less than unity. Certainly this approach is used by the most influential interpreters of Keynes' analysis, such as Klein, Hansen and Dillard.

Assuming a constant marginal propensity to consume allows the application of Keynes' investment and employment multipliers to be widened. For the investment multiplier can be used to define the relationship between aggregate investment and aggregate income and the

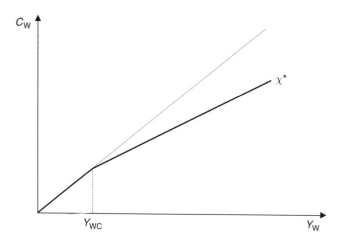

Diagram 4.A1   The real consumption function – a different perspective

employment multiplier is able to specify the association between total primary employment and total employment. In addition this treatment of consumption has implications for the analysis of saving. If the value of the propensity to consume is stable after the critical income level so too will the propensity save. In addition this approach changes the shape of the aggregate demand function, and, consequently, the analysis of aggregate effective demand. All these suggestions have no adverse implications; indeed they are beneficial by simplifying Keynes' model and making it more generally applicable.

There is however another rather more significant, yet rarely mentioned, omission in Keynes' analysis of the propensity to consume. This relates to his implicit assumption within the fundamental psychological law that *a community's ability to spend determines its willingness to spend*. This way of framing the issue is first set out by Katona (1960) who claims that just because a community has the ability to spend does not necessarily mean they will be willing to do so. Interestingly Keynes accepts that having a greater ability to spend does not necessarily lead to a steady increase in expenditure, especially as the prosperity of a community rises and the essentials of life are all met. As noted earlier Keynes recognises the possibility that the marginal propensity to consume will diminish as aggregate income rises. Moreover he accepts that when there are short-period changes in the level of aggregate income the community's initial marginal propensity to consume may be lower than its habitual propensity. The issue Keynes does not address is why do increasingly affluent people keep spending more as their incomes rise and the essentials of life are all more than satisfied.

Galbraith (1972) is the best-known economist to address the issue by looking at the ways corporations seek to persuade consumers to buy more, using advertising and other techniques to perpetually ratchet up tastes and habits for spending. Perhaps the most interesting contribution is that of Potter (1973) who claims that in an era of material abundance enjoyed in post-Second World War North America, the economic problem becomes how to convince the most affluent people in the world to keep spending on an ever-expanding scale to utilise the huge productive forces of American industry. Put another way Potter recognises that in an era of abundance:

> the productive capacity can supply new kinds of goods faster than society in the mass learns to crave these goods or regards them as necessities. If this new capacity is to be used, the imperative must fall upon consumption, and society must be adjusted to a new set of drives and values in which *consumption is paramount.*
>
> (Potter, 1973, p. 173; emphasis added)

Potter claims that an institution of advertising – whose purpose is to promote spending – spontaneously emerges in an era of abundance to address the problem. The institution of advertising is the social force that gives priority to consumption, by adjusting the drives and values (i.e. the tastes and habits) of Americans to make them consistent with abundant consumption. In the process the marginal propensity to consume does not decline, but is stabilised as aggregate income rises.

More recently two contemporary economists, Petrick and Sheehan (2004), have taken up the issue not just for America but for what they refer to as the system of abundance. The promotion of ever greater spending by the globally affluent is spontaneously promoted by what they call an institution of marketing. In broad terms the institution of marketing is:

> a gigantic, global economic network of diverse groupings whose overarching purpose is to give priority to consumption. The institution straddles all sectors of an economy – private, public and not for profit. The institution embraces, directly and indirectly, intentionally and unintentionally, in whole or in part, a multitude of corporations, media, agencies and talented professionals. Its "output" is the communication of a glut of commercial messages to buyers that are

partial rather than neutral, and convincing rather than balanced. But whatever the unique characteristics of the vast array of very different commercial messages, they all share one common purpose: they are intended to persuade buyers to spend more, both in volume and value terms.

(Petrick and Sheehan, 2004, p. 4)

In the realm of consumption the institution focuses its glut of commercial messages at consumers in order to persuade them to keep buying more. A by-product of the work of the institution is to spontaneously stabilise the marginal propensity to consume as aggregate income rises. Put another way the institution encourages consumers to be willing to spend as their ability to spend increases.

Incorporating the concept of the institution of marketing into the General Theory offers no insuperable problems. Indeed it greatly enhances Keynes' analysis of effective demand and is entirely consistent with his rejection of Say's law. It does however raise an issue about demand management. The institution of marketing at the macroeconomic level acts as a spontaneous demand manager. It perpetually ratchets up consumer spending, increasing prospective yields on assets and strengthening the inducement to invest.

In affluent nations demand management is predominantly concerned about containing the growth of effective demand due to rising consumer spending (often financed by greater debt). On the rare occasions when an abundant capitalist economy moves into recession the constraints on spending intensify – lower incomes, higher interest rates – causing consumption to dip. But the persuasive messaging of the institution does not cease. This encouragement to spend helps mitigate the recession. And when some of the constraints on spending are released (say due to lowered interest rates), there exists a significant backlog of pent-up spending intentions. This causes consumer spending to rebound quickly, leading the economy out of recession. Keynesians who ignore the pivotal role of the institution as a spontaneous demand manager tend to overestimate the fears of permanent recession and underestimate the inflationary threat of permanently cheap money.

5
Consumption and Effective Demand

a) Introduction

This chapter will explain how the consumption function underpins the derivation of aggregate effective demand in the General Theory model. The purpose is to make clear the connections between the materials in Chapters 3 and 4. Keynes alludes to these linkages in the *General Theory* but does not amplify them. The chapter will demonstrate that, given the level of aggregate investment spending, the value of the propensity to consume determines effective demand; it highlights the way in which changes in the propensity to consume influences the level of effective demand, and hence the volumes of employment, income and saving. The forces that determine investment spending and cause it to fluctuate are discussed in the forthcoming Chapters 6, 7 and 8.

Section (b) examines the ways real consumption function helps to specify the real aggregate demand function, and how changes in the propensity to consume influence the real aggregate demand price. Section (c) examines the relationship between the real consumption function and the levels of real aggregate effective demand. Section (d) outlines Keynes' famous concept of the *Paradox of Thrift*. Finally, Section (e) provides a causal map of the General Theory model to date. An appendix to this chapter considers the under-consumptionist theories of deficient demand, which can be seen as a special case of the General Theory model.

b) Consumption and the aggregate demand function

It is important to explain how the real consumption function [i.e. $C_w = \chi(Y_w)$ or $C_w = \chi(N)$] derived in Chapter 4 can be used to derive a real aggregate demand function [i.e. $D_w = F_w(N)$] defined in Chapter 3.

Table 5.1 Consumption, aggregate demand prices and aggregate income

Y_w (mills)	0	1	2	3	4	5	6
χ^*		1.0	1.0	0.9	0.9	0.7	0.5	0.5
C_w (mills)	0.0	1.0	1.9	2.8	3.5	4.0	4.5
I_w (mills)	1.0	1.0	1.0	1.0	1.0	1.0	1.0
D_w (mills)	1.0	2.0	2.9	3.8	4.5	5.0	5.5

Consider the following simple spreadsheet example set out in Table 5.1 which shows real expected consumption spending by a community (C_w), at a range of real income (Y_w) levels. The critical income level (Y_{wc}) is assumed to be 1 million wage units; up to that point the marginal propensity to consume (χ^*) is equal to unity.

After the critical income level the marginal propensity to consume diminishes in value. Consequently in Table 5.1 as aggregate income rises from 1 million wage units up to 3 million the marginal propensity to consume has a value of 0.9. This means that when aggregate income rises from 1 million to 2 million wage units aggregate consumption increases by 0.9 million units, and by the same amount as income rises from 2 million to 3 million units. When aggregate income rises from 3 million to 4 million units the marginal propensity to consume falls to 0.7, and consumption rises by 0.7 million units. Finally, when aggregate income rises above 4 million units up to 6 million units the marginal propensity declines to 0.5; consumption increases by 0.5 million units for each 1 million increase in aggregate income. To determine the aggregate demand price the expected real volume of fixed investment spending (I_w) must be specified; it is assumed that it has a constant value of 1 million wage units. Expected real consumption (C_w) plus expected investment spending determine the real aggregate demand price (D_w) at a range of real income levels.

In Table 5.1 it can be clearly seen that as real income varies, the change in aggregate demand price is specified by the marginal propensity to consume. This example can be illustrated by Diagram 5.1. The real aggregate demand price (D_w) is on the vertical axis, and real aggregate income (Y_w) is on the horizontal axis. The constant level of investment spending is represented by a horizontal dashed line.

On top of the dashed investment line is added the consumption function from Table 5.1. The two curves combined determine a function (F_{w0}) outlining real aggregate demand prices at a range of real income levels. Note, after the critical income level the marginal propensity to

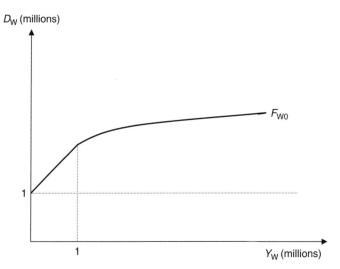

Diagram 5.1   The real aggregate demand function

consume, and, hence, the slope of the real aggregate demand function, begins to diminish. The problem with this aggregate demand function, however, is that it does not relate to labour units. It therefore needs to be amended. But this is not a great problem. Chapter 4 demonstrated that the consumption function relating to real income is interchangeable with the consumption function relating to labour units $[C_w = \chi(Y_w) = \chi(N)]$.

Table 5.2 is constructed showing the marginal propensity to consume (χ^*), real consumption spending (C_w), real investment spending (I_w) and the real aggregate demand price (D_w) for a range of employment units (N). The figures are identical to those used in Table 5.1 apart from the fact that employment is measured in millions of labour units. The critical employment level (N_c) is assumed to be 1 million labour units.

Table 5.2   Consumption, aggregate demand prices and employment

N (mills)	0	1	2	3	4	5	6
χ^*	1.0	1.0	0.9	0.9	0.7	0.5	0.5
C_w (mills)	0.0	1.0	1.9	2.8	3.5	4.0	4.5
I_w (mills)	1.0	1.0	1.0	1.0	1.0	1.0	1.0
D_w (mills)	1.0	2.0	2.9	3.8	4.5	5.0	5.5

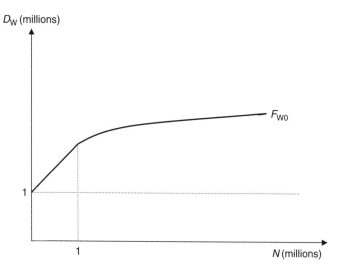

Diagram 5.2 The real aggregate demand function – alternative version

Note that in Table 5.2 as employment varies the change in the aggregate demand price is specified by the marginal propensity to consume. The information contained in Table 5.2 is illustrated in Diagram 5.2. On the vertical axis is the real aggregate demand price (D_w) and on the horizontal axis are labour units (N).

Real aggregate fixed investment spending is represented by a horizontal dashed line as before and to this is added the real consumption function relating to labour units. The two combined derive a function F_{w0} specifying real aggregate demand prices at a range of employment levels. Note that after the critical employment level, the marginal propensity to consume and hence the slope of the real aggregate demand function begin to diminish.

It follows that if any of the subjective or objective factors, which are assumed to be constant when deriving a consumption function, change this will have an impact on the aggregate demand function. Consider the information in Table 5.3 – which outlines three cases. In each case suppose that real investment spending is 1 million wage units and the critical employment level is 1 million labour units.

Case 1 replicates the information in Table 5.2 to represent an initial aggregate demand function. In Case 2 the marginal propensity to consume rises at all employment levels above N_c. As the volume of employment rises from 1 million labour units up to 3 million the

Table 5.3   Changing subjective or objective factors

	N (mills)	χ*	C_w (mills)	I_w (mills)	D_w (mills)
Case 1					
	0	1.0	0.0	1.0	1.0
	1	1.0	1.0	1.0	2.0
	2	0.9	1.9	1.0	2.9
	3	0.9	2.8	1.0	3.8
	4	0.7	3.5	1.0	4.5
	5	0.5	4.0	1.0	5.0
	6	0.5	4.5	1.0	5.5
Case 2					
	0	1.0	0.0	1.0	1.0
	1	1.0	1.0	1.0	2.0
	2	0.95	1.95	1.0	2.95
	3	0.95	2.9	1.0	3.9
	4	0.9	3.8	1.0	4.8
	5	0.6	4.4	1.0	5.4
	6	0.6	5.0	1.0	6.0
Case 3					
	0	1.0	0.0	1.0	1.0
	1	1.0	1.0	1.0	2.0
	2	0.8	1.8	1.0	2.8
	3	0.65	2.45	1.0	3.45
	4	0.55	3.0	1.0	4.0
	5	0.4	3.4	1.0	4.4
	6	0.4	3.8	1.0	4.8

marginal propensity to consume now has a value of 0.95. Between employment levels of 3 million and 4 million units the marginal propensity to consume is 0.9. When employment levels are between 4 million units and 6 million units the marginal propensity has a value of 0.6. In Case 3 the marginal propensity to consume falls at all employment levels above N_c. As employment levels rise from 1 million labour units up to 2 million units the marginal propensity to consume has a value of 0.8. When aggregate employment is between 2 million and 3 million units the marginal propensity is just 0.65. With employment levels ranging from 3 million to 4 million units the marginal propensity is 0.55. Finally, when employment rises above 4 million up to 6 million units the marginal propensity is as low as 0.4.

These numerical examples demonstrate that an increase in the propensity to consume will raise the aggregate demand price after the critical employment level and vice versa. These three cases are illustrated in Diagram 5.3 below. Initially real aggregate demand prices

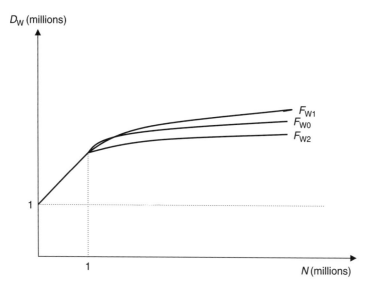

Diagram 5.3 Changes in the aggregate demand function

are illustrated by the F_{w0} function (Case 1). If any subjective or objective factors change such as to cause the real consumption function to swivel upwards, then the real aggregate demand function will swivel upwards after N_c – to F_{w1} (Case 2). Conversely, if any subjective or objective factors change such as to cause the real consumption function to swivel downwards, the real aggregate demand function swivels downward after N_c – to F_{w2} (Case 3). From this analysis it can be seen that once the values for the propensity to consume at each employment (or real income) are known, and expected real investment spending is specified, the aggregate demand price can be determined for each employment (and real income) level.

The nominal consumption function [i.e. $C = WU \; \chi(Y_w)$ or $C = WU \cdot \chi(N)$] defined in Chapter 4, can be used to derive the nominal aggregate demand function [i.e. $D = F(N)$] outlined in Chapter 3. Consider Table 5.4 which shows the same figures as those used in Tables 5.1 and 5.2. This time a range of real income (Y_w) and employment (N) levels are considered together. Moreover it is necessary to set the level of the wage unit. Suppose the wage unit paid to each unit of labour is £10. To complete Table 5.4, an additional four columns are included: the wage unit (WU), nominal expected consumption spending (C), nominal expected investment expenditure (I) and the nominal aggregate demand

Table 5.4 Consumption and nominal aggregate demand prices

N (mills)	0	1	2	3	4	5	6
Y_w (mills)	0	1	2	3	4	5	6
χ^*	1.0	1.0	0.9	0.9	0.7	0.5	0.5
C_w (mills)	0.0	1.0	1.9	2.8	3.5	4.0	4.5
I_w (mills)	1.0	1.0	1.0	1.0	1.0	1.0	1.0
D_w (mills)	1.0	2.0	2.9	3.8	4.5	5.0	5.5
WU £	10	10	10	10	10	10	10
C £mills	0	10	19	28	35	40	45
I £mills	10	10	10	10	10	10	10
D £mills	10	20	29	38	45	50	55

price (D), all measured in sterling. Investment spending is assumed to be set at £10 million (1 million wage units multiplied by £10) for all levels of income and employment. The inquisitive reader can construct a diagram to illustrate the nominal aggregate demand function from this table either for different volumes of Y_w or N. Of course there is no reason why in the General Theory model the wage unit cannot change. Clearly if the wage unit does vary in value then the nominal aggregate demand function will shift its position.

c) The consumption function and aggregate effective demand

It is now possible to outline the relationship between the propensity to consume and the real volume of aggregate effective demand, that is where $D_w = Z_w$. To do this Keynes' real aggregate supply function must be included in the analysis. This means amending Table 5.4 to include values for the real aggregate supply price (Z_w) over a range of real income and employment levels. Remember from Chapter 3 that the value of the aggregate supply relationship (ø) is always unity. This means that the real aggregate supply price function has a slope of one (that is a 45° line); therefore the value of Z_w (measured in wage units) can be equated with the volume of N (measured in labour units).

The amended information is shown in Table 5.5; aggregate investment spending is assumed to be constant at 1 million wage units; the critical income level is 1 million wage units; and the critical employment level is 1 million labour units. Table 5.5 also includes data relating to the values of the aggregate demand and supply prices measured in nominal terms (i.e. D and Z), assuming the wage unit is £10 per labour

Table 5.5 Consumption and aggregate effective demand

N (mills)	0	1	2	3	4	5	6
Y_w (mills)	0	1	2	3	4	5	6
χ^*	1.0	1.0	0.9	0.9	0.7	0.5	0.5
C_w (mills)	0.0	1.0	1.9	2.8	3.5	4.0	4.5
I_w (mills)	1.0	1.0	1.0	1.0	1.0	1.0	1.0
D_w (mills)	1.0	2.0	2.9	3.8	4.5	5.0	5.5
Z_w (mills)	0.0	1.0	2.0	3.0	4.0	5.0	6.0
WU £	10	10	10	10	10	10	10
C £mills	0	10	19	28	35	40	45
I £mills	10	10	10	10	10	10	10
D £mills	10	20	29	38	45	50	55
Z £mills	0	10	20	30	40	50	60

unit. The inquisitive reader should note that the value of Z is equal to $Z_w \times WU$ or $WU \times \phi \times N$.

Aggregate effective demand is defined at the volume of employment where the aggregate demand price equals the aggregate supply price (i.e. $D = Z$ or $D_w = Z_w$). On these figures, with a given real level of investment and a stable consumption function, the equilibrium volume of aggregate effective demand measured in wage units is 5 million, the equilibrium value of nominal aggregate effective demand is £50 million and the equilibrium level of employment is 5 million labour units.

The information in Table 5.5 is illustrated in Diagrams 5.4a and 5.4b. Diagram 5.4a has the real aggregate demand price (D_w), the real aggregate supply price (Z_w) and the real effective demand (AED_w) on the vertical axis, whilst the horizontal axis shows units of employment. With a given volume of real investment and a stable real consumption function, a real aggregate demand function (F_{w0}) is defined; the real aggregate supply function (ϕ) is represented by a 45° line. Where the two functions intersect both real aggregate effective demand (5 million wage units) and equilibrium employment (5 million labour units) are defined.

Diagram 5.4b has the nominal aggregate demand price (D), the nominal aggregate supply price (Z) and the nominal effective demand (AED) on the vertical axis and labour units (N) on the horizontal axis. With nominal investment spending given and a stable consumption function, a nominal aggregate demand function (F_0) is determined; whilst the nominal aggregate supply function ($WU \times \phi$) has a slope defined by the wage unit. When the aggregate demand price and aggregate supply price are equal this specifies the nominal volume of aggregate effective

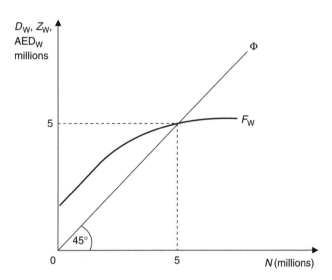

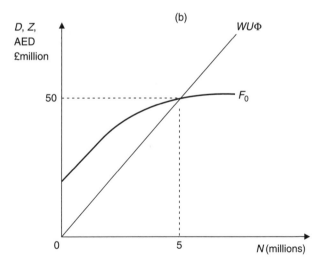

Diagram 5.4 Aggregate effective demand: (a) real terms and (b) nominal terms

Table 5.6 Changing subjective or objective factors and effective demand

	N (mills)	Y_w (mills)	χ^*	C_w (mills)	I_w (mills)	D_w (mills)	Z_w (mills)
Case 1							
	0	0	1.0	0.0	1.0	1.0	0.0
	1	1	1.0	1.0	1.0	2.0	1.0
	2	2	0.9	1.9	1.0	2.9	2.0
	3	3	0.9	2.8	1.0	3.8	3.0
	4	4	0.7	3.5	1.0	4.5	4.0
	5	5	0.5	4.0	1.0	5.0	5.0
	6	6	0.5	4.5	1.0	5.5	6.0
Case 2							
	0	0	1.0	0.0	1.0	1.0	0.0
	1	1	1.0	1.0	1.0	2.0	1.0
	2	2	0.95	1.95	1.0	2.95	2.0
	3	3	0.95	2.9	1.0	3.9	3.0
	4	4	0.7	3.8	1.0	4.8	4.0
	5	5	0.6	4.4	1.0	5.4	5.0
	6	6	0.6	5.0	1.0	6.0	6.0
Case 3							
	0	0	1.0	0.0	1.0	1.0	0.0
	1	1	1.0	1.0	1.0	2.0	1.0
	2	2	0.8	1.8	1.0	2.8	2.0
	3	3	0.65	2.45	1.0	3.45	3.0
	4	4	0.55	3.0	1.0	4.0	4.0
	5	5	0.4	3.4	1.0	4.4	5.0
	6	6	0.4	3.8	1.0	4.8	6.0

demand at £50 million; this in turn determines the equilibrium volume of employment of 5 million labour units. It is, of course, possible to derive two further functions with real income (Y_w), rather than labour units, on the horizontal axis, but the results are very similar.

If there are changes in any of the subjective or objective factors that cause either the real and nominal consumption functions to change this will influence the level of effective demand. This is shown in Table 5.6, which considers the impact on real aggregate effective demand resulting from an increase (Case 2) and a decrease (Case 3) in the propensity to consume, in comparison to an initial position (Case 1). It replicates and expands upon the data set out in Table 5.3.

Initially real effective demand is 5 million wage units and employment is 5 million labour units (Case 1). An increase in the propensity to consume will increase the level of real aggregate effective demand

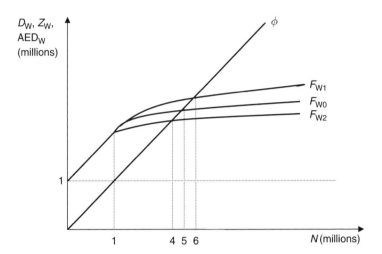

Diagram 5.5 Changing consumption and aggregate effective demand

to 6 million wage units (Case 2) and raise the volume of employment to 6 million labour units. A decrease in the propensity to consume will have the opposite effect, with real effective demand falling to 4 million wage units, and employment falling back to 4 million labour units (Case 3).

The contents of Table 5.6 are illustrated in Diagram 5.5. In Diagram 5.5 the real aggregate demand price (D_w), the real aggregate supply price (Z_w) and real effective demand (AED_w) are on the vertical axis and units of employment (N) are on the horizontal axis. With an initial aggregate demand function F_{w0} (consistent with Case 1), the level of real aggregate effective demand is 5 million wage units, and the equilibrium employment is 5 million labour units. When the propensity to consume increases, the real aggregate demand function swivels up to F_{w1} (Case 2); real effective demand rises to 6 million wage units; and employment increases to 6 million labour units. When the propensity to consume decreases the aggregate demand function swivels to F_{w2} (Case 3); real effective demand falls to 4 million wage units and the equilibrium level of employment declines to 4 million labour units.

d) The Paradox of Thrift

Keynes' treatment of the relationship between consumption expenditure and effective demand can be used to illustrate the famous concept

Table 5.7 The Paradox of Thrift

	N (mills)	Y_w (mills)	χ^*	C_w (mills)	I_w (mills)	D_w (mills)	Z_w (mills)
Case 1							
	0	0	1.0	0.0	1.0	1.0	0.0
	1	1	1.0	1.0	1.0	2.0	1.0
	2	2	0.9	1.9	1.0	2.9	2.0
	3	3	0.9	2.8	1.0	3.8	3.0
	4	4	0.7	3.5	1.0	4.5	4.0
	5	5	0.5	4.0	1.0	5.0	5.0
	6	6	0.5	4.5	1.0	5.5	6.0
Case 2							
	0	0	1.0	0.0	1.0	1.0	0.0
	1	1	1.0	1.0	1.0	2.0	1.0
	2	2	0.7	1.7	1.0	2.7	2.0
	3	3	0.7	2.4	1.0	3.4	3.0
	4	4	0.6	3.0	1.0	4.0	4.0
	5	5	0.4	3.4	1.0	4.4	5.0
	6	6	0.4	3.8	1.0	4.8	6.0

of the *Paradox of Thrift*. The Paradox can be summed up as follows: *any increase (decrease) in the propensity of a community to save leaves the total volume of saving unchanged; it will however cause the level of aggregate income to fall (rise)*. A simple example will illustrate why the Paradox exists in Keynes' model. Note that Table 5.7 relates to variables measured in wage units, although the arguments can be equally expressed in nominal terms.

Case 1 outlines the initial position previously set out in Table 5.6. The real level of effective demand is 5 million wage units (i.e. where $D_w = Z_w$), made up of 1 million wage units of expected investment spending and 4 million wage units of expected consumption spending. Assuming short-term expectations are correct the volume of real aggregate income (Y_w) is also 5 million wage units. The level of real aggregate saving (S_w), that is Y_w minus C_w, is equal to 1 million wage units; hence aggregate saving equals aggregate investment.

Now consider Case 2 where the community embarks on a thrift drive; this can be represented by a decline in the propensity to consume for each level of employment and aggregate income above the critical level. The lower expected consumption spending ensures that the values for D_w fall back; this in turn causes effective demand to decline to 4 million wage units. As a consequence real aggregate income declines to 4 million units; this is made up of 3 million units of realised consumption expenditure and 1 million units of realised fixed investment spending. The equilibrium volume of employment declines to 4 million labour units. The economy is experiencing a downturn. At this lower aggregate income, however, real aggregate saving is *unchanged* at 1 million wage units (i.e. 4–3 million); hence, *although the propensity to save of the community has increased the volume of aggregate savings remains unchanged.* This also suggests that even though the economy experiences an economic downturn the volumes of aggregate saving and aggregate investment are still equal at 1 million wage units each. It follows that any attempt by a community to save less in the aggregate will also fail. For although the propensity to save falls, this causes the propensity to consume to rise; consumption spending and aggregate income both increase, whilst aggregate saving is unchanged (yet it still equals investment spending).

It may be concluded that in the General Theory model the levels at which saving and investment are equal can be changed *if the rate of investment changes*, but not because of a change in the propensity to save. In the General Theory model investment and consumption spending *determine* the level of saving; Say's law is overturned and the Paradox of Thrift is identified.

e) A causal map of the General Theory model

It is appropriate to update the causal map of Keynes' model which was outlined in Chapter 3. Instead of referring broadly to aggregate expected consumption expenditure it is now possible to integrate the concept of the propensity to consume into the map. Expressing the causal map in nominal terms the ultimate independent variables are now the propensity to consume (χ), expected aggregate investment spending (I) and the wage unit (WU). The stable aggregate supply relationship (ϕ) is the last independent variable.

The propensity to consume (χ) and the wage unit (WU) combined define the level of nominal consumption expenditure (C). Nominal consumption and investment spending together constitute the nominal aggregate demand price (D). The wage unit and the aggregate supply relationship define the nominal aggregate supply price (Z). Nominal aggregate effective demand (AED) is set where D and Z are equal; and AED determines the equilibrium values for the dependent variables: nominal aggregate income (Y), nominal aggregate saving (S) and employment of labour units (N).

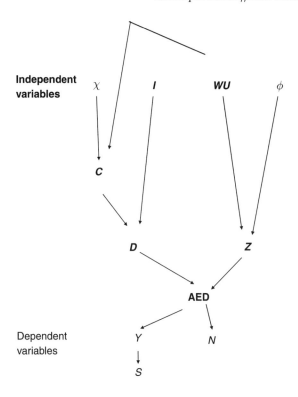

Independent variables χ I WU ϕ

C

D Z

AED

Dependent variables Y N

S

Map 6

The causal map in real terms has the propensity to consume (χ), real investment spending (I_w) and the stable aggregate supply relationship (ϕ) as the independent variables. The propensity to consume defines expected real consumption expenditure (C_w) at each possible level of employment and real income. Nominal investment spending deflated by the wage unit gives real investment spending (I_w). Real expected consumption and investment spending determine the level of the aggregate demand price measured in wage units (D_w). The aggregate supply relationship (ϕ) defines the real aggregate supply price (Z_w). Where D_w and Z_w are equal the volume of real aggregate effective demand (AED$_w$) is defined; AED$_w$ determines equilibrium values for three dependent variables – aggregate real income (Y_w), real aggregate saving (S_w) and total employment of labour units (N).

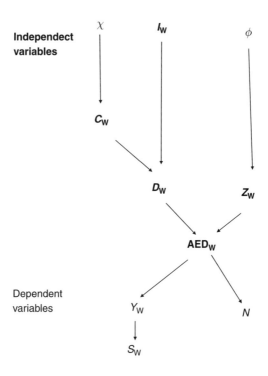

Map 7

f) Summary

This chapter has sought to amplify the relationship between the community's propensity to consume and the level of aggregate effective demand set out in Chapters 3 and 4. Once the values for the propensity to consume at each level of employment (or real income) are known, and expected investment spending is specified, the aggregate demand price can be determined for each employment (and real income) level. This shows why Keynes identifies the psychological propensity to consume as one of the ultimate independent variables in his model. If the subjective or objective factors change in such a way as to cause the consumption function to swivel, so too will the aggregate demand function.

The consumption function, along with fixed investment spending, defines the volume of aggregate effective demand in a macroeconomy.

If subjective or objective factors change such as to cause the consumption function to swivel, this will have an impact on the volume of effective demand and the equilibrium level of employment. But as noted in Chapter 4, Keynes argues consumption spending is likely to be the most stable component of effective demand, although he does not preclude the possibility that changes in the propensity to consume can cause economic fluctuations.

Keynes' treatment of consumption and effective demand allows him to identify the existence of the Paradox of Thrift. Keynes realises such a Paradox exists because in the General Theory model consumption and investment spending are independent variables. This means Say's law is rejected and aggregate saving becomes a dependent variable.

Appendix
Keynes and the Under-Consumptionists

The treatment of consumption and saving in the General Theory model might cause some to portray Keynes as another, perhaps more sophisticated, under-consumptionist. This perspective requires further discussion. It will be discovered that Keynes shares the under-consumptionist concern about the sufficiency of aggregate spending but departs from under-consumptionist analysis in important respects.

Under-consumption sentiment is originally evident in mercantilist thought and influential in early socialist thinking, especially in the writings of Sismondi, Owen and Bray (King, 1997; Keynes, 2007). Although under-consumptionist ideas were a very secondary aspect in Mercantilist writing, Keynes claims the work of Bernard Mandeville – and his allegorical poem the *Fable of the Bees* – popularises under-consumptionist thinking. Of the classical economists only the work of Malthus (1958) contains elements of under-consumptionism, especially the idea that a community might save too much for its own good. Despite some inconsistencies, Marx is also broadly sympathetic to the under-consumptionist viewpoint. But, for King the major advance in under-consumptionist *theory* comes with the publication of Hobson and Mummery's *Physiology of Industry* in 1899, a text to which Keynes devotes much attention when discussing under-consumption in *Chapter 23* of the *General Theory*.

The under-consumptionists argue, in their various ways, that the failure of a community to consume a sufficient amount is the ultimate cause of depression and high unemployment. When a community saves too much the result is *over-investment*. The productive capacity of an economy expands more than is required to match consumer spending, causing profits to fall off and the onset of a depression. As a corollary of this some under-consumptionists, like Mandeville, claim that economic activity and prosperity is promoted by high consumption spending. Hence the *private vice* of luxurious unproductive consumption leads to generalised economic prosperity – a *public virtue*. Mandeville also argues that large military expenditure by the State fosters economic well-being; this is analogous to what later writers call *military Keynesianism* (Fusfeld, 2002).

This argument goes against the grain of the austere classical economists. Starting with Adam Smith, the ultimate Presbyterian economist, the classical school argues that the private virtue of parsimony – saving – leads to the public virtue of national wealth accumulation. Prodigal spending by contrast is the surest way to national ruin. In moral terms Smith can simply not countenance the Mandevillian claim that prodigal consumption is a means to prosperity, or that private thrift is inimical to public well-being. Smith is greatly irritated by Mandeville's Fable precisely because for Smith it is not enough for capitalism to be the most advanced mode of production, the creator of the greatest degree of prosperity. Capitalism must also be morally virtuous.

There is however an intriguing moral consensus that Smith and early socialists share about under-consumptionism. Like Smith early socialists have a moral repugnance at the thought of the virtues of wasteful unproductive consumption spending. But from this common starting point they diverge. Rather than following Smith in denying that wasteful consumption is needed for capitalism to prosper the Socialists use this fact to criticise capitalism. If the capitalist mode of production can only succeed with wasteful consumer spending, suffering depressions when it is absent, then all the more the reason to be rid of capitalism.

Luckily for the sanity of later classical economists Say's law seems to square the circle. Savings leads to investment, and investment in more capacity is the foundation for greater economic growth. Mandeville must be wrong. The Ricardo–Malthus debate in the early nineteenth century is the last time that under-consumption thinking is seriously aired in classical circles (Dorfman, 1989). Because Ricardo is deemed to have won that particular joust, Say's law becomes an unquestioned classical shibboleth. By rejecting Say's law and allowing demand deficiency back into the picture, Keynes is the first mainstream economist since Malthus to see some value in the under-consumptionist case, although he is ultimately not convinced by its *theoretical* soundness.

King accepts that by the time of the publication of the *General Theory* under-consumptionist theory had not progressed beyond the work of Hobson and Mummery. Significant advancement only occurs in the 1940s with the formalised Bauer–Sweezy model. This model predicts that as capitalism develops there is a shift in the distribution of income from wages to profits, and as workers' propensity to consume is highest, this inevitably leads to a lagging of consumption behind income growth. As the propensity to save and invest increases so too does the productive capacity of the economy, well beyond what is required; moreover the most developed capitalist economies are the most likely to suffer from under-consumptionist tendencies. This perspective is further improved by the Baran and Sweezy model, outlined in the mid-1960s, which explains the shift in the distribution away from wages by the increasing tendency towards monopolistic market structures in capitalism; the market power inherent in monopoly allows capitalists to increase the profit share in national income. Both the Bauer and Sweezy and the Baran and Sweezy approaches share the view that private consumption has an inherent tendency to lag behind what is required to maintain growth and prosperity. Demand is deficient due to the inadequate growth of consumer spending. The solution – just as Mandeville suggests – is a "massive expansion of wasteful expenditures by the private sector and by civilian and military branches of the state" (King, 1997, p. 427).

King claims that this under-consumptionist theory has had beneficial influence on other writers. Notably Kalecki seems to share some sentiments about the possibility of economic crises being caused by over-investment (under-consumption). Moreover some of the intellectual insights contained in the Harrod-Domar Keynesian theory of growth (at least according to Domar) are based on under-consumptionist analysis. For King under-consumptionist theory, despite its deficiencies, is "vindicated, in effect, by the generalisation of the General Theory to the long period" (ibid., p. 428).

The General Theory model certainly contains an element of under-consumptionism with its idea of a diminishing marginal propensity to consume as aggregate income rises. This is the source of Keynes' claim about the existence of poverty in the midst of plenty, with an affluent nation experiencing a low marginal propensity to consume and small investment multiplier. The affluent nation caught in an economic depression will, according to Keynes, consequently find it more difficult to initiate a State-led economic recovery.

Keynes however departs from the Hobsonian version of under-consumptionism because it is deficient in two important respects. First, in the General Theory model changes in *both* the propensity to consume *and* investment spending can generate economic instability; furthermore variations in investment spending are the *most likely* cause of fluctuations in output and employment. Hobsonian under-consumptionism, therefore, is correct to be fearful of deficient demand, but it identifies *only one source* of demand deficiency, and that being of the least importance. What is true of the critique of Hobson is equally valid for other under-consumptionist approaches. The under-consumption theories, therefore, can be seen as another *special case* of the General Theory model. It sets out the special circumstances where fluctuating consumption spending alone causes changes in output and employment.

Secondly, the under-consumption theory is deficient in its treatment of saving and investment, and in particular in its implicit acceptance of the classical loanable funds theory of interest, based on Say's law. Keynes therefore claims that under-consumptionist theory is incomplete. The analysis has:

> no independent theory of interest.... [Hence it] laid too much emphasis...on under-consumption leading to over-investment, in the sense of unprofitable investment, instead of explaining that a relatively weak propensity to consume helps to cause unemployment by requiring and *not* receiving the accompaniment of a compensating volume of new investment, which, even if it may sometimes occur temporarily through errors of optimism, is in general prevented from happening at all by the prospective profit failing below the standard set by the rate of interest.
>
> (Keynes, 2007, p. 370)

To properly appreciate Keynes' critique of under-consumptionism the reader will, of course, have to work through the next three chapters in this book which explain Keynes' treatment of the inducement to invest. At this point you are advised to note Keynes' comments and return to the material after familiarising yourself with the analysis contained in Chapters 6, 7 and 8.

6
The Practical Theory of the Future

a) Introduction

With Say's law the classical school has little need for an explicit macroeconomic theory of investment. Moreover when the classical school does discuss investment demand, the calculus of probability means that they seriously underestimate the capricious nature of long-term profit expectations. Freed from such classical notions, Keynes' task in the *General Theory* is to outline a rigorous theory of *aggregate* fixed investment spending.

Because the objective of investment spending and other forms of wealth accumulation is to generate returns at comparatively distant dates, Keynes begins by considering how decisions-makers cope with the inherently uncertain future. To do this Keynes sets out a *practical theory of the future*. This practical theory underpins Keynes' key concept of the state of long-term expectation; the latter contributes to the determination of both the marginal efficiency of capital and the state of liquidity preferences – see Chapter 7. According to Keynes short-period changes in the state of long-term expectation are the ultimate cause of fluctuations in effective demand and employment.

This chapter begins by reminding the reader of the classical school's theory of the future and outlines Keynes' critique of it – Section (b). In Section (c) Keynes' alternative practical theory of the future – the *conventional method of calculation* – is considered. It explains how a state of long-term expectation is formed. Section (d) considers the linkages Keynes identifies between the precarious character of the conventional method of calculation and the operation of organised investment markets. Finally Section (e) examines Keynes' famous concept of *animal spirits* and relates it to the practical theory of the future.

b) The calculus of probability and Keynes' critique

The classical school analyses an economic system which is more or less stable at the full employment position. The system is subject to change but it is predictable, although the disappointment of expectations cannot entirely be ruled out. This allows the school to accept a "hypothesis of a calculable future", which Keynes summarises in the following way:

> [A]t any given time facts and expectations [are] assumed to be given in a definite and calculable form; and risks, of which, though admitted, not much notice [is] taken, [are] supposed to be capable of an exact actuarial computation.
>
> (Keynes, 1973a, p. 112)

With this perspective the classical school can argue that decision-makers do not find the inherently uncertain future unmanageable. Decision-makers calculate the future *consequences* of present investment decisions via the calculus of probability. Keynes claims that the theoretical application of this calculus by the classicals means they ignore all the important characteristics of an uncertain environment, thereby reducing uncertainty to the status of certainty. This leads the classical school to erroneously assume that wealth accumulation in a market economy is characterised by *a high degree of stability*.

A persistent theme of Keynes' thought is that the future is inherently uncertain and *not* capable of being reduced to a calculable status (Keynes, 1973e). Decision-makers do not have knowledge of the far future which might allow them to calculate precisely the consequences of present actions. Following the axiom of the philosopher G. E. Moore (Skidelsky, 1983), Keynes argues that decision-makers know little of the full consequences of their actions. They might be able to assess the direct and immediate consequences of an action but have only a hazy idea of the more distant consequences. This lack of future knowledge, Keynes contends, is particularly acute in the economic sphere. Keynes has a vision of the capitalist system being inherently dynamic in character, and in the *Treatise* Keynes approvingly quotes the arguments of Schumpeter on this subject. According to Mitchell the great heretic Joseph Schumpeter claims that capitalism is dynamic because of the actions of innovating entrepreneurs. In particular:

> their practical application of scientific discoveries and mechanical inventions, their development of new forms of industrial and

commercial organisation, their introduction of unfamiliar products, their conquests of new markets, exploitation of new resources, shifting of trade routes, and the like.

(Mitchell; quoted by Keynes, 1971b, pp. 85–86)

Given this vision of the capitalist system, it is not surprising that Keynes believes knowledge of the economic future is generally inadequate, changing and obscure. This, however, causes difficulties for those concerned with the accumulation of wealth. According to Keynes:

(t)he outstanding fact is the extreme precariousness of the basis of knowledge on which our estimates of prospective yield have to be made. Our knowledge of the factors which will govern the yield of an investment some years hence is usually very slight and often negligible. If we speak frankly, we have to admit that our basis of knowledge for estimating the yield ten years hence of a railway, a copper mine, a textile factory, the goodwill of a patent medicine, an Atlantic liner, a building in the City of London *amounts to little and sometimes nothing*; or even five years hence.

(Keynes, 2007, pp. 149–150; my emphasis)

Consequently, for Keynes the classical calculus of probability is likely to lead to flawed reasoning because it seriously understates the importance of uncertainty on wealth accumulation. This is not to say that the classical approach has no uses. The hypothesis of a calculable future may be applied to the special case of an economy dominated by immediate consumption, where the accumulation of wealth is insignificant. But as soon as the economy advances and wealth accumulation starts to play an important role in its development Keynes argues that the classical theory of the future requires considerable amendment. It is in these circumstances that the essential flaw in the classical approach – that it assumes that decision-makers have knowledge of the future they do not possess – does damage to economic theory. Specifically, it leads the classical school to a wrong-headed analysis of behaviour in an uncertain environment and an "under-estimation of the concealed factors of utter doubt, precariousness, hope and fear" (Keynes, 1973a, p. 122).

c) Keynes' practical theory of the future and the state of long-term expectation

In modern textbooks there is a great deal of confusion about how to treat risk and uncertainty. Risk is often conflated with uncertainty and vice versa. In this discussion Ramsey's and Knight's distinction between risk and uncertainty is applied. In which case the term *risk* applies to cases where a mathematical probability can be calculated for the likelihood of the occurrence of a particular future event. This often forms the basis for actuarial calculations in the insurance industry, for example the chance of a car accident for those aged under 25. An outcome is *uncertain*, by contrast, where the relevant knowledge does not exist to calculate a mathematical probability for a future event. Keynes ably clarifies what he means by the term uncertainty in the following manner:

> By *uncertain* knowledge, let me explain...The sense in which I am using the term is that in which the prospect of a European war is uncertain, or the price of copper and the rate of interest twenty years hence, or the obsolescence of a new invention, or of the position of private wealth owners in the social system [thirty years hence]. About these matters there is no scientific basis on which to form any calculable probability whatever.
>
> (Keynes, 1973a, pp. 113–114; my emphasis)

Given this uncertain knowledge of the economic future how do individuals form *long-term expectations*? According to Shackle (1967) the answer is that an agent acts irrationally, implying the use of any arbitrary method to make forecasts; indeed a person acting irrationally can use a different arbitrary method every time a forecast is made. This is *not* the approach taken by Keynes. He develops a *practical theory* to explain how agents cope, which deserves thorough attention. Keynes' practical theory is much influenced by the philosophy of David Hume (Hume, 1938, 1962). Faced with an uncertain future Hume argues that individuals must use customs or conventions to guide action – especially the "rule of thumb" that the future will be much like the past.

Keynes suggests, therefore, that decision-makers reach what he terms *probable forecasts* about the future by using a number of customs or *conventional techniques* to supplement their vague knowledge. Keynes outlines three main conventions which decision-makers apply when making forecasts. The first, not surprisingly, is related to the one suggested by Hume. That is we assume that the present is a reasonably good guide to the future, and in the process ignore future changes about which we know nothing. To this Keynes adds two further techniques which are generally utilised by entrepreneurs and wealth-holders. The second convention is that the existing state of knowledge in terms of asset prices, output levels and product prices is based on correct expectations of the future. The final convention is that when all else fails and decision-makers are unsure what to think they simply accept the *conventional judgement* of the rest of the world – that is they follow the crowd. Probable forecasts based on this *conventional* method of calculation allow decision-makers to behave in a *reasoned manner*, though without possessing the knowledge of the future that the classical school assumes.

However, decision-makers are always keenly aware that the conventional techniques are arbitrary. They know that the probable forecasts will, in hindsight, prove to be incorrect, to a greater or lesser degree. Hence Keynes supposes that probable forecasts are held by decision-makers with a particular *state of confidence*. This state of confidence may be strong or weak depending upon how reliable decision-makers believe the conventional techniques to be. If it is expected that there will be significant changes in the economy in the future, but it is unclear what precise form they will take, confidence in probable forecasts will be weak. Conversely, if few changes are expected in the future and the present is likely to be a good guide to the future, confidence will be strong. *The state of long-term expectation, therefore, has a twofold character: it incorporates a range of probable forecasts made by decision-makers held with a particular state of confidence.*

Keynes believes that the state of long-term expectation formed by these conventional techniques is likely to be reasonably stable, so long as decision-makers can rely on the maintenance of the conventions. He realises, however, that such arbitrary conventions will inevitably have grave weaknesses with respect to predicting the future. Keynes reasons that a practical theory of the future has one key attribute.

> In particular, being based on so flimsy a foundation, it is subject to sudden and violent changes. The practice of calmness and immobility, of certainty and security, suddenly breaks down. New fears and hopes will, without warning, take charge of human conduct. The forces of disillusion may suddenly impose a new conventional basis of valuation ... At all times the vague panic fears and equally vague

and unreasoned hopes are not really lulled, and lie but a little way below the surface.

(Keynes, 1973a, pp. 114–115)

With uncertain knowledge of the future, and an arbitrary conventional method of calculation, Keynes concludes that the state of long-term expectation *is liable to fluctuate* in the short period suddenly and violently. Instability need not be the norm, *but it is a continual threat.*

d) Calculations on organised 'investment' markets

An organised investment market is a stock exchange (like those that operate in the City of London or Wall Street) which is supposed to provide long-term finance for capital investment. Investment markets encourage wealth-holders to invest in capital assets, whilst giving them the guarantee that they can, at any time, sell their share of the asset in the market, and obtain liquid control over resources. Consequently, the individual wealth-holder can be convinced that a commitment to invest only really runs the risk of a change in the business environment in the *near future*. An investment market, therefore, helps to encourage additional capital investment which for a community is *fixed*, but for the individual is *liquid*. This is the main advantage of an organised investment market.

Keynes however recognises that an organised investment market, based around the need for liquidity, can increase the precarious character of the conventional method of calculation. Keynes identifies four ways in which conventional calculations are made more precarious.

1. As an organised investment market increases in size there emerges a larger *separation of ownership and control*. Those who own a business increasingly have no special knowledge about the firm and the investment activity it wishes to undertake. As ownership of shares are concentrated in a group of largely ignorant owners, insignificant changes in the day-to-day performance of a firm can have an excessive influence on its valuation on the stock exchange. Keynes provides an example of American ice companies[1] whose share valuation rises in the summer and falls in the winter. Clearly the actions of largely ignorant owners can only amplify the precarious character of uncertain knowledge in the realm of wealth accumulation.

2. *Stock market valuations of capital investments are often based on the conventional judgement of a large number of relatively ill-informed individuals.* Valuations based on such "mass psychology" are liable to change suddenly for reasons unrelated to the prospective yields of such assets. Keynes argues that valuations are influenced by unreasoning yet in some sense legitimate waves of optimism and pessimism because knowledge of the future is so insecure. Such shifts towards optimism and then pessimism will, yet again, amplify the unstable basis of investment decisions.

3. Given the influence of conventional valuations of firms and capital investments, Keynes notes that *organised investment markets can become overly interested in what he refers to as speculation,* that is the attempt by those active on a stock exchange to make forecasts about what the market will judge to be assets that rise or fall in value. The purpose is to foresee changes in conventional judgements about the valuation of assets just before everybody else. When successful such speculation allows a trader to buy assets cheap and sell them dear. Keynes contrasts speculation with what he calls *enterprise*; namely the labourious, but important, mental activity of making reasoned judgements about the likely yields on an asset over long time periods in order to calculate accurate asset values. If an organised investment market, and especially the actions of the skilled professional traders, is predominantly characterised by enterprise no great harm is done to the process of capital accumulation by some speculation. But Keynes notes that investment markets, and expert professional traders, can often be more attracted to speculation, which is a far more exciting activity. Seeking to outguess the rest, or outwit the crowd, is a battle of wits which can even be played by professional expert investors amongst themselves. This leads Keynes to make his famous references to such activity being like a game of snap or old maid or musical chairs. According to Keynes, if speculation dominates enterprise on investment markets the process of capital investment in a nation can be harmed.

> Speculators may do no harm as bubbles on a steady stream of enterprise. But the position is serious when enterprise becomes the bubble on a whirlpool of speculation. When the capital development of a country becomes the by-product of the activities of a casino, the job is likely to be ill-done.
>
> (Keynes, 2007, p. 159)

4. Often speculative investors who want to buy share holdings wish to borrow money from lending institutions (i.e. the private banking system), repaying the loans out of the successful capital gain made from buying shares cheap and selling them dear. This introduces another aspect of the state of confidence which has not been mentioned; namely the state of confidence of lending institutions towards those who wish to borrow, which Keynes calls the *state of credit*. That is a lending institution must make judgements about the credit worthiness of those who borrow; when banks think that borrowers are less credit worthy than before (i.e. less likely to repay outstanding debt) the state of credit deteriorates and vice versa. Keynes argues that a serious fall in equity prices (i.e. the valuation of the shares of a firm quoted on the stock market) may be generated by *either* a weakening of confidence by those who purchase shares *or* through a deteriorating state of credit, meaning speculators are refused bank credit in order to buy shares. This, in turn, may cause a decline in the demand by entrepreneurs to invest in capital equipment. For entrepreneurs are inevitably sensitive to falls in the share price of their firms when considering issuing new shares to finance additional investment spending; and banks are sensitive to the value of a company (as represented by its share price) when considering granting a new loan to finance capital equipment purchases. Keynes notes, however, that a recovery in equity prices requires a revival of *both* speculator confidence and the state of credit. Fluctuations in the state of credit and speculator confidence add yet another source of instability and uncertainty to decisions relating to the accumulation of wealth.

From this it is clear that although an organised investment market is a vital element in encouraging capital accumulation in a capitalist economy it does have a downside. Instability is amplified by the separation of ownership and control, stock market valuations determined with inadequate information, casino-led stock markets and the fluctuating character of both speculator confidence and the state of credit. These factors increase the already precarious character of the conventional method of calculation and strengthen the potential for short-period instability in the state of long-term expectation.

e) Animal spirits

Keynes' concept of *animal spirits* can only be explained in the context of uncertainty about the future. Keynes realises that it is unclear why, given gross uncertainty, decision-makers are motivated to invest in capital equipment at all; for if it is impossible to calculate the consequences of any action, decision-makers may be tempted not to act at all (Meeks, 1978). However, the reason why decision-makers still invest in capital equipment lies in the *instincts* of humankind.

There is, Keynes argues, an innate urge within individuals to act positively, to do something spontaneously rather than nothing. These innate urges to act, based on a spontaneous optimism that something good will result, are animal spirits. Actions motivated by animal spirits are *not* the result of the careful quantitative weighing up of benefits and probabilities. This viewpoint of human action is particularly attractive to those who realise that decisions-makers are people motivated by factors other than those that impel a rational economic man to act. It is a further characteristic of animal spirits that those most likely to be influenced by the spontaneous urge to action are entrepreneurs. As a result the animal spirits of business people, Keynes argues, have a crucial influence on wealth accumulation. For:

> individual initiative will only be adequate when reasonable calculation is supplemented and supported by animal spirits, so that the thought of ultimate loss which often overtakes pioneers, as experience undoubtedly tells us and them, is put aside as a healthy man puts aside the expectation of death.
>
> (Keynes, 2007, p. 162)

Keynes notes that animal spirits introduce a further source of instability into wealth accumulation, as the delicate flower of spontaneous optimism is always influenced by economic circumstance. In an economic boom, when profits are buoyant, the animal spirits of entrepreneurs may be very strong indeed. In fact spontaneous optimism may be such as to generate a greater rate of capital accumulation than cold calculation alone would advise. Conversely, in an economic downturn, as commercial indicators become adverse, animal spirits may be dimmed and falter. The business community may curtail capital investment to a larger degree than appropriate. Keynes also allows the animal spirits of entrepreneurs to be affected by general political and social considerations. For example, the spontaneous optimism of the business community may be influenced by the political colour of elected governments. The election of a "left of centre" government, which is not supportive of entrepreneurship, may dim the animal spirits of business people; whilst animal spirits can be buoyed up by the election of a "right of centre", pro-business, government.

Animal spirits therefore introduce yet another factor which makes the process of wealth accumulation inherently unstable. And in this case the instability is the *result of human nature*. To illustrate the point a little more the Economics Editor of *The Observer* newspaper writing during the long UK recession of the early 1990s can be quoted. When referring to the fluctuating optimism of the business community in 1991 he wrote "businessmen...tend to think that every point on the business cycle is unique – if times are good, they are here to stay; if they are bad, it is the end of the civilised world as we know it." The reason for this is the capricious character of animal spirits.

f) Summary

Without the classical notions of Say's law and the calculus of probability, Keynes has to formulate a new theory of aggregate fixed investment spending. Decisions today about investment spending and other forms of wealth accumulation depend upon estimates of profitable returns in the distant future. Hence macroeconomics must have a theory of how decision-makers calculate returns over the long term.

The classical school's treatment of the issue trivialises the problem by transforming uncertainty to the same calculable status as certainty. Keynes provides an alternative practical theory to explain how long-term expectations are formed. Decision-makers use conventions to make forecasts – the most important being that the present is a serviceable guide to the future. These probable forecasts are also held with a degree of confidence. The state of confidence measures how reliable decision-makers believe the conventional techniques to be.

Given uncertainty about the future, and the conventional method of calculation, the state of long-term expectation is *potentially* capricious in character. Short-period changes in the state of long-term expectation are further aggravated by the existence of organised investment markets and animal spirits. Hence wealth accumulation in Keynes' model is characterised by a high degree of *possible* instability (although it need not be the norm).

Keynes' practical theory of the future is the foundation for his explanation of why investment spending is so liable to fluctuate suddenly and violently in the short period. These matters are discussed in more detail in the following two chapters.

7
The Inducement to Invest – A Theory of Investment

a) Introduction

This chapter considers the theory of *aggregate* fixed investment spending that Keynes incorporates into his General Theory model. Having rejected Say's law Keynes begins by formulating an analysis of investment demand from the viewpoint of entrepreneurs. He introduces the marginal efficiency of capital schedule (or investment demand curve) that sets out the terms on which entrepreneurs *demand* funds in order to initiate investment projects. The marginal efficiency is largely dependent on the state of long-term expectation which is derived in ways outlined in the previous chapter. As durable capital equipment links the economic *present* to the *future,* the marginal efficiency capital schedule is the primary channel by which expectations of the *future* influence *present* day spending decisions in the General Theory model.

Having rejected the classical loanable funds theory Keynes replaces it with a monetary theory of the rate of interest – the liquidity preference theory. In the General Theory model the rate of interest is important as it governs the terms on which funds are *supplied* to entrepreneurs in order to undertake investment projects. The liquidity preference theory views wealth accumulation from the viewpoint of those who save referred to by Keynes as rentiers or wealth-holders. The theory emphasises the choices wealth-holders have between holding their accumulated wealth in liquid or illiquid assets. The state of long-term expectation influences wealth-holders' decisions about the holding of liquid assets, and this helps to determine the equilibrium long-term money rate of interest. This is a second channel by which expectations of the *future* influence *present* day spending decisions.

Keynes' analysis of the inducement to invest combines of the schedule of the marginal efficiency of capital and the liquidity preference theory of the rate of interest to determine the rate of aggregate investment spending. Armed with this theory Keynes can elaborate on his idea of poverty in the midst of plenty.

The chapter begins with some clarifications relating to the definitions of the capital stock and aggregate investment, the equality of investment and saving and the category of fixed investment that the General Theory model explains – Section (b). Sections (c) and (d) elucidate the derivation of the schedule of the marginal efficiency of capital and the reasons why the schedule is likely to be unstable. Section (e) precisely defines liquidity preference and money's role as a store of value, and then explains the liquidity preference theory of the rate of interest in some detail. The implications of Keynes' analysis for the classical loanable funds theory of interest are considered in Section (f). Finally in Section (g) Keynes' overall theory of aggregate investment spending is reviewed, and the concept of the paradox of poverty in the midst of plenty is revisited.

b) Aggregate investment – Further clarification

Any theory of investment must start with a definition of the capital stock, for investment is the incremental addition to the capital stock. In the *Treatise* Keynes provides a rigorous, but often neglected, definition of the stock of capital which is the bedrock of his approach in the *General Theory*. According to Keynes:

> The stock of real capital or material wealth existing at any time is embodied in one or other of three forms:
>
> 1. Goods in use, which are only capable of giving up gradually their full yield of use or enjoyment.
> 2. Goods in process, i.e. in the course of preparation by cultivation or manufacture for use or consumption, or in transport, or with merchants, dealers and retailers, or awaiting the rotation of the seasons.
> 3. Goods in stock, which are yielding nothing but are capable of being used or consumed at any time.
>   We shall call goods in use *fixed capital*, goods in process *working capital* and goods in stock *liquid capital*.
>   (Keynes, 1971a, pp. 115 – 116; Keynes' emphasis)

Keynes and the classics agree that fixed capital is an important component of the tangible capital stock. Moreover, Keynes clarifies the concept by distinguishing between *instrumental* fixed capital (e.g. plant and machinery) and *consumption* fixed capital (e.g. houses). Both instrumental and consumption fixed capital are "in use" for many years, if not decades. Beyond this not much can be added. The same is not true of working capital and liquid capital; for these categories of capital are largely neglected by the classical school. The main casualty of neglect is working capital.

The key to understanding Keynes' concept of working capital is to realise that production takes place through *time – it is a process*. If production *flows* through time it is necessary to have a *revolving fund* of raw materials and finished goods to sustain this continuous process. Moreover, time elapses between production and sale of commodities, so there is also a need for a *revolving fund* of finished goods in the distribution sector. In this context Keynes defines working capital:

> as being the aggregate of goods...in course of production, manufacture, transport and retailing, including such *minimum* stocks, whether of raw materials or of finished goods, as are required to avoid risks of interruption of process or to tide over seasonal irregularities...
>
> (Keynes, 1971b, pp. 103–104; my emphasis)

Note how Keynes defines working capital in terms of *minimum* stocks of raw materials and finished goods. It does not include *surplus* stocks of these items – which are dealt with later under the heading of liquid capital. Furthermore, Keynes is keenly aware that certain "goods in process" in one time period will eventually become the final output available for consumption and investment in a subsequent time period, which reinforces the idea of production as a process. According to Keynes the classical school fails to properly identify the concept of working capital because they do not conceive of production as a continuous process; in other words they treat items like raw materials as a stock rather than a flow.

Liquid capital in Keynes' schema is made up of two elements. First, there are "surplus" stocks of raw materials and unfinished goods above the minimum levels necessary to sustain production and distribution. Secondly, there are "surplus" hoards of final goods which entrepreneurs have not yet sold. It is, however, only possible to accumulate final goods that will keep. Yet the costs of warehousing and the interest charges for carrying them can be prohibitive, therefore entrepreneurs seek to reduce liquid capital stocks at the earliest opportunity. The existence of liquid capital is by far the most obvious signal that an economy is in a disequilibrium position; a position where expected results are not equal to realised results, that is $D_w \neq Z_w \neq Y_w$.

Keynes' definition of the aggregate physical capital stock allows him to proceed to a precise definition of what constitutes aggregate investment. Keynes explains that:

> aggregate investment in the popular sense coincides with my defini-tion of net investment, namely the net addition to all kinds of capital equipment, after allowing for those changes in the value of old capi-tal equipment which are taken into account in reckoning [aggregate] net income.

> Investment, thus defined, includes therefore, the *increment* of capi-tal equipment, whether it consists of *fixed capital, working capital and liquid capital* ...

> (Keynes, 2007, p. 75; my emphasis)

It is usual in equilibrium models to concentrate on fixed investment spending. Certainly this is true in the General Theory model in so far as it explains an economy experiencing different equilibrium positions. Liquid capital investment (or disinvestment) occurs when an economy is not in equilibrium; in the General Theory model it is possible that this can occur when the short-term expectations of entrepreneurs are erroneous. In the *General Theory* Keynes applies the working assumption that short-term expectations are always fulfilled, though there is no rea-son why this must be so as the appendix to Chapter 3 demonstrates. Working capital investment (or disinvestment), by contrast, takes place when the economy is moving between one equilibrium position to another. Hence if entrepreneurs in the aggregate enact plans to increase output they will initially have to build up the stock of goods in process (e.g. raw materials) to facilitate the higher production levels. Once pro-duction stabilises at the higher level there is no further need to increase the stock of working capital and working capital investment will cease. The reverse holds when there are plans to reduce production levels. The topic of working capital investment and disinvestment is taken up again in the next chapter.

There is one final point that should be made in this context. It is that in the General Theory model a fluctuation in spending on fixed capital equipment is a fundamental *cause* of variations in aggregate effective demand and employment. By contrast, investment (and disinvestment) in both working and liquid capital tend to be dependent upon variations in the volume of effective demand and output. This is one further reason why this chapter will focus on fixed investment spending.[1]

Next Keynes' definitions of aggregate income (Y) and aggregate net income (net Y) outlined in Chapter 4 allow him to specify an important relationship between aggregate investment spending and aggregate saving. As already noted Keynes solves the problem of what constitutes consumption expenditure by arguing it is the expenditure which is not made up of sales between entrepreneurs (i.e. $\Sigma A - A1$), where ΣA is the total sales made during a time period and $\Sigma A1$ is the total sales made between entrepreneurs. With this clarified Keynes can define aggregate saving (S), for it is equal to aggregate income (Y) minus consumption expenditure. In terms of a set of equations if:

$$Y = \Sigma(A - U)$$
and $$C = \Sigma(A - A1)$$
then $$S = \Sigma(A1 - U)$$

The definition of Y also allows Keynes to precisely define current aggregate investment spending (I). It is, for a specific time period, the incremental increase in the value of aggregate capital equipment as a result of productive activity during the period. The value of I relates to the sales of final investment goods plus changes in the stocks of raw materials, unfinished goods and final goods held by entrepreneurs at the end of a time period. Hence aggregate investment (I) relates to the part of income which is not consumed during a time period; that is I equals aggregate income (Y) minus consumption expenditure (C). The value of I can be derived using a set of equations. Therefore:

$$Y = \Sigma(A - U)$$
and $$C = \Sigma(A - A1)$$
then $$I = \Sigma(A1 - U)$$

These equations can all be reformulated in terms of aggregate net income, aggregate net investment and aggregate net saving, by introducing supplementary cost, but the essence of the argument remains the same. That is if:

$$\text{net } Y = \Sigma(A - U - V)$$
and $$C = \Sigma(A - A1)$$
then $$\text{net } S = \Sigma(A1 - U - V)$$
and $$\text{net } I = \Sigma(A1 - U - V)$$

From this Keynes reaches an important conclusion about the relationship between aggregate saving and aggregate investment measured in either nominal or wage units terms.

> Whilst, therefore, the amount of saving is an outcome of the collective behaviour of individual consumers and the amount of investment of the collective behaviour of individual entrepreneurs, these *two amounts are necessarily equal*, since each of them is equal to the excess of income over consumption…In short –
> Income = value of output = consumption + investment
> Saving = income – consumption.
> Therefore saving = investment.
>
> (Keynes, 2007, p. 63; abridged quotation; my emphasis)

c) The schedule of the marginal efficiency of capital

Keynes takes great care to precisely define the concept of the marginal efficiency of capital. This is because the classical school is confused on the topic, tending to subsume the marginal efficiency of capital into the rate of interest on the basis that both are in some sense the return on capital. Keynes subsequently reveals that when drafting the *General Theory* he found that the concept of the marginal efficiency of capital to be one of the most difficult parts of his new theory to get right; it was the last part of the jigsaw to fall into place. This chapter will show how Keynes distinguishes between the marginal efficiency and the rate of interest. Essentially the marginal efficiency of capital is the expected rate of profit from applying a capital asset to produce output, whilst the rate of interest is the reward for parting with liquid control over wealth.

To explain the marginal efficiency of a newly produced capital asset Keynes begins by defining two key concepts – the *prospective yield* and the *supply price* of a capital asset. Taking the former concept first, an entrepreneur purchasing a capital asset will hope to gain a series of profits – or an income stream – from the sale of the output of the asset over its lifetime. To calculate these profits over a period perhaps lasting as long as ten or 20 years, the entrepreneur will form a long-term expectation largely determined by the conventional method of calculation – outlined in Chapter 6. This series of expected profits – or annuities – (Q1, Q2,…, Qn) Keynes calls the prospective yield of an investment. The supply price of a capital asset Keynes defines as being equal to its replacement cost – that is the price that just induces a manufacturer to produce one more of the capital asset in question.

Armed with these two concepts Keynes defines the marginal efficiency of a capital asset as *the rate of discount which makes the total present value of the prospective yield of an investment just equal to its supply price*. To illustrate consider the case of an entrepreneur considering whether or not to invest in an additional unit of machinery. The machine has a supply price of £4926 and it is expected to generate a series of profits over a three-year period of £1000, £2000 and £2500, respectively.[2] By applying a simple formula for total present value (TPV) to three rates of discount, 4, 5 and 6 per cent, it is possible to determine which discount rate will equalise the total present value of the expected profits with the supply price. The following answer is forthcoming:

$$TPV = \frac{£1000}{(1.04)} + \frac{£2000}{(1.04)^2} + \frac{£2500}{(1.04)^3}$$

$$= £5035$$

$$TPV = \frac{£1000}{(1.05)} + \frac{£2000}{(1.05)^2} + \frac{£2500}{(1.05)^3}$$

$$= £4926$$

$$TPV = \frac{£1000}{(1.06)} + \frac{£2000}{(1.06)^2} + \frac{£2500}{(1.06)^3}$$

$$= £4823$$

It can be seen that only a rate of discount of 5 per cent equalises the TPV of the prospective yield and the supply price for this machine; the 4 per cent rate of discount is too low giving an TPV figure which is greater than the supply price, whilst the 6 per cent discount rate is too high causing the TPV value to fall below the supply price. Therefore the marginal efficiency of capital – or the expected rate of return – for this machine is 5 per cent per year. It is of course important to remind the reader that forecasts of future profits depend upon entrepreneur's expectations of future proceeds over long periods, which are inevitably based on flimsy and shifting foundations and liable to fluctuate suddenly. Moreover the longer that a capital asset can be applied (far longer than three years) the more unreliable will be the profit forecasts of entrepreneurs based on the conventional method of calculation. Therefore estimating the marginal efficiency of a capital asset is not an easy task and it requires specialised judgements to be made, which justifies why it is conducted by entrepreneurs.

Keynes then defines a marginal efficiency of capital *schedule* for each type of capital asset. With a given technique, Keynes suggests the schedule will be *downward sloping* assuming a given state of long-term expectation in the short period. In other words the greater the investment in a capital asset of a particular type, the lower will be the marginal efficiency of that asset. The first reason for this is that as the output of a capital asset is increased the law of diminishing productivity will set in and the supply price that will just induce a manufacturer to produce an additional unit of the asset must increase. Increases in the supply price will, *cet. par.*, lower the marginal efficiency of that asset. This is likely to have a powerful initial influence on the marginal efficiency. But Keynes argues a second factor has a more durable influence on the marginal efficiency ; namely that as investment in the asset increases its prospective yield will tend to fall. Why, with a given state of long-period expectation, will this occur? According to Keynes:

> the only reason why an asset offers a prospect of yielding during its life services having an aggregate value greater than its initial supply price is because it is *scarce*... If capital becomes less scarce, the excess yield will diminish without its having become less productive – at least in the physical sense.
>
> (Keynes, 2007, p. 213, Keynes' emphasis)

The reasoning behind this argument seems to be as follows. That as the number of capital assets of a particular type come into productive use they will collectively increase the output of a final product. As the supply of this final product increases so its price will tend to fall off, *cet. par.* This possible decline in sales revenue will cause entrepreneurs to downgrade expectations of future profits applying to each capital asset. Consequently as investment in a capital asset increases the prospective yields from that asset are expected to decline.[3]

If each capital asset faces a downward sloping marginal efficiency schedule the next steps are straightforward. First, the individual schedules for different types of capital can be aggregated together to develop a schedule relating the rate of aggregate investment to the marginal efficiency of capital in general. Second, with a given technique and a constant short-period state of long-term expectations, it can be supposed that the aggregated schedule is downward sloping – see Diagram 7.1. On the vertical axis is the marginal efficiency of capital measured in percentage terms; on the horizontal axis is aggregate investment measured in

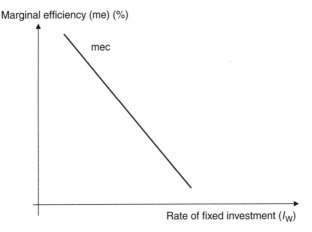

Diagram 7.1   The marginal efficiency of capital schedule

wage units. The diagram defines the aggregated schedule of the marginal efficiency for all capital assets.

According to Keynes, the aggregated marginal efficiency schedule is inherently *unstable*. The reason for this is that the position of marginal efficiency schedule is dependent on the short-period state of long-term expectation, which being based on such flimsy foundations is subject to sudden and violent fluctuation. This, in turn, causes the marginal efficiency schedule to become unstable.

Fluctuations in the marginal efficiency schedule are illustrated in Diagram 7.2. When the short-period state of long-term expectation

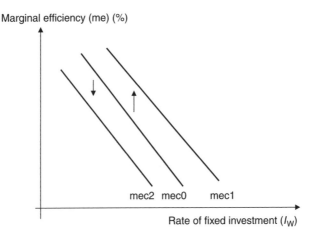

Diagram 7.2   Changes in the marginal efficiency

improves, entrepreneurs will become more optimistic about the future. In which case they will tend to revise upwards the prospective yields from the sale of output produced by new capital assets and make these forecasts with greater confidence. Therefore every capital asset will offer a greater marginal efficiency of capital than before, assuming supply prices are unaltered. This can be represented by an *upward* shift in the aggregated marginal efficiency of capital schedule for each rate of new investment (i.e. from mec0 to mec1). Conversely when the short-period state of long-term expectation deteriorates entrepreneurs will downgrade their profit forecasts from new capital assets, and the confidence with which these forecasts are made will weaken. In this case, assuming supply prices are constant, the marginal efficiency offered by each asset will fall, which is represented by a *downward* shift in the aggregated marginal efficiency of capital schedule for each rate of investment (i.e. from mec0 to mec2).

For Keynes it is primarily through the marginal efficiency of capital, therefore, that the General Theory model explains how unstable long-term expectations of the *future* influence spending on fixed capital assets *today*.

The schedule of the marginal efficiency of capital is of fundamental importance because it is mainly through this factor... that the expectation of the future influences the present. The mistake [of the classical school] of regarding the marginal efficiency of capital primarily in terms of the *current* yield of capital equipment... has had the result of breaking the theoretical link between today and tomorrow...

It is by reason of the existence of durable equipment that the economic future is linked to the present.

(Keynes, 2007, pp. 145–146; abridged quotation;
Keynes' emphasis)

Despite the central role that the marginal efficiency of capital plays in the General Theory model the concept has been the subject of substantial criticism, mainly from a Post-Keynesian perspective. These criticisms are discussed in some detail in Appendix A at the end of this chapter.

d) Other influences on the marginal efficiency of capital

It is important for completeness to consider the impact of other influences on the marginal efficiency of capital. It is relevant to return first to the role of saving in investment decisions, which has been touched on earlier, with specific reference to the marginal efficiency of capital. Then it is useful to consider how expected changes in the costs of producing capital assets in the future will influence the value of the marginal efficiency of capital assets produced today.

Propensity to save

The General Theory model rejects the classical idea that an individual act of saving creates a demand for future consumption goods and therefore encourages firms to invest in new capacity in order to meet this future demand. Keynes argues by contrast that an act of saving is a decision not to consume today but it implies very little in terms of specifics about future consumption. Certainly the decision to save implies a demand to hold wealth as noted above, and this wealth offers the potentiality of consuming an unspecified amount of an unspecified product at an unspecified time in the future. But beyond that the act of saving sends a message to entrepreneurs that consumption today will be lower. Of course entrepreneurs will wish to estimate future consumption demand especially when calculating the prospective yields from a new capital asset. They will tend to estimate future consumption trends based on present consumption demand, for there is very little else to go on. Hence if the present day propensity to consume weakens (as saving strengthens) this will if anything lower entrepreneurial expectations of future consumption demand. This leads to the conclusion that *an increase in the community's propensity to save, in so far as it lowers expectations of future consumption demand, will harm prospective yields and shift the schedule of the marginal efficiency of capital in general downwards, and vice versa.*

If you doubt the logic of the argument consider an enterprise faced with falling sales of its consumption goods (as the propensity to save strengthens) and a decline in the level of utilisation of its existing capital equipment. The classical idea requires us to believe that at the very moment this firm experiences increasing spare capacity it will bring forward plans to *add* to capacity in order to meet an unspecified future demand for its product at an unspecified future date. Frankly such an action is unlikely. Indeed it is reasonable to contend that an enterprise that acts in such a manner will not remain in business for long. By contrast the General Theory model suggests that a firm faced with declining sales and rising spare capacity will delay plans to add to its stock of equipment, which seems more in line with actual business behaviour.

Expected future reductions in the costs of producing capital assets

Keynes considers two ways in which future costs of producing a capital asset may decline; first due to an improvement in the technology of production allowing an asset to be produced more efficiently with other factor costs steady; and secondly due to a lowering of the wage unit thereby reducing costs with a given efficiency of production. Either way what affect might this have on the marginal efficiency of a capital asset which an entrepreneur is considering applying today? If an entrepreneur expects that the cost of producing a capital asset in the future will be lower than it is today, he/she will also expect that the final output of an existing capital asset will eventually have to compete with the final output of a future capital asset produced at a lower cost of production. Moreover the subsequently produced capital asset will probably be content with a *lower price* for the final output whilst still making a reasonable rate of return. If the price of the final output does fall under competitive pressure from the later capital assets, then profits (in money terms) from capital equipment, old or new, will decline. To the extent that such developments are thought to be probable, the prospective yields from capital assets produced today will be lower, which can be represented by a downward shift of the marginal efficiency of capital schedule.

From this Keynes goes on to contend that if there is an expectation that future prices in general will be lower than today this will tend to drag down the marginal efficiency of existing newly produced capital assets. The expectation of a rising future general price-level by contrast will if anything improve the marginal efficiency of capital in general and stimulate investment intentions. This in part explains why Keynes thinks capital accumulation is enhanced by a gently rising price-level.

e) The liquidity preference theory of the rate of interest

Knowledge of the prospective yields of capital assets or the marginal efficiency of capital in general does not allow either the rate of interest or the *actual* total present value of the prospective yield of an asset to be determined. It is only when the current rate of interest is known that entrepreneurs can deduce which capital assets will be sufficiently profitable to invest in and which will not. Therefore it is necessary to move on to explain how the rate of interest is determined in Keynes' schema. In earlier chapters it was shown that Keynes rejects the classical belief that the rate of interest is determined by saving and investment.

But this leaves Keynes with a problem: "[i]f the rate of interest is not determined by saving and investment in the same way in which price is determined by supply and demand, how is it determined?" (Keynes, 1973b, p. 212). To answer this question Keynes develops the liquidity preference theory of the rate of interest, where the money rate of interest is determined by the demand for, and supply of, money.

Keynes identifies four main reasons for the community to demand money – the finance, transactionary, precautionary and speculative motives to hold money. The finance and transactionary motives relate to what Keynes calls the demand for *active balances*. The precautionary and speculative motives relate to what he terms the demand for *inactive balances* that is the demand for money as a store of value. Using the terminology of the *Treatise* (see Chapter 2) the finance and transactionary motives refer to the demands for cash deposits plus overdrafts, whilst the precautionary and speculative demands relate to the demand for saving deposits.[4] Finally, note that the finance motive is not included in the *General Theory* itself. Keynes extends the analysis of the demand for money to include the finance motive in the debate that follows the publication the *General Theory* (Keynes, 1973b). It is included here as it constitutes a vital component of the liquidity preference theory, and one which is all too often overlooked by mainstream Keynesians.

The *finance motive* relates to the need for entrepreneurs to demand cash in the time lag between the planning and execution of decisions about profitable activity. For example an entrepreneur may decide to purchase a new machine or a new building, or to build up raw material stocks to facilitate an expansion of output or to purchase shares of another company. The entrepreneur will need to build up a sum of cash in order to finance these plans. This financial provision may be arranged via extending the entrepreneur's overdraft facilities or arranging a term loan with a bank or by the issue of new securities to attract cash.

This demand for money can be facilitated by a revolving fund, for as each bank loan or overdraft is repaid or security matures this frees money to finance the next round of planned activity. As long as economic activity is constant the finance demand for money will be stable. Of course if the level of planned economic activity changes, this will cause a change in the demand for money due to the finance motive. For example if entrepreneurs in general plan to purchase more investment goods or increase production of consumption goods, they will need a greater financial provision to move ahead with these plans with confidence. This means there will be an increase in the finance motive to hold money which will be associated with an increase in the revolving fund of cash to facilitate this activity. The reverse is true for a reduction in planned activity. In so far as investment spending is the most unstable component of effective demand *investment finance* is a particular component of the more general finance motive that is subject to significant fluctuations. This point is taken up again in Chapter 8.

The *transactionary demand* follows on from the finance motive. The latter relates to *planned* scales of activity and the former to the *actual* levels of activity. The transactionary demand comes from the need to conduct exchange with ease and convenience. For entrepreneurs it emerges due to the time lags between the receipts of sales incomes and the payment of expenses, for example, wages, raw material costs etc.; private households have a transactionary demand for money to bridge the time lags between the receipt and disposal of all forms of incomes. As actual activity rises the transactionary demand will strengthen and vice versa.

Crucial to Keynes' liquidity preference theory is the idea that individuals desire to hold a proportion of their *accumulated* wealth in liquid saving deposits. In Keynes' theory saving is a residual – it is the *result* of individuals' decisions to consume a particular amount of their income. However the savings accumulated represents a command over future consumption in *some form*. Therefore *after* a wealth-holder decides on the propensity to consume out of income "a further decision . . . awaits him, namely, in *what form* he will hold the command over future consumption which he has reserved" (Keynes, 2007, p. 166; Keynes' emphasis). For ease of exposition Keynes simplifies the choice for those who save to two asset classes. First, savings can be hoarded in liquid saving deposits – which represent the vast array of liquid and near liquid assets. Second, savings can be placed in non-liquid deep discount bonds – which act as a representative of all illiquid assets.

A further question remains to be addressed: why should a wealth-holder desire to hold savings deposits as a liquid store of wealth? If, as the classical school suggests, uncertainty can be reduced to the same calculable status as certainty itself, the desire to hoard saving deposits is difficult to explain. Keynes poses the question that in the classical world "why should anyone outside a lunatic asylum wish to use money as a store of wealth?" (Keynes, 1973a, pp. 115–116). In the General Theory model there is no problem explaining the demand for inactive balances, for *uncertainty* about future rates of interest is a precondition for holding money as a store of value.

Keynes clarifies why a community hoards money when the state of long-term expectation is *given*. First there is the *precautionary motive*.

That is wealth-holders may find that they need immediate access to cash to meet unexpected threats or opportunities before the expiry of a bond they may be holding. They can sell the bond on the stock exchange but for an uncertain value; it is possible that if stock market conditions are dominated by bears[5] the bond will be sold at a loss. Therefore to provide security in an uncertain world it makes sense to hold a proportion of total resources in liquid saving deposits. Secondly, given the existence of uncertainty and an organised investment market there will be a *speculative motive* to hold liquid saving deposits. This is because:

> different people will estimate the prospects [of future changes in the rate of interest] differently and anyone who differs from the predominant [or conventional] opinion as expressed in market quotations may have good reason for keeping liquid resources in order to profit...
>
> (Keynes, 2007, p. 169)

Specifically if a wealth-holder expects the future rate of interest to be greater than the present rate (and the future value of bonds to be lower), he/she will hoard liquid saving deposits. Hence the speculative motive comes from wealth-holders trying to out-guess each other, to sell when conventional wisdom says buy, and in the process gain additional "profit from knowing better than the market what the future will bring forth" (Keynes, 2007, p. 170).

Keynes also examines what happens to the propensity to hoard when there are short-period *changes* in the state of long-term expectation, which is of crucial importance to the overall theory of liquidity preference. He begins by reasoning that:

> partly on reasonable and partly on instinctive grounds, our desire to hold money as a store of wealth is a *barometer of the degree of distrust* of our own calculations and conventions concerning the future... The possession of actual money lulls our disquietude; and the premium which we require to make us part with money is the measure of the degree of our disquietude.
>
> (Keynes, 1973a, p. 116; my emphasis)

In other words the *strength* of the motive to hoard money (and especially the speculative motive) depends ultimately on the *lack of confidence* wealth-holders have in their long-term forecasts about the future. Therefore when the *state of confidence* about the future forecasts:

- *deteriorates*, a community will, *cet. par.*, *strengthen* its preference to hold money as a store of wealth
- *improves*, a community will, *cet. par.*, *weaken* its desire to hoard money.

It follows that a deteriorating (improving) state of long-term expectation will strengthen (weaken) the liquidity preferences of a community to hold money as a store of value at every rate of interest. This is an essential aspect of Keynes' treatment of money the importance of which is rarely appreciated within the mainstream Keynesian literature.

> The significance of this characteristic of money has usually been over-looked; and in so far as it has been noticed, the essential nature of the phenomenon has been mis-described. For what has attracted attention has been the quantity of money which has been hoarded. ... But the quantity of hoards can only be altered either if the total quantity of money is changed or if the quantity of current money-income (I speak broadly) is changed; *whereas fluctuations in the degree of confidence are capable* of having quite a different effect, namely, in modifying not the amount that is actually hoarded, but the amount of the premium which has to be offered to induce people not to hoard. And *changes in the propensity to hoard, or in the state of liquidity preference* as I have called it, primarily affect, not prices, but the rate of interest ...
>
> (Keynes, 1973a, p. 116; my emphasis)

Keynes utilises his concept of liquidity preference to derive a new theory of the rate of interest. More specifically Keynes seeks to explain the determination of the *long-term money rate of interest*. First, because the long-term rate is used to calculate the present value of a flow of future income that will influence the investment decisions of an entrepreneur. Second, because it is the money rate of interest which is compared with the aggregated marginal efficiency of capital schedule to decide the volume of capital assets that are newly produced. In these senses the money rate of interest is *significant*. Other reasons why the money rate of interest is significant are set out in Appendix B at the end of this chapter.

Keynes formalises his liquidity preference theory by deriving an equation to represent the total demand for money by a community, which is made up of a number of elements. First, there is the demand for deposits to satisfy the transactionary and precautionary motives ($Md1$), which is a positive function ($L1$) of aggregate income (Y), where income is used as a proxy for actual economic activity and total resources. With respect to the precautionary motive there is the *cet. par.* condition that the state of long-term expectation is stable; if there are short-period changes in the state of long-term expectation then the precautionary demand (and the value of $L1$) will fluctuate. Secondly, there is the demand for saving deposits due to the speculative motive ($Md2$), which is a negative function ($L2$) of the long-term money rate of interest (r). Once again the important *cet. par.* rule is that the state of long-term expectation is given; if there are short-period changes in the state of long-term expectation the value of $L2$ function becomes unstable. Finally there is the demand for deposits to satisfy the finance motive ($Md3$) which is a stable positive function ($L3$) of planned entrepreneurial activity (Ap), for example plans to increase production of consumer goods, plans to purchase and produce capital goods or plans to increase stock market turnover. If the level of Ap fluctuates so too will the finance motive.[6] The supply of total bank deposits (Ms) is largely determined by the private banking sector after assessing the state of credit and taking account of prudential cash and liquidity ratios. Chapter 12 will examine the ways in which the monetary authority can influence the supply of deposits by the banking sector.

In equilibrium the total demand and supply of money will be equal, hence:

$$Ms = Md = Md1 + Md2 + Md3 \tag{1}$$

The total demand for money (Md) is made up of the sum of the transactionary, precautionary, speculative and finance motives to hold money. Therefore

$$Md1 = L1(Y) \; \textit{cet. par.} \text{ the state of long-term expectation} \tag{2}$$

$$Md2 = L2 \, (r) \; \textit{cet. par.} \text{ the state of long-term expectation} \tag{3}$$

$$Md3 = L3 \, (Ap) \tag{4}$$

It follows that in equilibrium:

$$Ms = L1(Y) + L2 \, (r) + L3 \, (Ap) \tag{5}$$

Keynes directs his attention to Equation 3 and the speculative demand for money function (*L2*) which he regards as the component of liquidity preference *most likely to fluctuate widely and suddenly.*[7] The first task Keynes sets himself is to define the shape of the *L2* function assuming that the state of long-term expectation is *given*. Keynes supposes that the majority of wealth-holders reach a conventional judgement as to what they regard as a *safe* rate of interest. The safe long-term interest rate is, in the conventional view of the majority of wealth-holders, the rate which is sustainable for a specified period. For each state of long-term expectation a separate conventional judgement will emerge as to what is a safe interest rate. With a safe rate of interest for a given state of long-term expectation, Keynes supposes that the *L2* function will be negatively sloped. Why?

> [W]hat matters is not the *absolute* level of r but the degree of divergence from what may be considered a fairly *safe* level of r...Nevertheless, there are two reasons for expecting that, in any given state of expectation, a fall in r will be associated with an increase in M[d]2. In the first place, if the general view as to what is a safe level of r is unchanged, every fall in r reduces the market rate relatively to the 'safe' rate and therefore increases the risk of illiquidity; and, in the second place, every fall in r reduces the current earnings from illiquidity...
>
> (Keynes, 2007, pp. 201–202; Keynes' emphasis)

Keynes' reasoning about the relationship between the market rate of interest and the safe rate requires further explanation. If the market rate is well above the safe rate the vast majority of wealth-holders will expect future interest rates to fall towards the safe level. Wealth-holders will generally prefer to hold bonds to accumulate expected capital gains. Even at a relatively high market rate, however, a small minority of wealth-holders (i.e. those who are unconventional) will expect future interest rates to move upwards and be fearful of the risk of illiquidity and a capital loss. These individuals think they know better than the market and demand cash for speculative purposes. As the market rate falls relative to the safe rate, the wealth-holders sharing the unconventional view about future interest rates will swell. The speculative demand for money will increase, but this group will still represent a minority opinion in the market. Even when the market rate equals the safe rate, the expectation that future interest rates will be higher is still likely to be a minority, but growing, viewpoint. But once the market rate falls below the safe rate the sentiment of wealth-holders will change. It may quickly become the conventional/majority view that future interest rates will rise and the speculative motive will be strengthened discernibly; but even then a minority will disagree and still prefer to hold bonds.

Therefore Keynes concludes that with every fall in the market interest rate (r) the speculative demand for money will increase – which gives us a negatively sloped $L2$ function – see Diagram 7.3.[8] On the vertical axis is the rate of interest (r) and on the horizontal axis is the speculative demand for money ($Md2$).

With a downward sloping $L2$ function the equilibrium value of the rate of interest (for a *given* state of long-term expectation) can be derived. Assuming the levels of $Md1$ and $Md3$ are constant, the amount of money available to supply the speculative motive to hoard saving deposits ($Ms2$) is also defined. Furthermore, with a given conventional judgement about the "safe" rate of interest the liquidity function $L20$ may be specified – see Diagram 7.4. In equilibrium the role of the long-term money rate of interest (r^*) is to match the demand with the supply of hoards – point E. It should be noted that even at the equilibrium interest

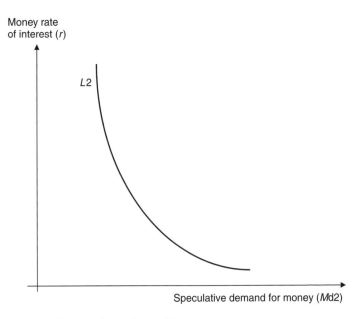

Money rate of interest (r)

$L2$

Speculative demand for money ($Md2$)

Diagram 7.3 The speculative demand for money

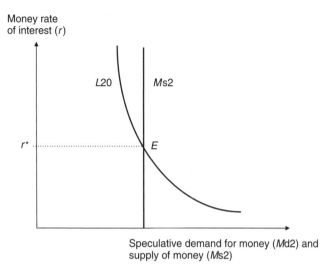

Diagram 7.4 The equilibrium rate of interest

rate r^* there is hoarding of inactive balances because the future is always uncertain and the calculations and conventions for judging the future are permanently distrusted.

Keynes then analyses the factors which might lead to a *change* in the rate of interest. He identifies two main factors; first, changes in the money supply with a stable liquidity function; secondly, changes "which are primarily due to changes in expectation affecting the liquidity function itself" (Keynes, 2007, p. 197). Followers of Keynes usually limit their analysis to changes in the supply of money. In what follows short-period changes in the state of long-term expectations which cause the *L*2 function to become *unstable* will be examined instead.

A short-period change in the state of long-term expectation which causes the value of the liquidity function *L*2 to fluctuate has a most important impact on the rate of interest. A sudden shift in the news (e.g. an Asian financial crisis, a global subprime emergency, a stock market meltdown, an improvement in profit rates) is likely to sharply alter the state of confidence and cause a shift in the *L*2 function. This will be followed by a discontinuous change in the rate of interest. With respect to the onset of an economic crisis and a decline in the state of confidence Keynes explains his argument in the following way:

> [L]iquidity preferences are sharply raised, this shows itself not so much in increased hoards.... as in a sharp rise in the rate of interest,

i.e. securities fall in price until those, who would now like to get liquid if they could do so at the previous price, are persuaded to give up the idea.... A rise in the rate of interest is a means alternative to an increase of hoards for satisfying an increased liquidity preference.

(Keynes, 1973a, p. 111)

The implications of Keynes' arguments must be clarified. Suppose initially an equilibrium interest rate r^0 compatible with liquidity function *L*20 in Diagram 7.5. Then, due to an adverse change in the news, the state of long-term expectation deteriorates. Wealth-holders generally experience a weakening in their state of confidence about their forecasts concerning the future. This increasing disquietude causes individuals to *desire* to hold more liquid saving deposits at *every* rate of interest. The *L*2 function shifts *outwards* – from *L*20 to *L*21. Another way of expressing this is that, due to a change in the news, wealth-holders perceive that the safe rate of interest has increased.

Assuming that the total money supply and other demands for money are given, the *quantity* of saving deposits available to satisfy the speculative motive (*Ms*2) is specified. To regain equilibrium after the outward

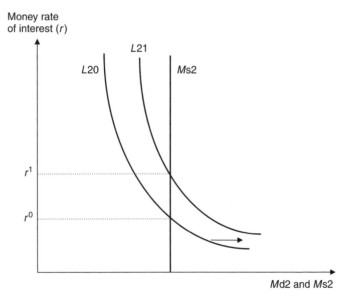

Diagram 7.5 Strengthening of liquidity preference and the rate of interest

shift in the liquidity function the rate of interest – the reward for parting with liquidity – must increase. A higher interest rate must be offered to individuals to induce them *not* to hoard saving deposits; the rate of interest rises in a *discontinuous* manner from r^0 to r^1. At this higher interest rate, the desire to hoard liquid assets is once again brought into equality with the available supply. The reverse is true if the state of long-term expectation improves and the liquidity function L2 shifts inwards. *Hence the L2 function is unstable because it depends on the state of long-term expectation which is subject to "sudden and violent" fluctuation.* It should also be noted that the unstable nature of the L2 function means that the money rate of interest will rise in response to a deterioration in the state of long-term expectation and fall in response to an improvement, *cet. par.* The implications of this for Keynes' treatment of investment spending are of the utmost importance and are taken up again in Chapter 8.

Therefore the liquidity preference theory of the rate of interest may be summed up as follows:

> The demand for liquidity can be divided between what we may call the active demand which depends on the actual and planned scales of activity, and the inactive demand which depends on the state of confidence of the inactive holder of claims and assets; whilst the supply depends on the terms on which the banks are prepared to become more or less liquid... [G]iven the state of expectation of the public and the policy of the banks, the rate of interest is that rate at which the demand and supply of liquid resources are balanced.
>
> (Keynes, 1973d, pp. 221–222; abridged quotation)

According to Keynes, therefore, the rate of interest is a *monetary phenomenon*. In the General Theory model the role of the rate of interest in a macroeconomy is to provide a reward, not for waiting or abstinence, but for parting with liquid control over resources for a specific period of time. It is because the rate of interest is the reward to wealth-holders for forgoing liquid control over their wealth that it also quantifies in concrete terms wealth-holders unwillingness to part with liquid control over their accumulated resources.

Finally note that Keynes' liquidity preference theory of the rate of interest has three important characteristics.

1. It derives a long-term money rate of interest which is *flexible* in responding to the market forces of the demand for and supply of *money*.
2. The equilibrium long-term money interest rate, so derived, need *not* be compatible with the full employment rate of interest. There is no reason to suppose that the price which equilibrates the demand and supply of money must *necessarily* be compatible with the full employment volume of investment.
3. The flexible interest rate responds to the deterioration in expectations by moving *upwards* (initially), thereby amplifying the degree of any depression.

For all these reasons the liquidity preference theory of the rate of interest marks a radical departure from the classical loanable funds theory.

f) Implications for the classical loanable funds theory

The liquidity preference theory of the rate of interest for Keynes puts the final nail in the classical loanable funds theory of interest. For when it is combined with Keynes' claim that it is the level of aggregate income which ensures the equality of aggregate investment and aggregate saving, the loanable funds theory of interest becomes redundant. Keynes is very clear on this radical point of departure from the classical theory. The following quotation shows this to be the case:

> [T]he initial novelty [of the General Theory model] lies in my maintaining that it is not the rate of interest, but the level of incomes which ensures equality between saving and investment. The arguments which lead up to this initial conclusion are independent of my subsequent theory of the rate of interest, and in fact I reached it before I had reached the latter theory. But the result was to leave the rate of interest in the air. If the rate of interest is not determined by saving and investment in the same way in which price is determined by supply and demand, how is it determined? . . . The resulting theory, whether right or wrong is exceedingly simple – namely, that the rate of interest on a loan of a given quality and maturity has to be established at the level which, in the opinion of those who have the opportunity of choice – i.e. of wealth holders – equalises the attractions of holding idle cash and of holding the loan.
>
> (Keynes, 1973b, pp. 212–213; abridged quotation)

Keynes' rejection of the loanable funds market allows him to jettison a key component of the classical theory of interest and employment. It allows attention in the General Theory model to be directed at the principle of effective demand to explain fluctuations in economic activity, rather than disequilibrium between saving and investment. The liquidity preference approach corrects a mistaken classical perception about interest, and defines the proper role which the money rate of interest rate plays in a macroeconomy.

In the *Treatise* Keynes still has a largely classical view of the rate of interest. In the *Treatise* he allows saving and investment to diverge and identifies a unique *natural* rate of interest which brings the rate of saving into equality with the rate of investment. The loanable funds market is not far away from such a conception. In the *General Theory* Keynes expresses two serious doubts about the concept of a natural rate of interest. The first relates to the already noted characteristic of the General Theory model that changes in aggregate income ensure that the volumes of aggregate saving and investment are always equal, therefore the rate of interest cannot directly preserve equality between these two aggregates.

The second doubt relates to the possibility that a macroeconomy may find itself in equilibrium below the full employment level, in which case the equilibrium rate of interest can diverge from the rate of interest compatible with the full employment level of aggregate income. Indeed Keynes' model suggests it is likely that there are a range of levels of employment where the macroeconomy is in equilibrium, and for each employment equilibrium there is a distinctive natural rate of interest. Therefore in the General Theory model there is nothing particularly special about the natural rate of interest beyond the fact that it is an *equilibrium* rate of interest. The possibility that an economy can experience both unemployment and full employment equilibria is a matter discussed in greater detail in Chapter 11.[9]

Keynes does, however, distinguish between natural rates of interest. He refers to the natural rate in the *special case* of fully employed economy as the *neutral*, or optimal, rate. This allows Keynes to make a further distinction between the General Theory model and the classical analysis. In Keynes' model the equilibrium rate of interest need *not* be compatible with the neutral rate; it is a possibility, but it is not inevitable. The classical macroeconomic analysis therefore relates to the *special case* where the equilibrium rate of interest is always at or tending towards the neutral rate.

g) The theory of fixed investment spending

The rate of investment in fixed capital is set by the relationship between the marginal efficiency of capital and the long-term rate of interest. Keynes argues:

> [t]he schedule of the marginal of capital may be said to govern the *terms* on which loanable funds are *demanded* for the purpose of new investment; whilst the rate of interest governs the *terms* on which funds are currently *supplied*.
>
> (Keynes, 2007, p. 165; my emphasis)

From the viewpoint of the wealth-holder the rate of interest is a reward for parting with liquidity, but it also sets the terms on which entrepreneurs can gain access to monies to finance capital investments. Investment spending on newly produced capital assets will be pushed to the point where the marginal efficiency of the last unit of equipment is just equal to the money rate of interest. The long-term money rate of interest sets a minimum standard which the marginal efficiency of any capital asset has to attain. No wealth-holder will purchase a capital asset providing a marginal efficiency of 5 per cent per annum, if, alternatively, he/she can lend money and receive a rate of interest of 6 per cent. Consequently Keynes concludes that there:

> will be an inducement to push the rate of new investment to the point which forces the supply-price of each type of capital asset to a figure which, taken in conjunction with its prospective yield, brings the marginal efficiency of capital in general to approximate equality with the rate of interest. That is to say, the physical conditions of supply in the capital-goods industries, the state of confidence concerning the prospective yield, the psychological attitude to liquidity and the quantity of money (preferably calculated in terms of wage units) determine, between them, the rate of new investment.
>
> (Keynes, 2007, p. 248)

This position is illustrated in Diagram 7.6. This diagram combines the aggregated marginal efficiency schedule (Diagram 7.6a) with the money market analysis (Diagram 7.6b) to define clearly the interactions. Once the rate of interest is defined in the money market (r^*) this is brought across to the marginal efficiency schedule to define the rate of fixed capital investment in the economy (I_{w^*}). The last unit of capital equipment brought into use therefore has a marginal efficiency just equal to the

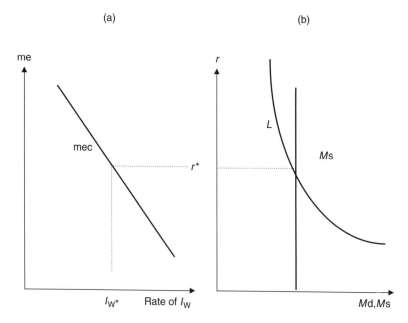

Diagram 7.6 Determining aggregate investment spending

current long-term money rate of interest. Another way of expressing this is that if Qr is the prospective yield from an asset at time r and dr is the present value of £1 deferred for r years at the current rate of interest, then $\Sigma(Qr.dr)$ is the *demand price* for the asset. Investment will therefore take place in this asset until the demand price of the investment equals its supply price. In terms of the numerical example given in Section (b) above this means that if the current rate of interest is 4 per cent then there will be investment in the machine in question as the demand price of the asset is clearly above its supply price; the same is true if the rate of interest is 5 per cent, for the demand price and supply price of an additional machine are just about equal; but at an interest rate of 6 per cent the demand price of an extra machine will fall below the supply price and the entrepreneur will not purchase another machine.

It is important to mention Keynes' constant concern that in wealthy advanced nations with a large stock of capital equipment, the opportunities for further profitable investment opportunities may be limited. As the volume of capital equipment becomes less scarce the profit from new investments will fall, and the marginal efficiency of capital in general will tend towards zero. The lack of investment opportunities in relatively wealthy nations, Keynes argues, aggravates the paradox of poverty in the midst of plenty noted in Chapter 4. An advanced nation not only has a relatively low marginal propensity to consume but the inducement to invest is weakened by the low marginal efficiency on additional capital assets.

This may become a particularly acute problem in an advanced nation suffering a high level of involuntary unemployment. Entrepreneurs in a capitalist system will have difficulty finding profitable reasons to embark on additional capital investment unless the rate of interest is very low indeed; and even if the investment is forthcoming the value of the multiplier is not likely to be large due to the relatively low marginal propensity to consume. The irony is enhanced when it is noted that a poorer nation faced with the same level of involuntary unemployment will find it easier to alleviate the situation with a much smaller reduction in the rate of interest. For with a scarcity of capital the marginal efficiency on new capital assets will be high; so a small reduction in the rate of interest may be sufficient to generate a substantial increase in private investment spending. Moreover with a relatively high marginal propensity to consume there will be a significant multiplier effect associated with the rise of investment.

From this it follows that a nation faced with both a relatively low propensity to consume and a weak inducement to invest will find it difficult to alleviate involuntary unemployment when it emerges. If there are limitations on the conduct monetary policy aimed at cutting the money rate of interest to very low levels in order to stimulate private investment spending, a strong case can be made for a State-led investment programme to stimulate sufficient effective demand to create full employment. This is a theme taken up again in Chapter 12.

Finally the reader needs to appreciate that Keynes' theory of aggregate investment implies a rejection of the classical dichotomy between the monetary and non-monetary sectors of the macroeconomy. In the classical theory money is simply a veil over actual decisions to produce and consume. In analytical terms the classics claim that it is possible to discover the workings of an economy without reference to monetary forces. Keynes disagrees with this perspective. *In his model the role of the money rate of interest in specifying the rate of investment in durable capital equipment emphasises the inextricable links between the monetary and non-monetary sectors of a macroeconomy. It is in this context, more than any other, that Keynes' General Theory model can be said to be a monetary theory of production.*

h) Summary

The rate of aggregate investment spending is determined by the relationship between the marginal efficiency of capital in general and the long-term money rate of interest. The marginal efficiency of capital of a capital asset is the rate of discount which brings the total present value of a stream of expected future profits from the sale of the output of the asset into equality with its supply price. For each capital asset a negatively sloped marginal efficiency schedule may be derived assuming a given state of expectation. The individual schedules can be aggregated into a marginal efficiency schedule for capital assets in general. The aggregated schedule will also be downward sloping.

The schedule of the marginal efficiency of capital is dependent on the state of long-term expectation. When there is a deteriorating short-period state of long-term expectations this will cause a downward shift of the schedule; an improvement in expectation will result in an upward shift. The general marginal efficiency of capital schedule is also affected by changes in the community's propensity to save and probable changes in the future costs of producing capital assets.

The long-term money rate of interest is the other main influence on the volume of fixed capital investment. The liquidity preference theory suggests that the rate of interest is the price which equilibrates the total demand to hold bank deposits with the available supply. The community demands to hold money to facilitate the planning of new activity (i.e. the finance motive) and actual exchange (i.e. the transactionary motive), and to store wealth in a liquid form (i.e. the precautionary and speculative motives). Uncertain knowledge of future is the precondition for the desire to hoard wealth in liquid money.

Keynes argues that the speculative motive to hoard money is potentially the most unstable element of total money demand because the motive depends heavily on the state of long-term expectation. A deteriorating short-period state of long-term expectation will increase the speculative demand for money and raise the rate of interest *cet. par.*; conversely an improvement in long-term expectation will reduce the strength of the speculative motive and lower the interest rate *cet. par.* In the liquidity preference theory the rate of interest is a monetary phenomenon; the rate of interest is the reward for parting with liquidity and it measures the unwillingness of the community to part with liquid control over resources.

The money rate of interest sets a minimum standard which the marginal efficiency of any capital asset must attain. For any given schedule of the marginal efficiency, the rate of interest defines the maximum volume of fixed capital investment (measured in wage units). The role of the money rate of interest in investment decisions shows the inextricable linkages between the monetary and non-monetary sectors of a macroeconomy.

Appendix A
Post-Keynesian Criticisms of the Marginal Efficiency of Capital Schedule

In Keynes' mind the specification of the marginal efficiency of capital – separate from the rate of interest – marks a considerable advance on classical theory. In addition for Keynes it is primarily through the marginal efficiency of capital that expectations of the *future* influence decisions about spending *today*. Yet Keynes' further contention that the aggregated marginal efficiency of capital schedule is downward sloping has been the subject of much Post-Keynesian criticism (Robinson, 1962; Kalecki, 1966, 1982; Asimakopulos, 1971). Keynes' justification for a downward sloping marginal efficiency schedule is based on two assertions. First, that as the rate of aggregate investment increases there will be upward pressure on the supply prices of a range of capital assets due to the law of diminishing returns. Secondly, that as the rate of investment increases the expected returns from new capital assets will inevitably decline as equipment available becomes relatively less scarce.

Robinson and Asimakopulos argue that that Keynes' treatment of supply prices is methodologically flawed. It mixes up ex ante investment decisions with ex post investment outcomes. An individual entrepreneur will make investment decisions ex ante based on a given supply price for a capital asset. Yet if there is a general recovery of investment, when a group of entrepreneurs decide to expand capacity at broadly the same time, then in the aggregate supply prices will increase ex post. But what is not legitimate is to assume that an individual entrepreneur can predict whether his investment decisions will or will not be associated with a general rise in investment spending. If the marginal efficiency schedule is supposed to be derived from the investment plans of businesses ex ante, methodologically it is inappropriate to explain its derivation by reference to results of investment decisions ex post.

When however ex post factors are included in the derivation of the schedule of the marginal efficiency of capital, then the impact on expected profits of changes in investment spending must also be incorporated into the analysis. Keynes does not do this. According to Kalecki the reason for this is that Keynes assumes the state of long-term expectation about profitability to be given when determining the rate of investment. Kalecki by contrast does consider the impact of changing levels of investment spending on the expected returns from investment. Kalecki accepts Keynes' analysis that higher aggregate investment will, with a multiplier effect, increase output prices and current profits earned by entrepreneurs. Then Kalecki claims that the *current* level of business profits is the most important influence on expected profits, a point to which Kalecki claims Keynes gives insufficient attention.

Kalecki goes on to consider an economy with a rate of investment (I_{w1}) where the marginal efficiency of capital (or the expected rate of profit, me^1) is greater than the rate of interest (r^2) – see Diagram 7.A1(a) and 7.A1(b). According to Keynes' analysis the rate of investment should increase to I_{w2} at which point the marginal efficiency and the rate of interest will be equalised ($me^2 = r^2$) due to the ex post increase in supply prices.

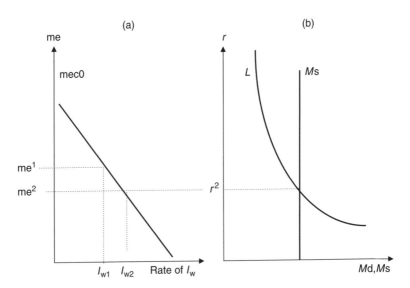

Diagram 7.A1   A disequilibrium rate of investment

Kalecki claims that the increase in investment will stimulate a wider economic recovery, with higher prices and outputs in all sectors, and a rise in current profits. As businesses enjoy higher current profits so they upgrade their expectations of future profits on new investment plans. This strengthening of profit expectations can be represented as an outward shift in the marginal efficiency schedule from mec0 to mec1 – see Diagram 7.A2 – caused by the higher rate of investment spending I_{w2}. In which case, at I_{w2} the marginal efficiency of capital (me^1) is once again greater than the rate of interest r^2.

If Kalecki is correct this means that Keynes' analysis cannot determine the actual rate of investment spending, which is a rather profound analytical deficiency. Additionally once it is allowed that current investment spending influences the expectations of profits on new investment, Kalecki can find little reason to justify Keynes' claim that the marginal efficiency schedule is downward sloping. In Diagram 7.A2, for example, the marginal efficiency (me^1) is the same for both rates of investment I_{w1} and I_{w2}. Indeed, once Kalecki's insights are considered, it is quite possible to conceive of circumstances where the marginal efficiency of capital increases as the rate of investment rises. The concept of a declining marginal efficiency of capital schedule will not do.

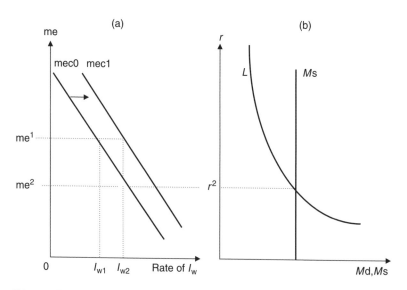

Diagram 7.A2   A Kaleckian view of Keynes' investment theory

Kalecki has one more, profound, methodological criticism of Keynes' analysis of investment. It is that Keynes attempts to constrain the inevitably *dynamic* process of investment spending within a *static* comparative equilibrium methodology. This has led Post-Keynesians such as Robinson and Asimakopulos to develop frameworks which treat investment spending as evolving dynamically through time as expected profits change, embracing the reciprocal determinist nature of such spending.

Joan Robinson, for example, accepts Kalecki's insight that increases in actual investment will increase current profits and the expectations of returns on new investment plans. Hence expected returns can be seen as a *positive* function of the present rate of investment spending. In addition capitalists have a *desired* rate of investment which is a function of *expected* returns; the higher the expected returns from investment decisions the greater the desired rate of investment spending and vice versa. It is quite possible to conceive an economy in which the expected rate of profit is such that the current and desired rates of investment are just equalised. But this position is by no means inevitable. If the current and desired rates of investment diverge from each other the economy will experience a process of dynamic change. Robinson's analysis is therefore not hampered by artificial assumptions about a declining marginal efficiency of capital. Clearly such an approach can be viewed as a Post-Keynesian advance upon Keynes' original theory of aggregate investment spending.

Appendix B
Why is the Money Rate of Interest the Most Significant?

In Keynes' theory of investment it is the *money* rate of interest which sets the standard which the marginal efficiency of any capital asset must, at least, attain before it is newly produced. But why does the *money* rate of interest play this important role? Put another way why does Keynes believe the money rate of interest to be the most significant? The answer for Keynes is that money has the important characteristic that it is the asset with the *greatest* own rate of interest which declines *more slowly* than the interest rate of any other durable commodity as its supply increases.

How does Keynes reach this conclusion? According to Keynes each durable commodity and asset, including money, has its "own" rate of interest expressed in terms of itself. Keynes gives the example of the own rate of interest of wheat where 105 quarters of wheat to be delivered one year hence can be exchanged for 100 quarters for spot delivery. In this case the wheat own rate of interest is 5 per cent. Similar examples can be given for houses, steel, machinery and, of course, money, each with their own rates of interest.

There is however no reason why own rates of interest on different assets or durable commodities should always be equal. Keynes provides an example where:

- the *spot* price for wheat is £100 per 100 quarters;
- the *future* price of wheat to be delivered in one year's time is £107 per 100 quarters;
- the money rate of interest is 5 per cent pa.

The wheat rate of interest in this case can be worked out in the following way:

- the £100 spot price (with a 5 per cent money interest rate) will buy £105 for forward delivery;

- £105 for forward delivery will buy 98 quarters of wheat (i.e. 105/107) for forward delivery;
- 100 quarters of wheat for spot delivery will buy 98 quarters for forward delivery and the wheat rate of interest is *minus* 2 per cent.

The next step of the argument is to determine the *significant* asset with the *greatest* own rate of interest. This is the asset with the own rate of interest that declines *most* slowly as the amount of investment in the capital asset increases. It is this interest rate which Keynes thinks appropriate to compare to the aggregated marginal efficiency of capital schedule to determine the rate of investment in newly produced capital assets. As already noted Keynes contends that this will be the *money* rate of interest. To understand Keynes' claim it is important to review the reasoning behind it.

Keynes argues that every capital asset possesses three attributes in different degrees. The three attributes of an asset are the:

1. *yield or output* (denoted by q) from assisting a production process or supplying a consumer service;
2. *carrying costs* (denoted by c) of holding the asset for example wastage and storage costs through time, whether or not they are being used;
3. *liquidity premium* (denoted by l) which is the sum people are prepared to pay to hold an asset which can be turned into (or is) a medium of exchange and thereby provides convenience and security to the holder.

The own rate of interest for any asset is equal to $(q - c + l)$, where q, c and l are measured in terms of the asset itself. Each asset will combine the three attributes in different ways. For example, a machine used in a production process has a larger yield than its carrying costs, whilst its liquidity premium is insignificant; a stock of liquid goods has a low yield, combined with significant carrying costs and some liquidity premium before the stock reaches an unreasonable level. Money, by contrast, will have no yield, negligible carrying costs, but a very large liquidity premium. Indeed it is an essential characteristic of money that l is greater than c, whilst for most other assets it is usually the other way around (i.e. $c > l$).

So what are the peculiarities which make money significant? Keynes identifies three peculiar characteristics.

1. Money tends, in both the short and long periods, to have a very low *elasticity of production*. By a low elasticity of production Keynes means that when the demand for money increases – and the money rate of interest rises – the supply of money does not increase by much (if at all). Moreover, there is no facility for entrepreneurs to apply more labour to produce money. By contrast an asset which can be easily produced (e.g. a machine or wheat) will find that as the demand for it increases its own rate of interest will decline as its stock rises (i.e. due to a falling level of q or an increasing level of c).

Keynes is, however, aware that a pure rent factor of production such as land will, just like money, has a small elasticity of production. Yet Keynes claims money has two further characteristics that make its own rate of interest significant.

2. The *elasticity of substitution* of money is zero or near to it. Money has utility in that it is a unit of exchange. Hence as the demand for money increases, and its interest rate rises, this demand is not usually diverted into other assets. Money is the most liquid asset which is the key to purchasing power whilst pure rent factors of production do not fulfil this role.

3. The "real" supply of money may, however, be increased if the wage unit falls. This may counter the low elasticity of production of money, in turn allowing the money rate of interest to fall. Yet Keynes notes that what is of importance is the *difference* between the marginal efficiency of capital on all other assets and the money rate of interest. Although a falling wage unit can allow the money rate of interest to fall, it will cause the marginal efficiency of all other assets to deteriorate. The reader will have to wait until Chapter 9 to fully appreciate this point; but after Chapter 9 is completed the reader is advised to come back and re-read this part of the appendix.

However, even if a reduction in the wage unit puts downward pressure on the money interest rate the extent to which this rate can decline is constrained by the existence of a so-called liquidity trap. The liquidity trap places a floor below which the money rate of interest will not fall, even when there are sizable increases in the money supply. The influence of the liquidity trap is reinforced by the fact that money has zero carrying costs which means that for money the value of 1 will always exceed c. Keynes claims a similar "trap" is unlikely to apply to other assets with significant carrying costs when a large stock is held. To fully appreciate this point the reader might wish to re-read this section again after completing Chapter 12.

All this allows Keynes to claim that the money rate of interest is likely to be the greatest own rate of interest when compared to other assets, and the rate which declines more slowly than the own rate of interest of other assets when supply increases. Keynes concludes that:

> a rise in the money-rate of interest retards the output of all the objects of which the production is elastic without being capable of stimulating the output of money.... The money rate of interest, by setting the pace for all other commodity-rates of interest, holds back investment in production of these other commodities without being capable of stimulating investment for the production of money...
>
> (Keynes, 2007, pp. 234–235)

Of course there is one solution to the problem of the money rate of interest being too high to generate full employment. It is a monetary authority under public control which increases the money supply when appropriate. As Keynes notes:

> [u]nemployment develops... because people want the moon; – men cannot be employed when the object of desire (i.e. money) is something which cannot be produced and the demand for which cannot be readily choked off. There is no remedy but to persuade the public that green cheese is practically the same thing and to have a green cheese factory (i.e. a central bank) under public control.
>
> (Keynes, 2007, p. 235)

This is a topic taken up again in Chapter 12 of this book.

8
Fluctuations in the Inducement to Invest

a) Introduction

Keynes uses short-period changes in the state of long-term expectation working through the marginal efficiency of capital and the money rate of interest to explain fluctuations in the inducement to invest. This chapter completes the explanation of why the inducement to invest is inherently unstable in character in a capitalist economy. The chapter also highlights the impact that changes in the level of fixed investment spending have on effective demand and employment.

Section (b) analyses a weakening of the inducement to invest caused by a deteriorating state of long-term expectation, which leads to a reduction in aggregate fixed investment spending. Section (c) examines a strengthening of the inducement to invest caused by an improvement in the state of long-term expectation and the consequent expansion in aggregate investment; this section highlights the role that bank *finance* plays in the process of capital formation. Section (d) provides a numerical and diagrammatic illustration of how unstable investment spending influences effective demand, employment and hence income. This section also applies the multiplier concepts developed in Chapter 4 to reinforce the arguments advanced. Finally, Section (e) updates the causal map of the General Theory model to take account of the analysis contained in this chapter and the two that precede it.

b) A weakening of the inducement to invest

The state of long-term expectation is conditioned by two important facts. First, decision-makers' utter ignorance of the future consequences of present actions; second, their *lack* of confidence in the precarious conventions available on which to base decisions about the future. Keynes, therefore, reasons that the state of long-term expectation is subject to sudden and violent changes in the short period. Sudden changes in the state of expectation influences both the schedule of the marginal efficiency of capital and the rate of interest. The former is influenced by changing opinions about prospective yields, the latter through changing the community's propensity to hoard liquid saving deposits as a store of value. Keynes concludes that there can be no surprise that fixed investment spending is so liable to fluctuate.

> For it depends on *two* sets of judgments about the future, neither of which rests on an adequate or secure foundation – on the propensity to hoard and on opinions of the future yield of capital assets... [Indeed] the same circumstances which lead to *pessimistic* views about the future yields are apt to *increase* the propensity to hoard.
>
> (Keynes, 1973a, pp. 118; my emphasis)

So say, due to adverse news, there is a sudden and significant *deterioration* in the state of long-term expectation. As disillusionment spreads through entrepreneurs the first consequence is a collapse in the marginal efficiency of capital in general. In Diagram 8.1a this may be represented by a *downward* shift of the marginal efficiency schedule (from mec0 to mec1). This will cause investment in fixed capital equipment (measured in wage units) to be curtailed (i.e. from I_{w0} to I_{w1}), even with no change in the rate of interest.

Keynes however identifies a further adverse effect on investment spending as expectations deteriorate. Namely that associated with the adverse change in the news the state of confidence of wealth-holders will be undermined, causing them to sharply increase their desire to hold money as a store of value. This strengthening of the state of liquidity preference will cause a rise in the long-term money rate of interest. In Diagram 8.1b above the sharp rise in liquidity preference is represented by the *outward* shift in the demand for money schedule (i.e. L0 to L1) and hence an increase in the interest rate (from r^0 to r^1).

The *cumulative* result of *both* the downward shift in the marginal efficiency of capital schedule *and* the rise in the rate of interest is that fixed capital investment spending will fall (from I_{w0} through I_{w1} to I_{w2}). This in turn will have an adverse impact on aggregate effective demand, amplified by the multiplier effect, causing a fall off in total output and employment.

The decline in fixed investment spending will have a further impact on liquid capital and working capital investment. After the initial

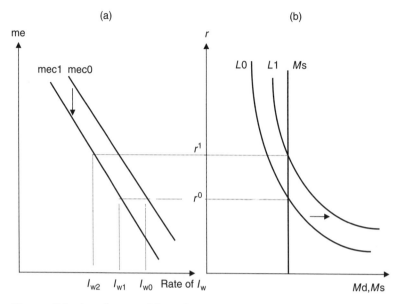

Diagram 8.1 A weakening of the inducement to invest

decline in the placing of orders for fixed capital equipment there will be a build-up of surplus stocks of both finished and semi-finished goods. As the multiplier effect takes hold and consumption spending starts to fall off, this build-up of surplus goods will extend to the consumption goods sector. In other words a decline in fixed investment spending will initially cause a temporary *increase* in liquid capital investment. But profit-maximising entrepreneurs will not keep surplus stocks for long and will initiate plans to reduce these stocks as a matter of urgency. As these surplus stocks are absorbed this represents a form of *negative investment* which has a further adverse impact on current output and total employment.

The reduction in output caused by the decline in fixed investment spending will, moreover, occasion some working capital *disinvestment*. In other words there will be a reduction in the stocks of raw materials and finished goods required to ensure a continuous process of production and distribution as the level of total output and sales declines. The decline in working capital may be significant, and once a slump has started it will create a cumulative downturn in output and employment in the raw material and manufacturing components sectors of the economy.

It should also be noted that as entrepreneurial plans to add new or replace old capital assets are shelved there will be a consequent decline in the finance motive to hold money. The revolving fund of finance will be under-utilised as old loans and debts are repaid but entrepreneurs decide not to seek access to new financial provisions. However in so far as the finance motive is met by loans and overdrafts drawn against the private banking system, any decline in the finance demand for money will be matched by a reduction in the bank money supply.

c) A strengthening of the inducement to invest

It is usual for followers of Keynes – both mainstream and Post-Keynesian – to focus attention on an economic downturn. But Keynes' model can be applied to consider an economic expansion as well. This occurs when, due to a change in news, there is a sudden and significant *improvement* in the state of long-term expectation. This strengthens the inducement to invest.

As confidence spreads the first consequence is a strengthening of the marginal efficiency of capital. In Diagram 8.2a this is shown as an *upward* shift of the marginal efficiency schedule (from mec0 to mec*). This will cause investment in fixed investment spending to rise (i.e. from

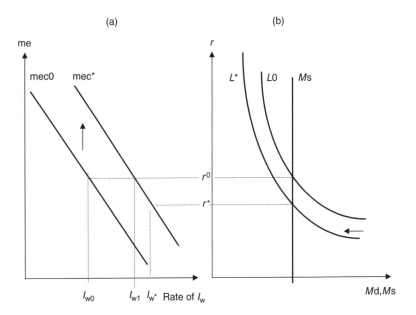

Diagram 8.2 A strengthening of the inducement to invest

I_{w0} to I_{w1}), even with no change in the rate of interest. But there is a further beneficial influence on the inducement to invest, for the improved news causes wealth-holders' state of confidence to improve, thereby reducing their desire to hold money as a store of value. The weakening of liquidity preferences will, *cet. par.*, lower the long-term money rate of interest. In Diagram 8.2b the decline in liquidity preference is represented by the *inward* shift in the demand for money schedule (i.e. $L0$ to L^*), meaning a decrease in the interest rate (from r^0 to r^*).

The *cumulative* result of *both* the upward shift in the marginal efficiency of capital schedule *and* the fall in the rate of interest is that fixed capital investment will increase (from I_{w0} through I_{w1} to I_{w^*}). This will have a beneficial impact on aggregate effective demand which, because of the multiplier effect, will rise by an even greater amount, causing total output and employment to move upwards.

An increase in fixed investment spending will again impact on working capital investment. For the increase in output caused by stronger fixed investment spending will require more working capital investment to maintain the continuity of production and distribution at a higher level. The expansion of working capital will occur first in the capital goods sector, but as the multiplier effect takes hold it will transfer to the consumption goods industries as well. Of course this will provide a further stimulus to total output and employment, at least initially.

Once the increase in fixed investment spending, and its associated multiplier effects, fully works through, the rise in aggregate income will generate a consequent increase in aggregate saving that just matches the additional investment spending.

This still leaves the question of how the additional investment spending is financed before the saving is generated. How can entrepreneurs make plans to increase investment activity whilst feeling sufficiently liquid to be able to place the orders for new machinery? According to Keynes the answer to these questions lies in the provision of finance to bridge the interregnum between businesses making plans to increase investment spending and conducting the actual transactions for new equipment. In other words associated with the planned rise in investment demand there is an increased finance motive to hold money, which can be met in a number of ways.

First, the private banking sector can increase its bank lending in order to finance the purchases of new capital equipment and it can extend the overdraft facilities of entrepreneurs to allow the latter to finance new working capital investment – both of which will increase in the bank money supply.[1] Or entrepreneurs can issue new securities hoping that wealth-holders will release previously inactive balances which entrepreneurs can then use to facilitate investment activity; that is there is a movement within the total demand for money from inactive towards active balances. Actually wealth-holders are most likely to release such inactive hoards (which Keynes calls dishoarding) precisely when the state of confidence in the future is improving and the demand for money as a store of value is weakening.[2]

Once the new investment in capital equipment has started aggregate income begins to rise and the associated saving will be forthcoming. If the additional saving takes the form of higher business profits (i.e. retained profits) this provides entrepreneurs with the money with which to repay the outstanding bank loans and reduce any overdraft obligations. As extra savings are accumulated by wealth-holders this will generate an additional demand for bonds. Entrepreneurs can then take advantage of the relative ease of obtaining money on the bond market by issuing new bonds in order to repay outstanding bank loans and other debt; in the process entrepreneurs replace short-term debt with debt that can be repaid over a longer time frame more in keeping with the expected profit stream from new capital assets.[3]

It should not be thought, however, that when the finance motive to hold money increases there is an inevitable increase in the supply of money available. Keynes is keenly aware that if the demand for new fixed investment rises very strongly the available revolving fund of finance may be exhausted, in which case the additional demand for money will cause a rise in the rate of interest and a slowdown in investment plans.[4] Hence for Keynes the private banking system plays a pivotal role in the transition from a lower to a higher level of economic activity. If, however, the lending policies of the private banking sector in any way inhibit the provision of finance to facilitate a process of expansion then the banks will act as a barrier to prosperity. The private banking system therefore has a pivotal role in the process of capital formation in a capitalist economy. *It should also be noted that the role of the finance motive in investment activity shows once again the inextricable linkages between the monetary and non-monetary sectors of a macroeconomy which Keynes is so concerned to emphasise.*

d) Aggregate effective demand revisited

In Chapter 3 it was shown that with a stable aggregate supply function the expected levels of consumption and investment spending determine the volume of aggregate effective demand. And, assuming short-term expectations are correct, the volume of effective demand equals the level of aggregate income. Hence:

$$Y_w = \text{AED}_w = D_w = C_w + I_w = Z_w$$

Keynes reasons that investment spending is likely to be the most unstable component of aggregate effective demand. It should be clear *why* Keynes reaches this conclusion. The two main independent variables which influence fixed investment spending – the marginal efficiency of capital and the state of liquidity preference – are both liable to fluctuate widely and suddenly. In addition variations in aggregate effective demand, caused by changes in fixed investment, lead to fluctuations in the volumes of working and liquid capital investment.

The impact that unstable investment spending has on effective demand and employment can be represented in a numerical example – see Table 8.1. Assume initially aggregate fixed investment spending is 1 million wage units. With a given consumption function that has a diminishing marginal propensity to consume after the critical income level, real effective demand is 5 million wage units. This means that aggregate income is 5 million wage units, and the equilibrium volume of employment is 5 million labour units. Table 8.1 then demonstrates the impact on effective demand and employment of first a decrease (Case 2) and then an increase (Case 3) of aggregate investment spending.

In Case 2 a decrease in fixed investment spending – in wage units from 1 million to 0.5 million – lowers the level of real aggregate effective demand – to 4 million wage units. This reduces aggregate income to 4 million wage units, and the equilibrium volume of employment falls to 4 million labour units. Conversely in Case 3 the increase in fixed investment spending – in wage units from 1 million to 1.5 million – raises the level of real aggregate effective demand – to 6 million wage units. Aggregate income rises to 6 million wage units, whilst the equilibrium volume of employment rises to 6 million labour units.

The contents of Table 8.1 are illustrated in Diagram 8.3. The real aggregate demand price (D_w), the real aggregate supply price and effective demand measured in wage units (AED_w) are on the vertical axis and labour units are on the horizontal axis. With a stable consumption function (F_{w0}) and a given level of aggregate investment spending equal to 1 million units as in Case 1 above, the aggregate demand function F_{w0} is defined. The economy is, therefore, in equilibrium with a volume of aggregate effective demand equal to 5 million wage units. This in turn determines that the equilibrium volume of total employment is 5 million labour units.

Table 8.1   Unstable investment spending, effective demand and employment

N (mills)	Y_w (mills)	χ^*	C_w (mills)	I_w (mills)	D_w (mills)	Z_w (mill)
Case 1						
0	0	1.0	0.0	1.0	1.0	0.0
1	1	1.0	1.0	1.0	2.0	1.0
2	2	0.9	1.9	1.0	2.9	2.0
3	3	0.9	2.8	1.0	3.8	3.0
4	4	0.7	3.5	1.0	4.5	4.0
5	5	0.5	4.0	1.0	5.0	5.0
6	6	0.5	4.5	1.0	5.5	6.0
Case 2						
0	0	1.0	0.0	0.5	0.5	0.0
1	1	1.0	1.0	0.5	1.5	1.0
2	2	0.9	1.9	0.5	2.4	2.0
3	3	0.9	2.8	0.5	3.3	3.0
4	4	0.7	3.5	0.5	4.0	4.0
5	5	0.5	4.0	0.5	4.5	5.0
6	6	0.5	4.5	0.5	5.0	6.0
Case 3						
0	0	1.0	0.0	1.5	1.5	0.0
1	1	1.0	1.0	1.5	2.5	1.0
2	2	0.9	1.9	1.5	3.4	2.0
3	3	0.9	2.8	1.5	4.3	3.0
4	4	0.7	3.5	1.5	5.0	4.0
5	5	0.5	4.0	1.5	5.5	5.0
6	6	0.5	4.5	1.5	6.0	6.0

Glossary: N = labour units; Y_w = aggregate income measured in wage units; χ^* = the marginal propensity to consume; C_w = expected aggregate consumption expenditure measured in wage units; I_w = expected investment spending measured in wage units; D_w = the aggregate demand price measured in wage units; Z_w = the aggregate supply price measured in wage units.

Suppose that the level of aggregate fixed investment spending falls to 0.5 million wage units. With a stable consumption function, this means that the aggregate demand function shifts downwards (from F_{w0} to F_{w1}). Furthermore, with a stable aggregate supply price function (ϕ), real effective demand falls to 4 million wage units and total equilibrium employment declines to 4 million labour units. Conversely, if aggregate fixed investment spending increases to say 1.5 million wage units, the aggregate demand function will shift up to F_{w2}; consequently

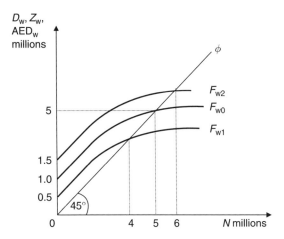

Diagram 8.3 Unstable investment spending and effective demand

effective demand increases to 6 million wage units and total equilibrium employment rises to 6 million labour units.[5]

The extent of the change in aggregate income is, of course, greater than the initial change in investment spending; just as the variation in total employment is greater than the fluctuation in employment in the investment industries. The precise relationship between these changes is specified by the investment and employment multiplier. Once the investment multiplier is determined so too is the employment multiplier, using the simplifying assumption that the two multipliers have the same value. In Case 2 where there is a decline in fixed investment spending there seems to be a complication in working out the investment multiplier as the marginal propensity to consume changes from a value of 0.5 to 0.7 as aggregate income declines. Actually the complication is more apparent than real, as the marginal propensity used to calculate the investment multiplier is that of the original level of aggregate income that is 0.5 at 5 million wage units. Therefore the value of the investment multiplier (k) is equal to:

$$k = \frac{1}{1 - \chi^*} = \frac{1}{1 - 0.5} = 2$$

The reduction in aggregate fixed investment spending by 0.5 million wage units leads to a decline in aggregate income of 1 million wage units – a multiplier effect of 2. A similar impact can be noted for the rise in investment spending by 0.5 million wage units as aggregate income increases by 1 million wage units. Assuming the employment multiplier also has a value of 2 this suggests that as a result of the decline in investment spending, primary employment falls by 0.5 million labour units causing a decline in total employment of 1 million labour units. Conversely an increase in investment spending adds to primary employment by 0.5 million labour units and to total employment by 1 million labour units. The reader can check for themselves that all the calculations work when the aggregates are expressed in nominal rather than wage unit terms.

Keynes' analysis of fluctuations in the inducement to invest leads him to a very important conclusion. In the General Theory model, with a given state of long-term expectation, the:

> level of output and employment as a whole depends on the amount of investment. I put it this way, not because this is the only factor on which aggregate output depends, but because... [it is the factors] which determine the rate of investment which are most unreliable, since it is they which are influenced by our views of the future about which we know so little.
>
> (Keynes, 1973a, p. 121; abridged quotation)

e) A causal map of the General Theory model

It is possible to update the causal map outlined at the end of Chapter 5 to take account of the analysis contained in Chapters 6, 7 and this chapter. Specifically the variables that determine the level of investment spending can be clarified. In the nominal model the ultimate independent variables in the model can be extended; to the propensity to consume (χ), the wage unit (*WU*) and the aggregate supply relationship (ϕ), can be added the expectation of prospective yields from capital assets (pyc), the demand for money (*Md*) and the money supply (*Ms*).

The overarching variable that will determine aggregate investment spending is the state of long-term expectation (SLTE). Short-period changes in this variable have an important influence on the prospective yields on newly produced capital assets (pyc), hence the marginal efficiency of capital (me), and on the liquidity preferences (*Md*) of the community. The demand to hold money combined with the money supply (*Ms*) defines the long-term money rate of interest (*r*). Comparing the rate of interest with the marginal efficiency of capital determines the nominal volume of fixed capital investment (*I*). Nominal consumption spending (C) is specified by the community's propensity to consume and the wage unit. Expected consumption and investment spending determine the level of the aggregate demand price (D). The wage unit and the aggregate supply relationship specify the aggregate supply price (Z). Where D and Z are equal the volume of aggregate effective demand (AED) is defined. Finally, nominal effective demand determines the nominal values for aggregate income (Y), aggregate saving (S) and total employment of labour units (N) – the dependent variables.

The causal map expressed in real terms follows a similar, but not identical, pattern. The propensity to consume alone defines the real level of consumption spending (C_w). Nominal investment spending (I) is determined by the forces of the state of long-term expectation, expected prospective yields on capital assets, the state of liquidity preference, the

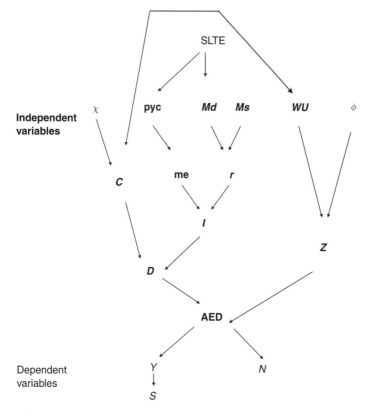

Map 8

marginal efficiency of capital and the long-term money rate of interest; and I is deflated by the wage unit to determine real investment spending (I_w).

Expected levels of C_w and I_w combined determine the real level of the aggregate demand price (D_w). The stable value for the aggregate

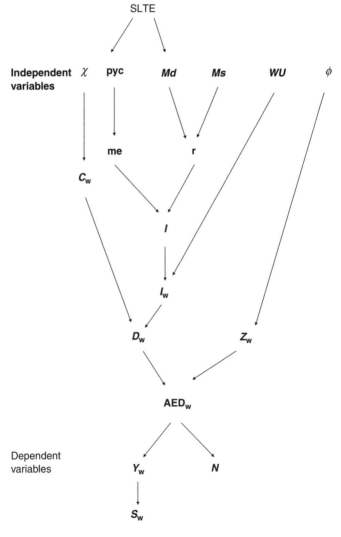

Map 9

supply relationship (ϕ) determines the real aggregate supply price (Z_w). When D_w and Z_w are equal the real level of aggregate effective demand is defined (AED_w). The level of AED_w in turn specifies the equilibrium values for the dependent variables – real aggregate income (Y_w), real aggregate saving (S_w) and employment of labour units (N).

f) Summary

This chapter reviews the primary *source* of instability in the inducement to invest – its reliance on the capricious state of long-term expectation. Keynes argues that short-period changes in the state of long-term expectation will influence both the marginal efficiency of capital and the rate of interest. Changes in both the marginal efficiency and the rate of interest will have a *cumulative* effect on the rate of investment in fixed capital. Hence if there is a deteriorating marginal efficiency of capital this will be accompanied by a rise in the rate of interest, *both* of which will reduce fixed investment spending. Alternatively, an improvement in the marginal efficiency will usually be associated with a fall in the interest rate, *both* of which will stimulate the rate of fixed investment. Both working and (to a lesser extent) liquid capital investment are subject to significant changes as well; these are largely a consequence of fluctuations in fixed capital investment spending and the associated variations in total output.

This chapter also shows the influence which a fluctuating inducement to invest has on effective demand and total employment (hence real income). A fall (rise) in investment spending will cause an amplified fall (rise) in the aggregate effective demand and total employment. The precise extent of any changes can be calculated using either the investment or employment multiplier.

9
Money Wages, Employment and Effective Demand

a) Introduction

So far in this book the analysis has been conducted assuming the general level of money wages – and the wage unit – is given. Keynes however *does* allow money wages to change and this chapter will explain the implications of this for the General Theory model. In the process the chapter explodes the most erroneous myth perpetrated by mainstream Keynesians: that Keynes' General Theory model *assumes* money wages are constant. Nothing is further from the truth. Indeed Keynes' treatment of the impact that a cut in the general level of money wage has on total employment is a crucial part of his claim that his model is more generally applicable than the classical analysis.

The reason why the *General Theory* considers the impact of wage cuts on employment is that this subject greatly exercised Keynes in the policy debates of the 1920s and early 1930s. In this period a debate raged about the role of wage cuts in resolving the high unemployment rates experienced in the United Kingdom. In the 1920s it related to the UK government policy of setting an overvalued exchange rate for sterling (by as much as 10–12 per cent) in the Gold Standard system, necessitating a 10 per cent cut in the general level of money wages. In the 1930s even larger wage cuts – of anything up to 30 per cent – were proposed as a cure for the impact of the Great Depression on the United Kingdom. Keynes throughout this period is an intuitive opponent of these wage-cutting policies, for in a free society he thinks them impractical, lacking in economic rationale and socially unjust. These objections form the basis for his policy writings before the *General Theory*.

With the General Theory model Keynes returns to the subject to reveal how a general money wage cut can generate both good and bad results for employment, depending on its impact on aggregate effective demand, and about which it is difficult to generalise. However in an open, decentralised society Keynes concludes that wage cutting will probably have adverse effects on employment. Furthermore, Keynes' analysis suggests that the most beneficial influence a wage cut can have on employment is through a reduction in the long-term rate of interest; but Keynes notes that the same effect can be achieved with an expansionary monetary stance and stable money wages. Touching on issues first raised by Keynes in the 1920s, this chapter outlines the criteria by which he chooses between a flexible monetary policy and a flexible wage policy.

Section (b) reviews Keynes' contribution to the policy debate about wage cuts in the 1920s and 1930s as part of his continual efforts to influence policy-makers. Section (c) considers a reduction in the general level of money wages and the numerous influences it has on effective demand and employment in the General Theory model. Section (d) includes a numerical and diagrammatic representation of Keynes' generalised approach to money wage cuts. Finally Section (e) examines Keynes' argument that both a flexible wage policy and a flexible monetary policy have much the same beneficial effects on employment, and that for a range of reasons the latter is preferable to the former.

b) Keynes' attitude to money wage cuts prior to the *General Theory*

The one policy proposal to which Keynes consistently objects is wage cutting. Whether as a remedy for the United Kingdom going onto the Gold Standard at an uncompetitive exchange rate in the 1920s, or as part of a *contractionist cure* to the international slump in the early 1930s, Keynes foresees huge problems with trying to reduce the general level of money wages. Indeed Keynes reserves his strongest objections to what he calls competitive international wage cutting during the Great Depression.

There is, however, some development in his ideas over time. In the *Economic Consequences of Mr. Churchill* (from now on referred to as *Economic Consequences*) Keynes objects to the policy of returning sterling to the Gold Standard in 1925 at an exchange rate which he claims is perhaps 10–12 per cent overvalued (Keynes, 1972a). The government's solution – offered by the then Chancellor of the Exchequer Winston Churchill – is to pursue a 'fundamental re-adjustment' aimed at lowering all money wages and hence prices by 10 per cent. But Keynes is quick to point out that before this happens the UK export sectors will find it very difficult to trade at such an uncompetitive exchange rate. Moreover he claims this will aggravate the problems of the export industries (especially the coal and textiles sectors) still dealing with the outstanding adjustments problems in the post-First World War global competitive environment.

Keynes argues that just because the exchange rate is overvalued and trade is imbalanced this does not mean that wages and prices fall automatically. Actually Keynes claims that money wages will only fall if unemployment is on a rising trend. Therefore a key element of adjusting to a trade imbalance is a contractionary domestic monetary policy (i.e. increasing the domestic interest rate and restricting bank lending) to increase unemployment. The increase in unemployment changes the bargaining positions of workers and entrepreneurs, allowing the latter to push for wage reductions. In addition the high domestic interest rate will attract short-term capital movements and counter the adverse trade balance resulting from the uncompetitive exchange rate.

Even then the process of engineering a reduction in the general level of money wages is not easy – for money wages must fall *first* in all sectors of the economy, both the export and domestic (or sheltered) industries, *before* the prices of products will fully adjust downwards. Moreover, in an open society with decentralised wage bargaining, it is impossible to implement a *simultaneous and uniform* cut in money wages for all classes of labour. Money wages for each group of workers have to be reduced as and when employers decide to re-negotiate labour contracts; with those in the weakest bargaining position being the first to have their wages lowered and those with the strongest industrial muscle being the last to comply. There is, of course, no obvious economic rationale for such a process and it must strike the general public as socially unjust, especially when other (often richer) groups in society (e.g. rentiers) are not asked to reduce their incomes, and in fact they gain from the lowered price-level.

Faced with the prospect of having their money and real wages cut, groups of workers "are bound to resist so long as they can; and it must be war, until those who are economically weakest are beaten to the ground" (Keynes, 1972a, p. 211). This is a remarkably prescient statement given what happened in the British coal mining dispute of 1926–1927. Keynes goes on to point out that the greater the resistance to wage cuts the more restrictive monetary policy must be, for only rising unemployment can weaken the bargaining position of workers sufficiently.

And when, in this messy and costly fashion, all wages are eventually reduced and the domestic price-level has fully adjusted downwards, what is the gain? The answer is that the economy is back where it started before the overvaluation of the exchange rate, with the real wage rate stabilised at its previous level. Not surprisingly given this analysis Keynes advocates a reversal of the Gold Standard policy and a relaxation of the monetary stance. The exchange rate must find a competitive level combined with lower interest rates and easier bank lending. This expansionary cure will restore prosperity and "encourage business men to enter new enterprises, not, as we are doing, to discourage them" (Keynes, 1972a, p. 220).[1]

By the start of the 1930s the Great Depression was in full force. In the United Kingdom the Macmillan Committee, with Keynes as a member, was established to consider the causes of the slump and possible remedies. One remedy considered by the committee is a competitive general money wage cut in the United Kingdom in order to insulate the economy from the global slump of demand. Keynes is again unconvinced about such a contractionist cure. He estimates that it might require general money wage cuts in the region of 20–30 per cent such is the decline in demand (Keynes, 1981a). Not surprisingly given Keynes' concern about the social and political upheaval associated with a 10 per cent general wage cut at the time of the re-entry to the Gold Standard, he fears wage cuts of a much larger magnitude must be seen as socially unjust, leading perhaps to violent resistance and social chaos. But what Keynes fears most during this period is competitive international wage cutting causing prices in the global economy to significantly decline. Keynes is distinctly aware of the very large debt burdens of certain nations, especially the German government as a result of borrowing to finance its post-war reparations. In such an environment falling world prices might dangerously increase debt burdens internationally, leading potentially to a deranged global financial structure of "widespread bankruptcy, default and repudiation of bonds" (Keynes, 1981b, p. 547). Not surprisingly therefore Keynes advocates an *expansionary cure* to the Great Depression, with governments, domestically and internationally, relaxing fiscal and monetary policy in order to stimulate effective demand and employment. However the theoretical justification for this expansionary cure is only subsequently provided with the publication of the *General Theory*.

Moreover in the final report of the Macmillan committee there is an early sign that *theoretically* Keynes has begun to realise that cutting money wages might not benefit employment at all. In rather simplistic terms he argues that wage cuts will not boost private sector profitability and domestic employment, as the gains in terms of lower costs of production are counteracted by the lower purchasing power of workers. This marks Keynes' departure from the classical *analysis* of how a general money wage cut will influence employment, but once again a fully worked out theoretical framework has to wait until the General Theory model evolves.

c) The General Theory model and money wage cuts

With the General Theory model Keynes is able to rigorously analyse the impact that changes in money wages have on aggregate employment (Keynes, 1973a, 1973b, 2007). What is not widely appreciated is the *context* in which Keynes discusses the issue in *Chapter 19* of the *General Theory*. Keynes clarifies the position in a 1939 *Economic Journal* article where he makes the following statement.

> First of all it is necessary to distinguish between two different problems. [In one part of the General Theory] I was dealing with the reaction of real wages to changes in output and had in mind situations where changes in real and money wages were a reflection of changes in the level of employment caused by changes in effective demand.... But there is also the case where *changes in wages reflect changes in prices or in the conditions governing the wage bargain which do not correspond to, or are not primarily the result of, changes in the level of output and employment* and are not caused by (though they may cause) changes in effective demand. This question I discussed in another part of my General Theory (namely *Chapter 19*, 'Changes in Money Wages').
>
> (Keynes, 2007, p. 395; my emphasis)

The circumstances which Keynes is discussing in *Chapter 19* can, of course, apply to the re-entry of sterling onto the Gold Standard at an uncompetitive exchange rate. For this policy will not only change the relative *price* competitiveness of the United Kingdom, it is associated with a contractionary monetary policy to increase unemployment and thereby strengthen the position of entrepreneurs over workers when *bargaining for wages*. It can also apply to the alleged remedy of government-induced *reductions in wages* as part of a contractionist cure for a generalised economic slump mentioned above. Therefore in *Chapter 19* Keynes is returning to the earlier policy debates to re-assess them in the light of the General Theory model. A change in effective demand that modifies the level of output and employment and subsequently alters money wages and prices is, by contrast, dealt with elsewhere in the *General Theory* – and elsewhere in this book, see Chapter 10.

The other intriguing aspect of *Chapter 19* is that Keynes explicitly rejects the classical *analysis* of how a change in the general level of money wages influences the volume of employment. In the classical model, for example, a general wage cut (that is either a money or real wage reduction for they came to much the same thing) stimulates employment on an aggregated labour market until the diminishing marginal revenue product of the last worker just equals the lower money wage, or to where the diminishing physical product of the last worker just equals the lower real wage rate.

In the General Theory model, by contrast, the volume of aggregate effective demand measured in wage units determines total employment. When real effective demand falls, so too will employment, and vice versa. Aggregate effective demand is itself dependent upon the community's propensity to consume the marginal efficiency of capital and the state of liquidity preferences. Both the marginal efficiency of capital and the state of liquidity preferences are very much influenced by the state of long-term expectation. *Therefore for Keynes a change in the general level of money wages only influences the volume of employment in as far as it changes the propensity to consume, the marginal efficiency of capital and the rate of interest.*

There is a further aspect of Keynes' analysis of flexible money wages requiring clarification. Keynes considers *two* ways in which the general money wage level can adjust to the emergence of unemployment. First, a generalised money wage cut which is immediate and significant, after which wages are expected to move on an upward trend. This can be referred to a *wage adjustment speed A* and is likely to apply in a society with a strong central government which imposes changes by administrative decree (e.g. in a fascist state). Second, a gradual diminishing of the general level of money wages in response to a gradual increase in unemployment that sets in motion expectations that wages will sag down even further in the future – in what follows referred to as *wage adjustment speed B*. This adjustment process is more Marshallian in character and most likely to occur in an open democratic state, where wage bargaining between entrepreneurs and workers is free and de-centralised.

Armed with the General Theory model Keynes considers the impact of a decline in the general level of money wages by posing the following question:

[W]hilst no one would wish to deny the proposition that a reduction in money wages *accompanied by the same aggregate effective demand as before* will be associated with an increase in employment, the precise question at issue is whether the reduction in money wages will or will not be accompanied by the same aggregate effective demand as before measured in money, or, at any rate, by an aggregate effective demand which is not reduced in full proportion to the reduction in money wages (i.e. which is somewhat greater measured in wage units).

(Keynes, 2007, pp. 259–260; Keynes' emphasis)

Using the General Theory model Keynes considers the impact of a general money wage cut on a number of key variables; they are the *propensity to consume, the marginal efficiency of capital, the money rate of interest, the state of confidence and open economy influences on effective demand*. It is necessary to consider each of these variables in turn.

The propensity to consume

The propensity to consume shows the relationship between aggregate income and aggregate consumption both measured in wage units. In an advanced nation Keynes supposes that as the level of aggregate income increases aggregate consumption will rise by a lesser amount and at a diminishing rate; that is the marginal propensity to consume is less than unity and falling. A consumption function is derived for a given wage unit assuming that the distribution of income is stable. However a reduction in the general money wage level (i.e. a fall in the wage unit) will change the distribution of income. Specifically income will shift from wage earners towards rentiers whose income (i.e. interest, dividends and rents) is unchanged in money terms. Moreover in so far as the prices of outputs are reduced as wages fall income shifts from entrepreneurial profits towards rentier income as well. Keynes claims that workers, being those on the lowest incomes, will have the highest propensity to consume. He is less confident about whether rentier or entrepreneur consumption patterns will differ markedly, although he is prepared to propose that the rentiers, who represent in general the richest section of the community, have the lowest propensity to consume.

In general then the redistribution of income resulting from the reduction in wages will have a number of effects, but on balance Keynes asserts the overall influence on the propensity to consume is likely to be unfavourable. Hence the impact of a general money wage reduction on the propensity to consume, if anything, tends to *reduce* aggregate effective demand, no matter what wage adjustment speed applies.

The marginal efficiency of capital and the money rate of interest

The marginal efficiency of a capital asset is the rate of discount which brings the total present value of the prospective yield (i.e. a stream of expected future profits) from the sale of the output of the asset into equality with its supply price (i.e. its replacement cost). The greater the prospective yields from a capital asset the greater the marginal efficiency of capital, and vice versa. The marginal efficiency of capital is dependent on the state of long-term expectation, and the latter being based on such flimsy foundations can change violently and rapidly. A schedule for the marginal efficiency of capital in general is derived for each rate of fixed investment spending. An improvement in prospective yields on capital assets causes the marginal efficiency schedule to move upwards illustrating increasing demand for investment goods. A deteriorating state of long-term expectation will cause the marginal efficiency schedule to shift downwards suggesting reduced investment demand.

According to Keynes a reduction in the general level of money wages will not have an unambiguous impact on the marginal efficiency of capital; it depends on whether wage adjustment speed A or B applies. With wage adjustment speed A the reduction in the general level of money wages relative to its level in the future is likely to be *beneficial* to the marginal efficiency of capital. This occurs because the output of a capital asset produced today is expected to compete for part of its life with subsequently produced assets produced at higher costs of production due to rising wage rates. These later assets will have to charge a higher price for their final outputs to make a reasonable return. This means that the output of a capital asset produced today can be sold at higher prices in the future than would otherwise have been the case, boosting the prospective yields of such assets. This will cause the marginal efficiency of capital schedule to shift upwards, strengthening investment spending, and, via the multiplier effect, consumption expenditure. The overall impact on aggregate effective demand is positive.

By contrast with the second adjustment speed there is an expectation that money wages will sag down slowly over time. This is likely to bring about a deterioration in the general marginal efficiency of capital, for the output of capital assets produced today, even after the initial wage reduction, will have to compete in the future with the output of capital assets produced at even lower costs of production due to the sagging down of wages. The subsequently produced capital assets will be content with lower prices for their final outputs whilst still making a reasonable return. In so far as competition forces down the prices of outputs of all capital assets, old and new, the prospective yields from capital assets

produced today will be that much lower.[2] This causes the marginal efficiency of capital schedule to shift downwards, which is detrimental to
investment spending and, due to the multiplier, consumption spending
as well. In this case the consequences for effective demand are adverse.

The long-term money rate of interest is the other main influence
on the volume of fixed capital investment. The rate of interest is the
price which equilibrates the total demand to hold bank deposits with
the available supply. The supply of money is largely determined by the
lending policies of the private banking sector. The community demand
money to facilitate the planning of new activity (i.e. the finance motive)
and actual exchange (i.e. the transactionary motive) and to store wealth
in a liquid form (i.e. the precautionary and speculative motives). Uncertain knowledge of the future is a precondition for the desire to hoard
wealth in liquid money.

A reduction in the finance and transactionary demand for money
associated with lower planned and actual activity lowers the rate of
interest, *cet. par.* Conversely, a deteriorating state of long-term expectation increases the demand for money as a store of value and raises the
rate of interest, *cet. par.* Finally, the money rate of interest sets a minimum standard which the marginal efficiency of any capital asset has to
attain. Therefore, for any given schedule of the marginal efficiency, the
rate of interest defines the maximum volume of investment demand.

As money wages, prices and money incomes fall there is inevitably a
weakening of the community's demand to hold cash for transactionary
purposes. Assuming the nominal money supply is given, the long-
term money rate of interest therefore moves downwards, and, with a
steady marginal efficiency schedule, this will increase investment spending and effective demand. Clearly using wage adjustment mechanism
A the favourable effect on money demand and the rate of interest is
only short-lived as wages and prices subsequently move upwards again;
whilst with adjustment mechanism B the reduction in interest rates is
long lasting as wages sag slowly downwards.

Combining the analysis of the effects on the marginal efficiency and
the rate of interest Keynes uncovers an interesting result. Using wage
adjustment speed A there is a beneficial impact on the marginal efficiency of capital, but only a short-lived benefit of a lower interest
rate after which the rate rises. By contrast adjustment speed B tends
to undermine the marginal efficiency of capital whilst providing more
long-lasting benefits in terms of a falling money interest rate. As Keynes
notes the overall influence on aggregate effective demand, either way,
is difficult to determine. However, he thinks adjustment speed A has

probably the most beneficial influence on effective demand due to its positive impact on the marginal efficiency of capital.

The state of confidence

The state of long-term expectation held by a community is made up of two parts. First, entrepreneurs and wealth-holders make probable forecasts about various important elements of the economic system for example the anticipation of prospective yields, the unfolding trend of the rate of interest and the future political stability of a nation. Second, the probable forecasts are held with a particular state of confidence, depending on whether the conventions that guide judgements about the future are thought to be reliable or otherwise.

Just as an individual entrepreneur always looks positively on a reduction in his/her own wage costs, so a once and for all reduction in the general level of money wages can lead to a general improvement in business confidence. It might be thought that the general wage cut presages a more pro-business economic environment stimulating greater confidence in estimating future profitability. This improvement in the state of business confidence might break an otherwise pessimistic cycle and shift the marginal efficiency of capital schedule upwards. Of course such a generalised reduction in money wages is hard to arrange unless one lives in a centralised state where wages can be changed by administrative decree; for example in fascist Italy in 1927 Mussolini issued a decree reducing all money wages by 20 per cent overnight.

If however the political environment allows free trade unions and decentralised wage bargaining negotiated by employers and unions, the effect of an attempt to achieve a once and for all money wage reduction may be quite different. Inevitably the wage reductions will have to be negotiated on an industry by industry basis. As each group of workers face wage cuts they will almost certainly resist thereby generating widespread industrial action by organised labour. Political instability will inevitably result. In these circumstances business confidence far from improving might quickly and seriously deteriorate, as the unstable present is projected by entrepreneurs into the future. The result is a deteriorating state of confidence about likely prospective yields on investments and a downward movement of the marginal efficiency of capital schedule. This must have an adverse impact on investment spending and lower effective demand. Indeed the political instability might be serious enough to strengthen wealth-holders' desire to hoard money as a store of value and counteract the previously noted reduction in money interest rates.

Ironically this scenario is most likely to occur in a democratic state. For example in Britain in 1926 in response to an effort to lower wages in the coal industry there was both a long-lasting miners strike and a General Strike which seemed to threaten the political system. The wage cuts in the coal industry were eventually implemented, but the political and business establishment had by then lost the appetite for further tests of strength with organised workers.

The burden of debt

In any advanced economy there is always a large pool of accumulated debt in money terms associated with past investment and saving. Entrepreneurs (and the government) have issued a range of financial instruments (e.g. bills and bonds) to finance past activity which are held by wealth-holders (i.e. rentiers) but have not as yet matured. Moreover entrepreneurs and households have outstanding loans, mortgages, hire purchase agreements and leasing arrangement with the private banking sector. Taken together this constitutes the debt liability and debt structure of private firms, households and the government to be repaid in money terms.

If the general level of money wages and prices fall the real burden of this accumulated debt inevitably increases. This has a depressing influence on business expectations of profits as entrepreneurs have to sell more output just to finance the interest and principal repayments to rentiers and financial institutions. It follows that if prices and wages fall far enough some entrepreneurs will find the extra burden of debt too great and file for bankruptcy. Most certainly all entrepreneurs will face pressure on their profit margins; the impact on profit margins being exaggerated if the government increases the burden of taxation to finance a larger real burden of the National Debt. The impact of all this undermines prospective yields on new investments and the state of confidence; as a result the marginal efficiency of capital is adversely effected, meaning a further decline in fixed capital investment spending – even assuming the rate of interest is constant. However the adverse state of confidence engendered by this rising debt burden can conceivably lead to an increased demand by the wealth-holders for money as a store of value. This, in turn, puts pressure on the rate of interest to rise (or halt the tendency for interest rates to fall noted earlier) and lower investment demand.

Furthermore, a rise in debt burdens, which causes an increase in the bad debts of the private banks, will eventually cause the banking sector to revise the state of credit. The private banking system will be forced to re-assess its loans policy; the sector may also prefer to hold more of its assets in a liquid form and this will, via the money multiplier, reduce the volume of bank money in the system. A fall in the money supply, *cet. par.*, increases the interest rate and reduces investment spending and effective demand.

Open economy influences

The analysis so far has been limited to a closed economy model. Keynes does however consider the influence on employment of a money wage reduction in an open economy. In doing so he identifies two further influences which a general money wage reduction *relative to wages abroad* (*i.e. a competitive wage cut*) can have on domestic effective demand. In the case of a competitive wage cut this will:

(a) improve the *balance of trade* and investment in export sectors which tends to stimulate effective demand;

(b) worsen the *terms of trade* causing export revenues to decline thereby reducing real income in the export sectors; however as real income falls this will tend to increase the propensity to consume of the community.

Any positive influence from a competitive wage cut applies as long as it is confined to *one country* and other nations do not respond in kind. If wage cuts become generalised across nation states they tend to cancel each other out; the balance and terms of trade then remain unchanged between countries. When wage cuts are international in character it seems more likely that money wage reductions will not stimulate effective demand; if anything the reverse is true. For global effective demand will probably fall significantly as the worldwide downward trend in wages and prices massively increases debt burdens (and bankruptcy) across the international economy.

There is of course another way in which other countries can neutralise the efforts of a specific nation to gain competitiveness by wage cutting. They do this by raising tariffs on the exports of that nation. In this circumstance there is no benefit of wage cutting for the specific nation in terms of the balance of trade, although its terms of trade may be changed. Finally Keynes notes that the extent of the gain from competitive wage cutting by one nation is conditioned by the degree of openness in the economy. The more open (closed) to trade the national economy is the greater (less) the potential for improving the net export position by cutting money wages.

It may be concluded that in the General Theory model the impact on employment of fluid money wages is quite a complicated thing to assess. It depends on various factors, in particular:

- the volatility of the state of long-term expectations; hence
- the instability of the marginal efficiency of capital and the state of liquidity preference;
- the elasticity of both the marginal efficiency and liquidity preference schedules;
- the relationship between the distribution of income and the propensity to consume of a community;
- the debt liability and debt structure of private firms, households and the government;
- the relationship between the bank money supply and changes in the wage and price-levels;
- the extent to which the wage reduction is confined to one country or generalised across the global economy;
- the degree of openness of the economy.

Keynes summarises his conclusions in the following way:

> [in *Chapter 19* of the General Theory] I reached the conclusion that wage changes, which are not in the first instance due to changes in output, have complex reactions on output which *may be in either direction according to the circumstances* and about which it is difficult to generalise.
>
> (Keynes, 2007, p. 395; my emphasis)

It is quite possible therefore that the General Theory model can generate a *classical* result where a general money wage cut leads to an increase in employment. For Keynes this *special* circumstance is most likely in an authoritarian state which has the administrative power to enact by decree wage adjustment speed A. It is also helpful if the wage cut in one nation is not compensated by wage cuts, or the imposition of tariffs, in other nations, and that the economy is relatively open so that it can maximise the benefits of its price competitiveness. In this scenario the positive influences on aggregate effective demand of a money wage reduction counteract the negative factors mentioned above. The cut in money wages leads to an increase in effective demand measured in wage units which causes aggregate employment to rise. This increase in employment counteracts, to some degree, the rise in unemployment which initiated the general money wage reduction in the first place.

But Keynes claims that in the most *generally applicable* circumstances a reduction in money wages will cause nominal effective demand to decline by a greater proportionate amount. The circumstances in which generalised wage cuts generate this adverse reaction are an open democratic state with independent trade unions conducting wage bargaining on a decentralised basis leading to wage adjustment speed B. Moreover the adverse reaction is strongest in a relatively closed economy where any competitive wage cut has an insignificant influence, or where the wage cut in one nation is matched by competitive wage cutting or the imposition of tariffs elsewhere. The sagging down of the general money wage rate causes effective demand measured in wage units to decline and aggregate employment to decrease as well. This decline in employment is in addition to the rise in unemployment which instigated the wage cut in the first place, and the economy is pushed further into a slump.

d) A numerical and diagrammatic illustration of Keynes' arguments

In this section Keynes' analysis is treated in a more systematic way by considering various numerical examples. Three cases will be examined below. First an initial Case 1 where due to a contractionary monetary policy or a generalised slump there is pressure to cut the general level of money wages in order to stimulate employment, but the wage cuts have not yet been enacted. Case 2 then looks at the classical case where, assuming wage adjustment speed A is applied by an authoritarian state, both real effective demand and employment increase. Finally Case 3 considers what Keynes regards as the generalised case with wage adjustment speed B applicable to a democratic state with free collective bargaining. This time the reduction in money wages overall has a strongly adverse impact on the propensity to consume, the marginal efficiency of capital and the rate of interest, causing both real effective demand and employment to decline.

Table 9.1 shows Case 1 which outlines the initial position of the economy before any change in the general level of money wages. The wage unit is constant at £10 per labour unit throughout. With a range of marginal propensities to consume for various hypothetical levels of real aggregate income (Y_w), the levels of real expected consumption expenditure (C_w) can be calculated. Given the marginal efficiency schedule and

Table 9.1   Case 1: The starting point

Y_w mills	0	1.0	2.0	3.0	3.5	4.0	4.5	5.0	6.0
χ^*	1.0	1.0	0.9	0.9	0.7	0.7	0.5	0.5	0.5
C_w (mills)	0	1.0	1.9	2.8	3.15	3.5	3.75	4.0	4.5
I £mills	5	5	5	5	5	5	5	5	5
WU £	10	10	10	10	10	10	10	10	10
I_w (mills)	0.5	0.5	0.5	0.5	0.5	0.5	0.5	0.5	0.5
D_w (mills)	0.5	1.5	2.4	3.3	3.65	4.0	4.25	4.5	5.0
Z_w (mills)	0	1.0	2.0	3.0	3.5	4.0	4.5	5.0	6.0
N mills	0	1.0	2.0	3.0	3.5	4.0	4.5	5.0	6.0

Glossary: N = labour units; Y_w = aggregate income measured in wage units; χ^* = the marginal propensity to consume; C_w = expected aggregate consumption expenditure measured in wage units; I_w = expected investment spending measured in wage units; D_w = the aggregate demand price measured in wage units; Z_w = the aggregate supply price measured in wage units; WU = the wage unit; I = nominal expected aggregate investment spending.

the rate of interest, suppose that expected aggregate investment spending measured in nominal terms is set at £5 million. With a wage unit of £10 real aggregate investment spending is 0.5 million wage units. Real values for the aggregate demand price and the aggregate supply price can then be derived for various hypothetical levels of aggregate income.

The economy is in equilibrium with effective demand of 4 million wage units. This generates an aggregate employment of 4 million labour units that is felt to be too low; the employment target (or full employment position) is assumed to be 5 million labour units. Using this as a starting point it is possible to consider Keynes' *analysis* of the impact of lowering the general level of money wages (represented by the wage unit) on effective demand and employment.

In Table 9.2 the classical special case – Case 2 – is considered where the sudden and uniform money wage cut of 10 per cent does influence aggregate demand in such a way that the impact overall is to *increase* the real volume of effective demand and employment. Note first how the wage cut, via its influence on the distribution of income, generally lowers the marginal propensity to consume in comparison to Case 1. But this is more than made up for because wage adjustment speed A has a beneficial impact on fixed investment spending. Assume that the nominal value of this aggregate rises strongly to £8.325 million (a very optimistic figure in order to be ultra-fair to the classical case) – an increase of 67 per cent. With the lower level of money wages, the real volume of fixed investment spending rises to 0.925 million wage units – a rise of 85 per cent.

Table 9.2 Case 2: The classical special case

Y_w mills	0	1.0	2.0	3.0	3.5	4.0	4.5	5.0	6.0
χ^*	1.0	1.0	0.85	0.85	0.65	0.65	0.45	0.45	0.45
C_w (mills)	0	1.0	1.85	2.7	3.025	3.35	3.575	3.8	4.25
I £mills	8.325	8.325	8.325	8.325	8.325	8.325	8.325	8.325	8.325
WU £	9	9	9	9	9	9	9	9	9
I_w (mills)	0.925	0.925	0.925	0.925	0.925	0.925	0.925	0.925	0.925
D_w (mills)	0.925	1.925	2.775	3.625	3.95	4.275	4.5	4.725	5.175
Z_w (mills)	0	1.0	2.0	3.0	3.5	4.0	4.5	5.0	6.0
N mills	0	1.0	2.0	3.0	3.5	4.0	4.5	5.0	6.0

In this special case the economy finds its equilibrium at a higher level of effective demand of 4.5 million wage units. This generates an increase in aggregate employment, up to 4.5 million labour units, but this is still below the employment target of 5 million units. In this case Keynes' model can explain the classical contention that a reduction in money wages leads to an increase in employment. Yet Keynes' *analysis* that reaches this conclusion is very different from that of the classical aggregated labour market (see Chapter 2).

Keynes' general case – Case 3 – is outlined in Table 9.3. This relates to a democratic state with free collective bargaining and wage adjustment speed B. This time the slow sagging down of money wages by 10 per cent lowers real effective demand and the level of employment. Assume the consumption function is influenced in the same way as in Case 2. But this time wage adjustment speed B causes a decline in nominal fixed investment spending as well – down to £4.275 million. With the lower level of money wages, the real volume of fixed investment spending declines to 0.475 million wage units.

Table 9.3 Case 3: The general case

Y_w mills	0	1.0	2.0	3.0	3.5	4.0	4.5	5.0	6.0
χ^*	1.0	1.0	0.85	0.85	0.65	0.65	0.45	0.45	0.45
C_w (mills)	0	1.0	1.85	2.7	3.025	3.35	3.575	3.8	4.25
I £mills	4.275	4.275	4.275	4.275	4.275	4.275	4.275	4.275	4.275
WU £	9	9	9	9	9	9	9	9	9
I_w (mills)	0.475	0.475	0.475	0.475	0.475	0.475	0.475	0.475	0.475
D_w (mills)	0.475	1.475	2.325	3.175	3.5	3.825	4.05	4.275	4.725
Z_w (mills)	0	1.0	2.0	3.0	3.5	4.0	4.5	5.0	6.0
N mills	0	1.0	2.0	3.0	3.5	4.0	4.5	5.0	6.0

In the most generally applicable case the level of real effective demand declines to 3.5 million wage units, meaning total employment falls, in comparison to Case 1, by 0.5 million labour units. Far from achieving the employment target the reduction in money wages is *counter-productive; it makes the employment position even worse.* Clearly Case 3 is a scenario that the classical school never considers.

The preceding numerical examples can be illustrated by using an aggregate demand and supply price diagram – see Diagram 9.1. On the vertical axis are the real aggregate demand price (D_w), the aggregate supply price in real terms (Z_w) and real aggregate effective demand (AED_w) and on the horizontal axis are units of labour (N). Whatever the change in the wage unit the aggregate supply relationship remains stable at unity; hence the aggregate supply price function is represented by a 45° line. Initially the aggregate demand function F_w^* intersects the aggregate supply function bringing forth a level of real aggregate effective demand equal to 4 million wage units; the latter in turn generates an equilibrium level of employment at 4 million labour units. In the special case the cut in the general level of money wages creates a rise in real effective demand up to 4.5 million wage units. The real aggregate demand function moves up to F_{w1}; not only does it shift upwards due to higher investment spending but the slope of the new function changes due to the lower community propensity to consume at each level of employment. Consequently, the equilibrium level of labour units rises to 4.5 million units.

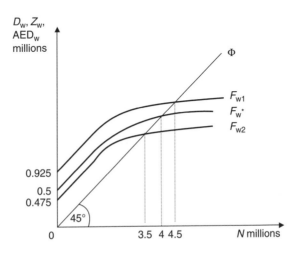

Diagram 9.1   Changing money wages – the special and general cases

The general case is where a slow sagging down of wages causes real effective demand to decline to 3.5 million units. In this general case the wage cutting causes the real aggregate demand function to move down to F_{w2}; the shift downwards this time is due to a decline in private investment spending, plus the slope of the function changes due to the fall in the community's propensity to consume. Consequently, the equilibrium level of employment falls to 3.5 million labour units.

Therefore the General Theory model allows Keynes to rigorously examine the efficacy of reductions in the general level of money wages, and to demonstrate that far from making the employment situation better it can make it far worse. The analytical reservations about wage reductions contained in *Chapter 19* of the *General Theory* can be added to the more intuitive objections based on grounds of impracticability, social injustice and the dangers of social chaos contained in the *Economic Consequences* and the *Macmillan Report*. As with other aspects of Keynes' policy recommendations his proposals with regard to wage cutting preceded the development of the General Theory model; the model subsequently justifies and strengthens the policy conclusions he had intuitively reached.

e) Wage cutting versus expansionary monetary policy

The policy implications of the General Theory model is something properly left to Chapter 12. It may however be useful now to consider one policy debate that preoccupied Keynes after writing the *Economic Consequences*. Armed with the General Theory model he returns in *Chapter 19* to discuss whether a policy of money wage cuts or a policy of monetary expansion is the best way to promote prosperity and increase total employment. As noted above Keynes claims that a money wage cut can only influence employment through its influence on the ultimate independent variables – the propensity to consume, the marginal efficiency of capital and the rate of interest. In terms of the propensity to consume the impact on the distribution of income is adverse and tends to lower effective demand and employment. In a democratic society with free collective bargaining the sagging down of wages has a detrimental impact on the marginal efficiency, and hence on effective demand and employment.

But in terms of the rate of interest there is more hope. For, assuming the nominal money supply remains fixed, as wages and prices fall so too will the demand for money (especially the transactionary demand), and this allows the long-term rate of interest to fall. Such a fall, *cet. par.*, stimulates investment demand, effective demand and employment. Keynes concludes that it is on the impact that a wage reduction has in lowering the rate of interest that "those who believe in the self-adjusting quality of the economic system must rest the weight of their argument" (Keynes, 2007, p 266).

If the money supply is related to the level of wages and prices, so that a reduction in wages and prices leads to a fall in the money supply a further complication with wage cutting emerges. For example if, as a result of falling wages (and production costs), entrepreneurs feel that they can hold less cash to cover planned activity there is a decline in the finance motive to hold money, and a consequent reduction in the revolving fund of bank loans to facilitate such financial provisions. In other words the finance demand for bank loans will decrease, causing a decline in the bank money supply. If, moreover, the reduction in money wages leads to greater insolvency and a deteriorating state of credit the banks might increase their liquidity ratios and refuse to grant loans to new customers (i.e. the value of the bank money multiplier falls). This means the money supply contracts as wages and prices fall and the rate of interest is unlikely to decline.

But supposing, for the sake of the argument, that the money supply is fixed as wages and prices fall, Keynes notes that this has analytically exactly the same effect as keeping money wages stable and increasing the money supply. Both policies have a beneficial influence on employment through lowering the rate of interest; the former is effectively monetary policy implemented by wage bargainers, the latter monetary policy implemented by the monetary authorities.

According to Keynes, however, the limitations of monetary policy as a method of stimulating effective demand apply equally to a policy of reducing money wages. For just as a moderate increase in the money supply might not lower the long-term interest rate sufficiently to make any significant impact on effective demand and employment, the same applies to a small reduction in the general level of money wages. Moreover, just as an excessive increase in the money supply can undermine the state of confidence of wealth-holders and strengthen their demand for money as a store of value, the same applies to an immoderate reduction in money wages. Consequently, for a *closed economy*, Keynes argues that a flexible wage policy is as unlikely to be able to promote continuous full employment as a flexible monetary policy pursued in isolation.

Having accepted that theoretically a flexible wage policy and a flexible monetary policy comes to much the same thing Keynes then poses the following question: for *practical purposes* which policy is the most preferable? He considered four criteria by which to assess the two policies.

Taking up a theme from the *Economic Consequences*, Keynes notes that a uniform reduction in money wages across all sectors and classes of labour is impossible to achieve in a free society. In this case wage reductions can be achieved but only after a process of "wasteful and disastrous" industrial disputes; with the wages of each group of workers in turn being lowered after an inevitable struggle, and with those in the weakest bargaining position being the first to succumb. Keynes suggests such a process not only lacks economic rationale it is socially unjust. Far better then to increase the money supply and achieve the same result with comparative ease.

Again returning to a theme of the *Economic Consequences*, Keynes argues that on grounds of social justice if some classes of society have their incomes fixed in money terms (e.g. rentiers, those on fixed salaries), better that all enjoy relatively fixed money remuneration, including workers. This is achieved if money wages and all other classes of income are held stable, and a flexible monetary policy is pursued instead.

As the wage unit declines and the price-level falls the burden of accumulated debt increases; and, as noted above, if the wage and price-levels fall far enough the resulting scale of bankruptcy and insolvency can have a disastrous impact on effective demand. Much better then to increase the money supply in order to increase effective demand; for part of the extra demand will increase output and employment, and part will tend to raise the general price-level (see Chapter 10 for further details). As the price-level increases the burden of accumulated debt *decreases*, giving an important advantage to the innovative entrepreneurs who borrow over the large institutions and rentiers who lend.

Finally if a downward trend in the long-term interest rate is gained by the slow sagging down of money wages then, as noted above, this will place a drag on the marginal efficiency of capital. The consequence of this will be a postponement of some investment spending and an adverse outcome for effective demand and employment. It is much more preferable then to increase the money supply slowly in order to gain long-lasting reductions in the rate of interest without the negative influences on the marginal efficiency of capital in general.

Therefore Keynes is convinced that a flexible monetary policy is for practical purposes and on grounds of social justice much preferable to a flexible wage policy. It is in this context that Keynes argues that:

the maintenance of a stable general level of money wages is, on a balance of considerations, the most advisable policy for a closed system; whilst the same conclusion will hold good for an open system, provided that equilibrium with the rest of the world can be secured by means of [a fluctuating exchange rate].

(Keynes, 2007, p. 270)

The latter point in the preceding quotation is of some importance, although Keynes does not labour the point. In the General Theory model Keynes accepts that a competitive wage reduction can have a beneficial trade impact on effective demand and employment. If for domestic reasons, however, a competitive wage cut is ill-advised the same beneficial trade effect can be generated by a competitive devaluation of the nominal exchange rate. Indeed such a policy has the same limitations as a competitive wage cut, for it relies on the devaluation not being replicated by other nations or neutralised by the imposition of tariffs. Therefore Keynes in the circumstances of the interwar period suggests that for an open economy the most preferable policy mix is a stable general money wage level, combined with a flexible monetary policy and a fluctuating exchange rate in order to retain international price competitiveness. This interpretation is reinforced when, in *Chapter 23* of the *General Theory*, Keynes takes another side-swipe at the Gold Standard policy he had objected to a decade earlier. In that chapter Keynes explains that:

Under the influence of [the classical] theory the City of London gradually devised the most dangerous technique for the maintenance of equilibrium which can be possibly imagined, namely, the technique of the bank rate coupled with a rigid parity of the foreign exchanges [i.e. the Gold Standard policy]. For this meant that the objective of maintaining a domestic rate of interest consistent with full employment was wholly ruled out. Since, in practice, it is impossible to neglect the balance of payments, a means of controlling it was evolved which, instead of protecting the domestic rate of interest, sacrificed it to the operation of blind forces. Recently, practical bankers in London have learnt much [the UK left the Gold Standard in 1931], and one can only hope that in Great Britain the technique of the bank rate will never again be used to protect the foreign balance in conditions in which it is likely to cause unemployment at home.

(Keynes, 2007, p. 339)

This quotation may lead the reader to think of Keynes as a die-hard opponent of the Gold Standard system. Actually what Keynes opposes is the operation of the Gold Standard system in the interwar period. During this time stronger nations with trade surpluses built up huge hoards of gold reserves putting the onus on weaker states with trade deficits to deflate their economies in order to establish a trade balance. Yet as the weaker nations contracted their economies this in turn lowered the trade surpluses of stronger states. The overall impact of such a system being that trade imbalances between nations were resolved by lowering the volume of world trade and increasing global unemployment. This is what Keynes subsequently refers to as the *contractionist* cure to trade imbalances about which he has strong objections (Keynes, 1980b, c). This topic is taken up again in Chapter 12.

f) Summary

Keynes is a consistent opponent of all proposals to cut the general level of money wages during the 1920s and 1930s in the United Kingdom, and is an even harsher critic of the process of competitive international wage cuts during the Great Depression. In his policy writings of the period Keynes repeatedly argues that in a free society, where wage bargaining is decentralised, such policies are impractical, lack economic rationale and are socially unjust in that they require the poorest to make the first and greatest sacrifice.

With the General Theory model Keynes explains how a general money wage cut can only influence employment by changing the volume of effective demand, that is by changing the propensity to consume, the marginal efficiency of capital and the rate of interest. Keynes also considers two ways in which the general level of money wages might adjust to the advent of unemployment. First, a significant and uniform wage cut across all classes of labour (presumably by government decree) after which wages are expected to rise – adjustment speed A. Second, a slow sagging down of wages in response to gradually rising unemployment (because wage bargaining is decentralised), giving an expectation that wages will fall further in the future – adjustment speed B.

By looking at a range of influences on effective demand Keynes concludes that in a special case – of an authoritarian state imposing wage adjustment speed A – the classical conclusion that a money wage cut will increase total employment could apply; but that in more generally applicable circumstances – of an open and democratic society with wage adjustment speed B – a money wage cut will make the employment position even worse. Therefore, unlike the classical theory, the General Theory model generates conclusions which can go either way depending on a number of factors.

Finally, Keynes argues that an expansionary monetary policy has much the same beneficial affect on employment as a reduction in the general money wage level, and that for a closed economy there are good practical reasons why an expansionary monetary policy is preferable. This conclusion applies to an open economy as long as the expansionary monetary policy is combined with a fluctuating exchange rate to maintain price competitiveness.

10
Prices and Real Wages

a) Introduction

The previous chapter examines the impact on employment of changes in money wages and prices that are *not* due in the first instance to changes in the level of effective demand. This chapter considers a separate issue: namely the changes in money wages, prices and real wages that *are* in response to variations in effective demand and output. The classical theory of money and prices is of little use in examining these responses, for it only applies to the special circumstances of a fully employed economy with effective demand assumed constant. In addition Keynes has severe reservations about the classical dichotomy between the theories of prices and value. In contrast Keynes' General Theory model provides a generalised explanation of the response of money wages, prices and real wages to changes in effective demand. In doing this Keynes integrates the theories of value and prices, and this provides a springboard for his generalised analysis of prices and inflation.

Keynes' general theory of prices and inflation has to explain two price-levels. The first is the general price-level that covers a large number of goods and services – *both wage goods and investment goods* – combined together in an inevitably subjective form of weighting that can never be exact. The second price-level relates just to *wage goods* – what the classicals call the consumption standard. It is this price-level, along with the money wage, that determines the real wage rate in the General Theory model. In this Chapter it is assumed that both price indexes respond to changes in effective demand by moving in the same direction, although the percentage changes of the two might not be uniform.

Furthermore it is useful to clarify what Keynes means by the term *inflation*. In the *General Theory*, Keynes usually uses the term to refer to a *once and for all* rise in prices. This contrasts with modern parlance whereby inflation means a *persistent and continuous* rise in prices. The change in meaning is perhaps the result of decades of persistent inflation in the post-Second World War period. It is important to realise that prior to 1945 the general price-level rose in a boom and often fell in a slump – referred to as *deflation* – and this should be kept in mind when considering Keynes' analysis. Moreover Keynes' more general analysis explains *two* types of inflation – semi and true. *Semi-inflation* occurs in an economy operating below full employment where an increase in nominal effective demand partly increases output and employment and partly raises the price-level. *True inflation* occurs at the full employment position where an increase in nominal effective demand only increases prices with no impact on output and employment. The classical theory of money prices is, of course, a special case that seeks to explain true inflation.

The chapter also reviews Keynes' treatment of the real wage rate. The real wage is a *dependent* variable in the General Theory model, just like the volume of employment. This is one of the least appreciated parts of the General Theory model, but it is a necessary corollary of Keynes' rejection of the classical aggregated labour market. The chapter also explains a seeming paradox of the *General Theory*, that whilst Keynes *rejects* the classical labour market analysis and the second classical postulate, he *accepts* the first classical postulate. This has probably confused followers of Keynes more than anything else, but its solution is quite straightforward.

Section (b) first explains Keynes' general theory of prices and inflation, which is an aggregated version of classical value theory extended to include the influence of effective demand. The influence of changes in nominal effective demand on the general and wage good price-levels is examined from various starting points. In the process three cases – those of semi-inflation, true inflation and deflation – are outlined in some detail. The implications of Keynes' theory for the derivation of real wages and the classical postulates are considered in Section (c). This section resolves an apparent paradox that whilst Keynes rejects the classical aggregated labour market he accepts the first classical postulate; it also makes transparent why Keynes rejects the second classical postulate. A labour association curve is derived to represent Keynes' viewpoint about the "relationship" between real wages and employment. Section (d) revisits the interwar debate between Keynes and the classics (represented by Professor Pigou) about the capacity of an investment programme to stimulate employment. The section highlights the analytical differences between Keynes and Pigou although they come to similar policy conclusions. Finally, Section (e) updates the causal map of the General Theory model generated in earlier chapters.

b) Keynes' theory of prices and inflation

In any discussion of Keynes' general theory of prices and inflation it is important to understand the economic data on prices that influences Keynes' thinking prior to the Second World War. During the Second World War and since 1945 advanced economies have experienced continuous inflation. In boom periods inflation accelerated, and in recessions it decelerated, but the movement was persistently upward. An increasing price-level has become an axiom of economic life. It has not always been so. Before 1940 the usual trend was for the general price-level to rise in a boom and often *fall* during a downturn. When prices in general fell it was said the economy was experiencing a deflation. Cecchetti (1992) provides conclusive evidence that in each of the five economic downturns in the United States in the 60 years between 1872 and 1933 the consumer and wholesale price-levels and the GNP deflator fell by quite considerable amounts. It was only during the downturns of 1892–1894 and during the Great Depression of 1930–1933 that total output actually declined; during the other periods output continued to grow, though at a slower pace than normal. The evidence provided by Cecchetti also clearly illustrates the exceptional character of the Great Depression when not only did the two key price-levels – the consumer price index and the GNP deflator – decline by a greater amount than ever before, but output declined by nearly one-third, or about 10 times as great as in the downturn of 1892–1894. The deflation of 1930–1933 was however not just an American phenomenon, although the epicentre of the Great Depression was the United States (Hobsbawm, 1995). The Great Depression was a global phenomenon, with perhaps only Russia and Japan being exceptions to the general rule. Moreover as Feinstein et al. (1997) note both the primary *and* secondary sectors of the global economy were greatly affected by the deflation of prices; the prices of world manufactured goods fell by over 50 per cent between 1929 and 1935. Indeed all prices continued to fall even after output levels had turned upwards from 1932 onwards; the world prices of food, raw materials and manufactures did not universally turn upwards until 1936.

Finally it is important to appreciate that in the immediate aftermath of the First World War inflation, not deflation, was the key economic problem. The post-war dislocation, combined with stored up purchasing power from the wartime being unleashed, led to massive inflationary pressures in the advanced nations of the world. However as Feinstein et al. note European economies were differently affected by the post-war inflation. In the United Kingdom the general price-index rose significantly so that by 1920 it was 150 per cent higher than it had been in 1914. But the experience of the United Kingdom was nothing to that of Austria. In Austria during and after the First World War there was massive hyper-inflation; a price index of 100 in 1914 rose at staggering rates to become 263,938 by 1922. The value of the Austrian currency fell dramatically and the currency system was debauched. Having lived through such tumultuous times Keynes is keenly aware of the systemic dangers of runaway inflation for "[t]here is no subtler, no surer means of overturning the existing basis of society than to debauch the currency" (Keynes, 1972e, p. 57). The reader should therefore appreciate that Keynes is acutely aware of the possibilities of both rapid inflation as well as serious deflation and hence his General Theory model is designed to explain both phenomena.

Before proceeding it is important to realise that Keynes' theory of prices and inflation contained in the *General Theory* is somewhat limited in scope. Keynes claims his theory only examines the relationship between changes in the quantity of money and changes in the price-level, a perspective perhaps overly influenced by the classical tradition. It may be argued that a genuinely general theory needs to explain how the general price-level (and the price-level for wage goods) responds to changes in aggregate effective demand *for whatever reason*. This more generalised approach is included in this chapter; but care is taken when doing this, for it is essential that the approach remains faithful to the basic principles of Keynes' price theory.

With the quantity theory put aside, Keynes takes as a starting point the classical theory of value to develop his theory of prices as a whole. Keynes provides the following explanation.

> In a single industry its particular price-level depends partly on the rate of remuneration of the factors of production which enter into its marginal cost, and partly on the scale of output. There is *no reason to modify this conclusion* when we pass to industry as a whole. The general price-level depends partly on the rate of remuneration of the factors of production which enter into marginal cost and partly on

the scale of output as a whole, (i.e. taking equipment and technique as given) on the volume of employment.

(Keynes, 2007, p. 294; my emphasis)

In other words the price of a single commodity depends on the cost of factors of production used to produce it and the productivity of these factors. Given the law of diminishing productivity the efficiency of factors of production depends on the level of output of the commodity, for as output increases the marginal productivity of each factor declines. Keynes argues that prices as a whole are determined in a similar way. General prices depend on the aggregated cost of factors of production and the productivity of these factors. Applying again the law of diminishing productivity the efficiency of aggregated factors of production depends on the level of *total* output; and as aggregate output increases (decreases) the productivity of each aggregated factor declines (rises). There is however an additional influence on the price-level that marks it out from the theory of value. In the latter theory it is legitimate to assume that aggregate effective demand is given, *cet. par.*, *whilst in the theory of prices as a whole the level of effective demand can vary*. This is important as effective demand determines the scale of total output, and *changes* in effective demand will cause aggregate output to vary, and hence the productivity of aggregated factors to alter. This is in essence the general theory of prices that brings into close connection the theories of prices and value. Finally note that what is true of the general price-level also holds for the wage good price-level.

Now let us consider the influence that a change in nominal effective demand has on the level of general prices and wage good prices in different circumstances. First, there is the case of an *increase* in nominal effective demand in an economy operating below the full employment level that creates *semi-inflation* (Case A). Next is the case of an *increase* in nominal effective demand in an economy operating at full employment that generates *true inflation* (Case B). Finally, a *decline* in effective demand in money terms is considered. Starting from either full employment with stable prices or a below full employment position, this causes a *deflation* of the price-level (Case C). Once again Keynes' model considers a wider range of circumstances than the classical theory (that only relates to Case B) and as such is a more generally applicable analysis. Finally suppose throughout, for ease of exposition, that *all factor costs change in the same proportion to the money wage*. This simplifying assumption is used by Keynes in the *General Theory*.

Semi-inflation (Case A)

Starting from a below full employment position increasing nominal effective demand, via an increase in the money supply and lower interest rates, has three major effects on the general price-level and the wage good price-level. *First* the wage unit will increase before full employment is reached. For as groups of workers press for higher money wages entrepreneurs are more likely to grant such increases when sales and output are on an upward trend. As factor costs rise entrepreneurs will pass on these cost rises to the customer in terms of higher prices. Consequently some part of rising nominal effective demand will be absorbed by a rising wage unit, which will push up the general price-level. But Keynes supposes the percentage increase in nominal effective demand will outstrip the rise in money wages. Real effective demand will rise and generate an increase in total output and employment.[1]

Secondly, as effective demand in real terms rises the scale of aggregate output increases. As output increases the supply price of output will rise due to the law of diminishing productivity. Diminishing productivity causes the efficiency of factors of production in the aggregate to decline, meaning it takes longer to produce an extra unit of aggregate output. The extra costs associated with this declining productive efficiency causes the general price-level to rise.

Thirdly, factors of production in reality are not interchangeable, meaning for example that more capital equipment cannot replace some form of specialised skilled labour or a specific raw material that is needed for production. Given this lack of interchange, as total output rises certain sectors of the economy experience *bottlenecks* as specialised labour or raw materials becomes very scarce. Another way of describing a bottleneck is that it occurs when the supply of a commodity becomes very, if not perfectly, inelastic, for no matter how much the price rises no extra supply is forthcoming. This does not happen to all commodities at the same time; usually only a few will experience these bottlenecks, though as effective demand rises more enter this category. In so far as a rise in effective demand causes some bottlenecks to emerge the prices of certain commodities will rise sharply. Once again this will cause the general price-level to rise.

As effective demand increases there is no reason why the upward trend in money wages and the two price-levels need to be smooth and continuous. Indeed Keynes suggests that as effective demand increases there may be a number of *semi-critical points* prior to full employment, where wages and prices jump sharply upwards. This means that at certain output levels a given percentage increase in nominal effective demand is associated with broadly stable prices even though costs are rising, whilst at other output levels the same percentage increase in nominal effective demand breaks through a psychological barrier (a semi-critical point) and entrepreneurs push up prices. Keynes therefore argues that up to the final critical point of full employment:

> we have a succession of earlier semi-critical points at which an increasing effective demand tends to raise money wages though *not fully* in proportion to the rise in price of the wage goods; and similarly in the case of a decreasing effective demand.
>
> (Keynes, 2007, p. 301; my emphasis)

Consequently, in an economy starting below the full employment position, an *increase* in nominal effective demand will spend itself partly in increasing output and employment, and partly in increasing money wages and the general and wage good price-levels. This is what Keynes terms an economy experiencing *semi-inflation*.

Finally note that the analysis of Keynes can easily be extended to cover the impact on prices of an increase in nominal effective demand *for any reason*. Indeed this exactly what happened after the Great Depression in the United Kingdom when a recovery of private consumption expenditure, and later Government military spending, increased output and employment and pulled up money wages and prices (Glynn and Booth, 1996).

True inflation (Case B)

Eventually there must come a time where a further expansion of the money supply causes the level of nominal effective demand to reach a *final critical point* consistent with the full employment level of output. Once this final critical point is reached a further increase in nominal effective demand will fail to bring about a higher level of aggregate output and employment. The technical conditions are such that output cannot respond to higher demand; in effect aggregate supply becomes perfectly inelastic. Instead at this final critical point an increase in nominal effective demand induces an equi-proportionate increase in prices and money wages. This means that a 10 per cent increase in nominal effective demand causes both prices and money wages to rise by 10 per cent, whilst real effective demand, hence output and total employment, remains constant. This is what Keynes calls a situation of *true inflation*. In other words the conditions of the classical quantity theory of money apply in Case B. This clearly demonstrates that the classical theory is only applicable to a *special case* of an economy operating at full employment.

But it should also be noted that in conditions of full employment an increase in nominal effective demand *for whatever reason* (not just an increase in the money supply) will lead to true inflation in the General Theory model. This is important as these circumstances faced the United Kingdom in the Second World War. Britain experienced a war-driven economy operating at maximum capacity due to very high Government armaments expenditure, with little room for consumption production. Full employment and rising wages was a recipe for huge inflationary pressures, just as in the First World War. In order to avoid a repetition of the high inflation between 1914 and 1918 Keynes writes *How to Pay for the War* in the early months of the Second World War. This pamphlet greatly influences UK Government policy at the time and is the first practical (and largely successful) application of the General Theory model (Skidelsky, 2000). This topic is discussed in more detail in Chapter 12.

Deflation (Case C)

Finally it is necessary to examine what happens to prices when nominal effective demand falls, due to a decline in the money supply and a higher rate of interest, with the starting point being either at full employment or below the full employment position. The three effects on the general price-level identified in Case A above can be applied once again, but in reverse.

First, as nominal effective demand declines this hits the revenues of entrepreneurs. When entrepreneurs face weakening trading conditions they respond by seeking to lower costs of production and press workers to accept lower money wages. As wages normally make up the largest part of aggregate costs this movement down of money wages will allow prices to move downwards as well. In the generally applicable circumstances where money wages are fairly stable, the fall in money wages is likely to be limited, and certainly less than the decline in nominal effective demand. This means that effective demand measured in wage units falls in value resulting in a decline in the scale of total output and employment. *Secondly*, as effective demand pulls down the level of total output, prices generally decline as the pressure of diminishing productivity eases. Therefore as fewer factors of production are employed their efficiency increases and the time taken to produce an extra unit of aggregate output declines. The resulting lower costs of production allow prices to fall. *Thirdly*, as effective demand declines the prices of commodities that are in inelastic supply will fall off rapidly as bottlenecks ease. Therefore, in an economy experiencing a reduction in nominal effective demand, there will be a fall in output and employment and a pulling down of money wages and prices.

Finally, it is possible to generalise Keynes' conclusion by extending it to cover the impact on prices of a decrease in nominal effective demand *for any reason*. When this is done the performance of the UK economy during the Great Depression becomes explicable. The decline in private investment spending and net export spending in the early 1930s generated a significant decline in effective demand, causing huge falls in output and employment. This then generated a decline in money wages and prices, with the latter declining by a greater amount than the former (Glynn and Booth, 1996). An even more extreme pattern of performance occurred in the United States in the early 1930s; the downturn in output and employment was far more severe than in the United Kingdom, as was the decline in the consumer price index which fell by nearly 30 per cent.

c) Real wages and the classical postulates

With Keynes' theory of general prices in place the reasons for his rejection of the classical treatment of the real wage rate become fully transparent. In the classical aggregated labour market the real wage rate is the key determinant of total employment; the volume of employment can only change if the real wage rate varies. More specifically the first classical postulate implies (with the law of diminishing productivity) that for entrepreneurs to demand more workers the real wage rate must fall and vice versa; there is an *inverse* relationship between real wages and employment.

In the General Theory model the analysis is very different in character with total employment and the real wage rate both being *dependent variables*. Total employment is determined by the volume of effective demand measured in wage units. The real wage rate is derived from the general level of money wages, established by wage bargaining between entrepreneurs and workers, deflated by the wage good price-level, determined by the level of nominal effective demand and the scale of output. In other words, because the wage good price-level is influenced by effective demand, the real wage rate is determined by money wage bargains *plus* the marginal efficiency of capital, the propensity to consume and the rate of interest.

Keynes finds that this new approach to real wage determination reveals important insights when considering changes in effective demand. First in Case C a decline in nominal effective demand causes employment to decline but it also has a threefold influence on the wage good price-level. Money wages will fall back reducing costs of production and wage good prices; the supply price of wage goods will fall even further as the pressure of diminishing productivity eases; and bottlenecks are removed causing the prices of particular commodities to fall rapidly. Hence the wage good price-level falls *by a greater amount* than the money wage rate and there is an increase in the real wage rate. This increase in real wages is not caused by the workers pushing for higher money wages (in fact money wages fall) but it is *associated* with a decline in aggregate employment. Indeed workers do not determine real wages by agreeing money wage rates as the classical analysis implies, for real wages are determined by forces beyond the workers' immediate influence.

In Case A an increase in effective demand causes money wages to rise and the wage good price-level to increase by an even greater amount. Rising money wages increase costs of production and wage good prices; the supply price of wage goods will rise even further due to the pressure of diminishing productivity; and an expansion of bottlenecks must mean that the prices of particular wage goods will rise rapidly. Overall as employment and output expand, money wages will *increase* but the prices of wages goods will increase even more, meaning that there is a *reduction* in the rate of real wages. Once again workers are not masters of the real purchasing power of their money wages. It is *only* in conditions of full employment – Case B – that Keynes accepts that money wages and wage good prices increase in exact proportion in response to a rise in nominal effective demand. In this special case the rate of real wages remains constant.

Therefore Keynes accepts that there is an inverse *association* between employment and the real wage rate up to the full employment position. Keynes' model predicts that as employment rises (falls) the real wage rate will decrease (increase). The seeming paradox that Keynes both argues that employment is determined by effective demand and accepts the first postulate has led many to conclude that Keynes must accept the aggregated labour market analysis. The latter contention is false. Keynes comes to a similar conclusion to the classical school about the inverse relationship between real wages and employment, but for different *analytical* reasons. In particular in the General Theory model Keynes claims that both employment and real wages are dependent variables; real wages do not determine employment, rather both are determined by other ultimate independent variables (Davidson, 1983).

It is possible to derive a diagram which shows how the General Theory model *associates* changes in the real wage rate and the volume of employment which may be referred to as the *labour association curve* – see Diagram 10.1. Great care has to be taken with this diagram as it does not appear in the *General Theory*, or any other subsequent writings of Keynes. Yet the labour association curve does I think represent the essence of Keynes' argument whilst keeping true to the methodology of a historical reconstruction of Keynes' ideas.

The labour association curve (NAC) clearly shows the inverse relationship between the response of the real wage rate and total employment *to variations in aggregate effective demand*. The NAC is compatible with the first classical postulate but for reasons very different to those provided by the classical school. The NAC also looks similar to a classical labour demand schedule but it is not the same thing.[2] A classical labour demand schedule represents the *causal* relationship between the real wage, which is an *independent* variable, and the volume of employment, which is a *dependent* variable. The NAC, by contrast, shows the *association* between two *dependent* variables of the General Theory model which are both determined by the level of effective demand.[3]

Keynes' treatment of the real wage in the General Theory model also throws light on his rejection of the second classical postulate. The second classical postulate claims that for the last worker employed the

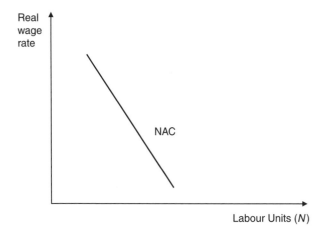

Diagram 10.1 The labour association curve

disutility of providing the last unit of labour just equals the real wage obtained by this unit of labour. From the classical perspective a worker can determine the real wage rate received by bargaining for money wages alone. As already noted in Chapter 2 when the first and second postulates are satisfied the aggregated labour market is in equilibrium and the full employment of labour is achieved, although voluntary and frictional unemployment can exist.

As will be shown in the next chapter Keynes attempts to show that an economy can be in equilibrium below the full employment position with demand-deficient unemployment in existence. In this case Keynes argues that the real wage rate can be greater than the disutility of the last unit of labour employed, but not because workers have bargained for higher money wages. This means that Keynes' rejection of the second postulate follows on from disputing the classical claim that workers, when bargaining for money wages, must determine the level of real wages. In other words Keynes claims that workers are not masters of the real wage they receive.

Keynes' analysis of real wage determination explains why he rejects the second classical postulate. The postulate depends on an implicit assumption that aggregate effective demand (and hence total output and employment) does *not* influence the wage good price-level. But fluctuations in effective demand and output do change the wage good price-level for reasons beyond workers control, and it is possible for the real wage rate to be *greater* than the disutility of the last worker employed. Further discussion of this subject will have to wait until the next chapter.

d) Keynes and the classics revisited – the stimulation of employment

In the interwar period Keynes and the classics were constantly having policy debates about how to stimulate employment. From a classical labour market perspective the only way that employment can increase is if the real wage rate falls. Keynes by contrast argues that employment can be increased through a public investment programme as proposed by Lloyd George in the 1929 election. Keynes' policy recommendations are examined in Chapter 12, but in this section an attempt can be made to appreciate the *theoretical* differences between Keynes and the classics with regard to stimulating employment.

Actually the leading British classical economist of the time, Professor Pigou, accepts that an investment programme increases employment, but for reasons very different from those of Keynes. To illustrate this point it is necessary to quote Keynes' comments on his mid-1920s debate with Pigou on the effect of expansionist policies on employment.

I was already arguing that the good effect of an expansionist investment policy on employment, the fact of which no one denied, was due to the *stimulant which it gave to effective demand.* Prof. Pigou, on the other hand, and many other economists explained the observed result by the reduction in real wages covertly effected by the rise in prices which ensued on the increase in effective demand. It was held that public investment policies... *produced their effect by deceiving, so to speak, the working classes into accepting a lower real wage, effecting by this means the same favourable influence on employment which, according to these economists, would have resulted from a more direct attack on real wages.*

(Keynes, 2007, pp. 400–401; my emphasis)

So for Pigou the impact on the real wage rate is crucial to determining whether an investment programme will increase employment. And the increase in effective demand will only increase employment in so far as it reduces the real wage rate by generating what is now called money illusion in the minds of workers. Workers can be deceived, or as Friedman claims "fooled", into the labour market. Indeed what is striking is the similarity of the analysis of Pigou on the one hand and Milton Friedman and mainstream Keynesians on the other about how an expansionist policy works. It is not a surprise, however, as all accept the classical postulates with an economy operating at full employment. Starting at full employment the only way an investment programme can raise employment is through the creation of money illusion to lower the real wage.

By contrast Keynes' analysis of the impact of an investment programme on stimulating employment is quite different. First, the analysis does not include an aggregated labour market, as effective demand determines total employment. Second, the starting point for considering an expansionist investment programme is an economy operating below the full employment position. This makes far more sense as calls for special investment measures are most likely to emerge in an economy operating with heavy unemployment. In Keynes' model effective demand determines the overall level of output and the output for specific sectors (e.g. construction, manufacturing, services etc). The level of sector output specifies the derived demand for labour in each industry.

Given demand conditions bargaining between entrepreneurs and workers set money wage rates in each industry. Effective demand, the scale of output and costs of production taken in the aggregate determine the general and wage good price-levels. With money wages and wage good prices specified the real wage rate is determined.

In the General Theory model part of any increase in effective demand due to an expansionist investment programme is absorbed by an expansion in output and employment. Another portion of the increase in effective demand is absorbed by rises in money wages and wage good prices, with prices rising more than wages. Therefore as the investment programme stimulates employment this is *associated* with a decline in the real wage rate. There is no money illusion[4] and no workers are deceived or fooled into the labour market. The previously demand-deficient unemployed workers are more than willing to take up the new jobs offered as a result of the expansionist investment programme. Moreover, as noted in the previous chapter, any direct effort to lower real wages through cutting money wages will at best have an ambiguous influence on employment.

In this context it is possible to understand Keynes' claim that in an economy with involuntary unemployment:

> it will be possible to increase employment [and output] by increasing expenditure in money terms until real wages have fallen to equality with the marginal disutility of labour, at which point there will, by definition, be full employment.
>
> (Keynes, 2007, p. 284)

Therefore although both Pigou and Keynes agree on the need for an investment programme in the interwar period, it is in the *analysis* of its impact on the economy where the two economists disagree. In the interwar period Keynes and Pigou were not talking to each other but past one another. Even in the 1920s Keynes intuitively feels that Pigou's analysis is misguided, but armed with the General Theory model Keynes can demonstrate why Pigou's approach is flawed.

e) A causal map of the General Theory model

The causal map can be updated from that outlined in Chapter 8. In this chapter the causal map expressed in nominal terms will not be set out as it is unduly complex, although the interested reader can seek to construct one. Here the causal map in real terms will be utilised

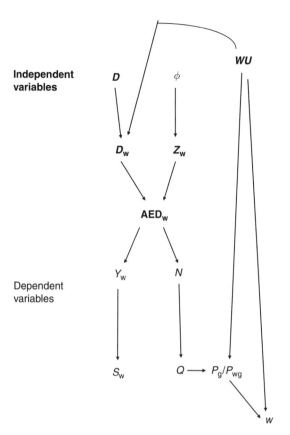

Map 10

to provide an overview of the General Theory model. The causal map expressed in real terms can be reduced to where there are three independent variables: the nominal aggregate demand price (D) derived in the way outlined in previous maps, the wage unit (WU) and the aggregate supply relationship (ϕ).

The levels of D and WU define the real aggregate demand price (D_w). The aggregate supply relationship determines the real aggregate supply price (Z_w). Where D_w and Z_w are equal the real volume of aggregate effective demand (AED_w) is specified. AED_w determines the equilibrium values for real aggregate income (Y_w), real aggregate saving (S_w) and total employment (N). The equilibrium level of total employment will have associated with it a volume of total output (Q). The levels of AED_w, WU

and Q combine to determine the general and wage good price-levels (P_g and P_{wg}, respectively). Finally WU and P_{wg} combined determine the real wage rate per labour unit (w) from the viewpoint of wage and salary earners.

f) Summary

The price of a single commodity depends on the cost of factors of production used to produce it and the productivity of these factors. The efficiency of factors of production depends on the level of output of the commodity. Prices as a whole are influenced by the aggregated cost of factors of production, the level of *total output* and changes in the level of effective demand. What is true of the general price-level also holds for the wage good price-level. This is how the general theory of prices brings together the theories of prices and value.

In an economy operating below full employment an *increase* in nominal effective demand is partly absorbed by increases in output and employment and partly by higher money wages and prices – an instance of *semi-inflation*. In a fully employed economy an *increase* in nominal effective demand is completely absorbed by rising money wages and prices – generating *true inflation*. Finally starting from a position of full employment with stable prices or a below full employment position, a *decline* in nominal effective demand will partly lower output and employment and partly reduce money wages and prices – leading to a *deflation* of the price-level.

In the General Theory model total employment and the real wage rate are both *dependent variables*. Employment is determined by the volume of effective demand measured in wage units. The real wage rate is derived from the general level of money wages, established by wage bargaining between entrepreneurs and workers, deflated by the wage good price-level which is determined by the level of nominal effective demand and the scale of output. A decline in nominal effective demand causes employment to fall, and wage good prices to fall further than money wages. Therefore a decline in employment is *associated* with an increase in the real wage rate. The reverse is true for an increase in effective demand, and an increase in employment is *associated* with a fall in the real wage rate. This means that Keynes accepts the first classical postulate whilst at the same time rejecting the classical aggregated labour market *analysis*. All this is represented by the labour association curve. Keynes' analysis demonstrates that workers are not masters of the real wage rate they receive. Hence Keynes rejects the second classical postulate.

For Pigou an investment programme increases employment if it reduces the real wage rate, by generating what is now called money illusion in the minds of workers. By contrast Keynes has a quite different analysis of the impact of an investment programme on employment. It does not include an aggregated labour market. Moreover, the starting point for the analysis is an economy operating below full employment. Keynes argues that the investment programme increases nominal effective demand. Part of this increase is absorbed by a direct rise in output and employment; another portion is absorbed by rises in money wages and wage good prices, with the latter rising by more than the former. Consequently the increase in employment is associated with a decline in the real wage rate. The rise in employment is not due to any money illusion or deception of workers, but due to workers previously demand-deficiently unemployed being only to willing to take up the new jobs on offer.

11
Employment and Unemployment

a) Introduction

This chapter brings together a range of themes about employment and unemployment in the General Theory model. First the chapter focuses directly on the relationship in the General Theory model between the key independent variable of aggregate effective demand and the main dependent variable of employment. This can be represented by what Keynes calls an *employment function*, which is strongly related to the aggregate supply function outlined in Chapter 3. The employment function allows Keynes to define different equilibrium volumes of employment generated by different levels of effective demand; it can additionally be used to define a full employment position free from reliance on the classical postulates.

Secondly the chapter examines the concept of the *elasticity of employment* – that is the change in employment in response to a change in real effective demand. Discussion of the elasticity of employment allows Keynes to revise his model to allow the *composition* of a change in effective demand to influence the volume of employment. The elasticity of employment helps clarify the time dimensions associated with the multiplier process, and hints at reasons why the values for the investment and employment multipliers will diverge.

Thirdly the chapter examines Keynes' contentious idea that a capitalist economy may be in *equilibrium* with less than full employment. This implies that demand-deficient (or involuntary) unemployment is persistent and long term in character. In the process Keynes' rather torturous definition of involuntary unemployment will be clarified. The chapter concludes by proposing that the employment function can be used to define an unemployment equilibrium free from reliance on the classical postulates.

Section (b) explains the employment function, how it is derived and its relationship with the aggregate supply function. The employment function is used to define the concept of full employment free from reliance on the classical postulates. Section (c) considers the idea of an elasticity of employment, and how the composition of a change in effective demand influences the value of the elasticity. Section (d) reviews Keynes' claim that it is possible for an economy to be in an equilibrium position with involuntary unemployment. This section goes on to apply the employment function in order to analyse how involuntary unemployment responds to changes in real effective demand. Finally, Section (e) provides the complete causal map of Keynes' model. An appendix to this chapter discusses how the concept of *equilibrium* requires amendment to cope with Keynes' analysis of unemployment.

b) The employment function

To begin with it is necessary to derive the employment function.[1] In the General Theory model this represents the relationship between the main independent variable, aggregate effective demand, and the ultimate dependent variable, the volume of aggregate employment. Keynes begins with some micro-foundations; that is he defines an employment function for each industry. This relates real effective demand for the output of a given industry ($ED_w r$) to the level of employment within that sector (N_r). A single industry employment function may be written as:

$$N_r = Fr(ED_w r) \tag{1}$$

Keynes asserts that single industry employment functions can be added together to define an employment function for the economy. The economy-wide employment function can be written as:

$$N = F(AED_w) \tag{2}$$

In Equation 2 N is total employment of labour units and AED_w is real aggregate effective demand.[2]

The employment function (F) is positive, with higher levels of aggregate effective demand generating higher levels of employment and vice versa. But what is the value of F for different levels of effective demand? As noted in Chapter 3 the employment function is the inverse of the aggregate supply function. Therefore an employment function can be derived from the interaction between the changing level of aggregate demand prices and the constant aggregate supply relationship.

The derivation of the employment function can be illustrated using the numerical example used in Chapter 8. Suppose that initially aggregate fixed investment spending is 1 million wage units. With a given consumption function, suppose real effective demand is 5 million wage units. This means that aggregate income is 5 million wage units and the equilibrium volume of employment is 5 million labour units. Table 11.1 then outlines the impact on effective demand and employment of first a decrease (Case 2) and then an increase (Case 3) of fixed investment spending.

Table 11.1 Unstable investment spending, effective demand and employment

	N (mills)	Y_w (mills)	χ^*	C_w (mills)	I_w (mills)	D_w (mills)	Z_w (mills)
Case 1							
	0	1.0	0.0	1.0	1.0	0.0	
	1	1.0	1.0	1.0	2.0	1.0	
	2	0.9	1.9	1.0	2.9	2.0	
	3	0.9	2.8	1.0	3.8	3.0	
	4	0.7	3.5	1.0	4.5	4.0	
	5	0.5	4.0	1.0	5.0	5.0	
	6	0.5	4.5	1.0	5.5	6.0	
Case 2							
	0	0	1.0	0.0	0.5	0.5	0.0
	1	1	1.0	1.0	0.5	1.5	1.0
	2	2	0.9	1.9	0.5	2.3	2.0
	3	3	0.9	2.8	0.5	3.3	3.0
	4	4	0.7	3.5	0.5	4.0	4.0
	5	5	0.5	4.0	0.5	4.5	5.0
	6	6	0.5	4.5	0.5	5.0	6.0
Case 3							
	0	0	1.0	0.0	1.5	1.5	0.0
	1	1	1.0	1.0	1.5	2.5	1.0
	2	2	0.9	1.9	1.5	3.4	2.0
	3	3	0.9	2.8	1.5	4.3	3.0
	4	4	0.7	3.5	1.5	5.0	4.0
	5	5	0.5	4.0	1.5	5.5	5.0
	6	6	0.5	4.5	1.5	6.0	6.0

Glossary: N = labour units; Y_w = aggregate income measured in wage units; χ^* = the marginal propensity to consume; C_w = expected aggregate consumption expenditure measured in wage units; I_w = expected investment spending measured in wage units; D_w = the aggregate demand price measured in wage units; Z_w = the aggregate supply price measured in wage units.

In Case 2 a decrease in fixed investment spending, from 1 million to 0.5 million wage units, lowers the level of real aggregate effective demand to 4 million wage units. This reduces aggregate income to 4 million wage units and the equilibrium volume of employment falls to 4 million labour units. Conversely in Case 3 an increase in fixed investment spending – in wage units from 1 million to 1.5 million – raises the level of real effective demand – to 6 million wage units. Aggregate income rises to 6 million wage units, whilst the equilibrium volume of employment rises to 6 million labour units.

The data in Table 11.1 can be illustrated in Diagram 11.1 that has the real aggregate demand price (D_w), the real aggregate supply price (Z_w) and real aggregate effective demand (AED_w) on the vertical axis, and labour units on the horizontal axis. The aggregate supply function (ϕ) is a constant 45° line, for reasons explained earlier. In Case 1 the economy is, therefore, in equilibrium with a volume of aggregate effective demand equal to 5 million wage units and equilibrium employment of 5 million labour units. In Case 2, with a stable aggregate supply price function (ϕ), real effective demand falls to 4 million wage units and total equilibrium employment declines to 4 million labour units. Conversely, in Case 3 effective demand increases to 6 million wage units and total equilibrium employment rises to 6 million labour units.

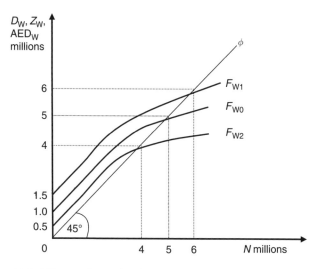

Diagram 11.1 Effective demand and employment

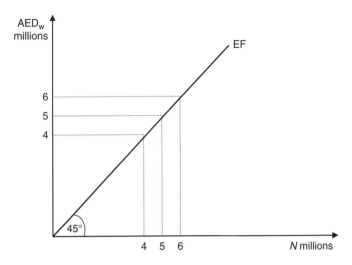

Diagram 11.2　The employment function

If the different levels of real aggregate effective demand (AED$_w$) and the employment levels (*N*) are charted out this will define the employment function (*F*) – see Diagram 11.2. On the vertical axis is effective demand measured in wage units and on the horizontal axis are units of labour. As real effective demand increases so too does total employment. It follows that if the real aggregate supply function is represented by a 45° line, so too is the employment function. As real effective demand rises and falls, employment changes by equivalent amounts.

The employment function can clearly cope with an economy operating below the full employment level. But for it to be consistent with a general theory it must also be capable of examining the full employment position. The employment function is used by Keynes to derive a definition of full employment free from reliance on the classical postulates. As such it is an effort by Keynes to break free from the frame of reference provided by the classical labour market theory.

Keynes accepts that successive increases in nominal effective demand will eventually generate a full employment position in an economy. Once full employment is attained what impact will further increases in nominal effective demand have on employment? Keynes claims that it will:

> be impossible to increase employment by increasing expenditure in terms of money; for money wages [will] rise proportionately to the

increased money expenditure so that there would be no increase of expenditure in terms of wage units and consequently no increase in employment.

(Keynes, 2007, p. 284)

In other words in a fully employed economy a 10 per cent increase in nominal effective demand will be associated with a 10 per cent rise in general prices and money wages, meaning real effective demand remains constant. This means that the employment function has an upper limit which it cannot surpass, defined by the full employment position. Consequently *when full employment is attained, and demand-deficient unemployment is eliminated, further increases in nominal effective demand will prove ineffectual in increasing output and employment.*

This may be shown in Diagram 11.3. Suppose the real level of aggregate effective demand of 6 million units generates the full employment level of 6 million labour units – point C. Therefore up until the point of full employment an increase in nominal effective demand will raise real effective demand and expand employment – see points A and B. Once, however, full employment is attained any increase in money expenditure will simply inflate all the *nominal* aggregates, whilst real effective demand, output and employment remain unchanged – point C. If nominal effective demand is increased to try to raise employment beyond the full employment position only true inflation will be created. Put

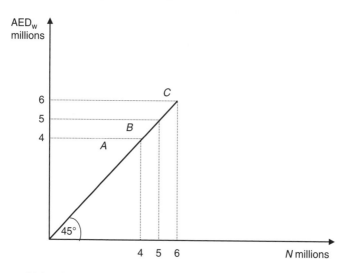

Diagram 11.3 The employment function and full employment

succinctly, the employment function cannot extend beyond point C. Keynes' model suggests that *demand creates its own supply, up until the point of full employment.* When full employment is reached, however, the conditions of aggregate supply place an upper limit on real effective demand.

The analysis of the employment function again demonstrates the *generalised* nature of Keynes' model which contrasts with the *special* character of the classical analysis. The applicability of the classical model is effectively restricted to point C on the employment function – the full employment position. Keynes' more generalised model explains the whole employment function *including* point C.

Using the employment function allows Keynes to outline a definition of full employment that is not reliant on the classical postulates. For Post-Keynesian economists who wish that Keynes had broken more completely free from classical notions when writing the *General Theory* this definition of full employment has the greatest value.

c) The elasticity of employment

The next question to address is how responsive is total employment to changes in real effective demand? To answer this question Keynes develops the concept of the *elasticity of employment* for the economy (e_e). This may be defined as:

$$e_e = \frac{\text{percentage change in total employment of labour units } (N)}{\text{percentage change in real effective demand } (AED_w)} \quad (3)$$

Equation 3 defines the elasticity of all points along the employment function.[3] Assuming that every change in real effective demand is foreseen by entrepreneurs some time ahead, the elasticity of employment will tend towards its maximum equilibrium value of unity. According to Keynes there are instances where the elasticity of employment will, for short periods, have a value below its maximum value. Keynes argues that this occurs because consumption good industries tend to have a lower *initial* elasticity of employment than investment good industries.

To explain this Keynes develops the concept of a *period of production* which he defines as the *number of time units of notice (n) that must be given to entrepreneurs of a change in demand for a product in order to generate the maximum elasticity of employment.* Keynes claims that entrepreneurs producing consumption goods have the longest periods of production (i.e. the highest values for *n*). The consumption industries have a low initial elasticity of employment since they are located at the final stage of the production process. Entrepreneurs in the investment goods industries, by contrast, will tend to have shorter periods of production. Consequently the initial elasticities of employment in investment industries will be closer to the maximum value. Clearly if entrepreneurs are given little prior notice of a change in effective demand, the initial elasticities of employment in both consumption and investment good industries will be that much lower. However, Keynes is clear that as time elapses, and entrepreneurs are able to respond to the change in effective demand, the elasticities of employment in both consumption and investment sectors will approach unity.

The concept of the elasticity of employment allows the treatment of the investment and employment multipliers to be revisited. As defined in Chapter 4 both concepts are of equal value and have no time dimension. The analysis of a production period suggests that new employment emanating from an increase in investment spending will only slowly emerge over time, implying that the value of the employment multiplier will initially be lower than that for the investment multiplier. This divergence lasts until the maximum values for the elasticity of employment are attained in all sectors.

With the elasticity of employment concept Keynes suggests an amendment to his earlier simple conclusion that changes in employment depend solely on changes in the *level* of effective demand. For the *composition* of any change in effective demand additionally influences the initial change in employment. In this context the composition of a change in effective demand is defined by how much of it is made up of expected consumption expenditure and how much of it is of expected investment spending.[4] As Keynes argues:

> if the first impulse towards the increase in effective demand comes from an increase in consumption, the initial elasticity of employment will be further below its eventual equilibrium level than if the impulse comes from an increase in investment.
>
> (Keynes, 2007, p. 287)

Furthermore, with an increase in real effective demand directed towards sectors with an initially low elasticity of employment the associated increase in aggregate income will be skewed towards entrepreneurs and rentiers and away from workers in those sectors. To the extent that entrepreneurs and rentiers have lower marginal propensities to consume than workers, this reduces the initial value of the investment multiplier, and provides a further reason why the values of the employment and investment multipliers may diverge in the short period.

This analysis allows Keynes to reach an important conclusion. Namely:

> that the assumption upon which we have worked hitherto, that changes in employment depend solely on changes in aggregate effective demand (in terms of wage units), is no better than a first approximation, if we admit that there is more than one way in which an increase in income can be spent. For the way in which we suppose the increase in aggregate demand to be distributed between different commodities may considerably influence the volume of employment. If, for example, the increased demand is largely directed towards products which have a high elasticity of employment, the aggregate increase in employment will be greater than if it is largely directed towards products which have a low elasticity of employment.
>
> (Keynes, 2007, p. 286)

d) The unemployment equilibrium

One of the most contentious ideas in the *General Theory* is that a capitalist economy can be in equilibrium below the full employment level – the *unemployment equilibrium*. This intriguing idea has met with very great resistance within the economics profession, especially from those who accept the general equilibrium model. Part of the problem is that Keynes applies the term "equilibrium" in a different sense to those trained in the insights of Arrow and Debreu (1954). Moreover Keynes' argument has not been helped by the rather peripheral character of his references to the idea in the *General Theory*. Therefore this section brings together a number of different references related to involuntary unemployment and the concept of equilibrium to shed greater light on this key insight. The possible revision of the concept of equilibrium in the light of Keynes' analysis is considered further in an appendix to this chapter.

Keynes' main direct reference to the unemployment equilibrium occurs when he is examining two variations of the classical theory of the rate of interest. These being the Wicksellian notion of a natural rate of interest which promotes stable prices and Keynes' idea, contained in the *Treatise*, that there is a natural interest rate which ensures equality between saving and investment. In rejecting both these variations on the classical theme, Keynes gives the following explanation.

> I had, however, overlooked the fact that in any given society there is, on the [Wicksellian] definition, a different natural rate of interest

for each hypothetical level of employment. And, similarly, for every rate of interest there is a level of employment for which that rate is the 'natural' rate, in the sense that the system will be in *equilibrium* with that rate of interest and that level of employment. Thus it was a mistake [in the *Treatise on Money*] to speak of the natural rate of interest or to suggest that the above definition would yield a unique value for the rate of interest irrespective of the level of employment. I had not then understood that, in certain conditions, the system *could be in equilibrium with less than full employment.*

(Keynes, 2007, pp. 242–243)

The next stage of the argument relates to how an economy finds an equilibrium position. This can be gleaned from Keynes' realisation that a very fluid market system, with flexible prices and wages, can create great uncertainty and instability. Indeed the instability may become so violent that all forms of business expectations and calculations are undermined. The production plans of entrepreneurs will be greatly harmed as they will have no idea at what prices they can sell products or what costs of production they will face. Yet Keynes acknowledges that thankfully capitalist economies do not behave in a fluid and unstable manner, indeed they are quite durable in the face of economic fluctuations. As Keynes notes:

it is an outstanding characteristic of the economic system in which we live that, whilst it is subject to severe fluctuations in respect of output and employment, it is not violently unstable. Indeed it seems capable of remaining in a chronic condition of sub-normal activity for a considerable period without any marked tendency either towards recovery or towards complete collapse.

(Keynes, 2007, p. 249)

So what saves a capitalist economy from severe instability and allows it to find an equilibrium position? To answer this Keynes claims that there are four key *psychological propensities* that save an economy from violent instability and promote stable equilibrium positions. They are:

1. The general level of money wages is relatively stable in response to variations in total employment; that is small changes in the volume of employment will not be associated with significant changes in money wages. A stronger form of this condition is that money wages should be more stable than real wages.

2. The value of the multiplier is greater than unity but not very large. The multiplier value is of course lowered in value through the withdrawals of savings, taxation and imports and is in most circumstances not likely to exceed a value of two.

3. Moderate changes in prospective yields or in interest rates will not create very great changes in investment spending. In essence this means that any shifts in the marginal efficiency of capital schedule are unlikely to be large and the slope of the schedule is not likely to be very elastic. Hence fluctuations in the inducement to invest will not generate very large changes in investment spending.

4. A higher (lower) rate of investment will eventually react unfavourably (favourably) on the aggregate marginal efficiency of capital if it continues for a number of years. In other words when investment plans have been curtailed for a number of time periods the depreciation of existing capital equipment makes the case for new investment progressively stronger and stronger. Conversely when investment spending has been rapid in the recent past the opportunity for new investment opportunities is curtailed.

If a capitalist economy is disturbed by a short-period change in the state of long-term expectation these psychological propensities will tend to bring the economy to a resting place. This resting place may be described as an equilibrium position in the Marshallian sense that there are no forces for change present. Moreover for each state of long-term expectation an equilibrium volume of employment (or long-period employment level) can be identified.[5] In so far as the level of long-period employment level is less than the full employment level (as defined in the previous section) an equilibrium volume of involuntary unemployment is specified. This is the context in which Keynes' claim to have identified the unemployment equilibrium may be understood. Moreover, each unemployment equilibrium position will be associated with a determinate level of output, a natural rate of interest, a specific general level of money wages and prices and a particular real wage rate. In conditions of full employment the equilibrium level of involuntary unemployment is zero and a *neutral* rate of interest applies.

Keynes' definition of the unemployment equilibrium is illustrated in Diagram 11.4. *Great care must be taken with this diagram as it is not a classical aggregated labour market.* It simply combines a labour association curve (NAC) – that shows the relationship between two dependent variables (real wages and employment) as the level of real effective demand varies – with an aggregate labour supply curve (N_s). The N_s

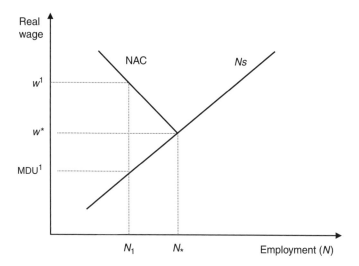

Diagram 11.4 Real wages and employment – two dependent variables

curve represents the aggregate real world supply curve of labour, which has embedded in it all the rigidities and imperfections which the classical school identified – see Chapter 2. It is an implicit assumption in the derivation of the N_s curve that the disutility of various types and intensities of employment and the supervisory structure and organisation of labour are given. The reader must remember when considering Diagram 11.4 that *the real wage rate does not determine the volume of employment*. In Keynes' model aggregate effective demand determines employment.

If effective demand is sufficient to generate the full employment position (N^*) this will be associated with real wage rate w^*. At real wage rate w^* the first and second classical postulates are equalised. This is the full employment position. Suppose however that a lower level of real effective demand determines the long-period volume of employment as N_1, below the full employment position. The equilibrium volume of involuntary unemployment is equal to the difference between the full employment level and the actual level of employment – that is N_* minus N_1. Associated with employment N_1 is real wage rate w^1. The latter is defined by the wage bargaining of entrepreneurs and workers and the wage good price-level; the wage good price-level is specified by real effective demand and the scale of aggregate output.

Note that in Diagram 11.4 at employment N_1 the real wage rate (w^1) is greater than the marginal disutility of the last labour unit (MDU^1); hence the second classical postulate does not hold. These are the circumstances in which to understand Keynes' argument that:

> If the propensity to consume and the rate of new investment result in deficient effective demand, the actual level of employment will fall short of the supply of labour potentially available at the existing real wage, and the equilibrium real wage will be *greater* than the marginal disutility of the equilibrium level of employment.
>
> (Keynes, 2007, p. 30; Keynes' emphasis)

This diagram can also be used to consider the impact of *increasing* real effective demand on employment and involuntary unemployment. Starting from a volume of employment, N_1 and real wage rate, w^1, as effective demand increases so too will output, money wages and the wage good price-levels. In generally applicable circumstances, the rise in the wage good price-level will outstrip the increase in money wages and the *real wage rate will fall*. Total employment will rise towards N_* and the level of involuntary unemployment will decrease. If the increase in effective demand is pushed far enough, eventually the full employment level of real wages (w^*) will emerge.[6] This analysis explains Keynes' famous, but rather tortuous, definition of involuntary unemployment. For Keynes:

> Men are involuntarily unemployed, if, in the event of a *small rise in the price of wage goods relatively to the money wage*, both the aggregate supply of labour willing to work for the current money wage and the aggregate demand for it at that wage would be greater than the existing volume of employment.
>
> (Keynes, 2007, p. 15; my emphasis)

Keynes' attempt to define an unemployment equilibrium position in terms of the rejection of a classical postulate – the inequality of the real wage rate and the disutility of labour – is the one serious misstep in the *General Theory*. Admittedly Keynes is simply attempting to demonstrate how his theory departs from that which preceded it. An unintended consequence however has been that Keynes' followers have engaged in intense, but ultimately fruitless, debates about his theory. Luckily a solution is at hand, for Keynes also uses the concept of the

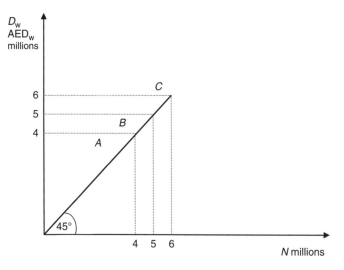

Diagram 11.5 The employment function revisited

employment function to define unemployment equilibrium positions. Using the employment function means that an unemployment equilibrium position can be defined free from reliance on the two classical postulates.[7]

In Diagram 11.5 (which repeats the earlier Diagram 11.3) real aggregate effective demand is on the vertical axis and labour units are on the horizontal axis. In this case the level of real effective demand of 6 million wage units is consistent with the full employment position of 6 million labour units. Any level of effective demand lower than 6 million wage units will bring forth a below full employment equilibrium position. For example with effective demand of 5 million wage units the volume of employment is 5 million labour units. The equilibrium level of *unemployment* can then be easily calculated at 1 million labour units by comparing the full employment position with the actual level of employment – that is 6 million minus 5 million labour units. Of course if effective demand were even lower at 4 million wage units then aggregate employment is that much lower, at 4 million labour units, whilst the equilibrium volume of *unemployment* rises to 2 million labour units.

Therefore in the General Theory model it is possible to define a *range* of employment and unemployment equilibria that are illustrated by the employment function. Each equilibrium position is the result of the operation of persistent market forces. The modern conception of having *one* full employment position and *one* natural rate of unemployment (or NAIRU) towards which an economy gravitates is quite alien to the General Theory model. For Keynes there is any number of resting places for an economy. Yet there is nothing desirable or inevitable or necessary about below full employment resting places.

> [W]e must not conclude that the mean position [of employment] thus determined by `natural' tendencies, namely, by those tendencies which are likely to persist, failing measures expressly designed to correct them, is, therefore, established by laws of necessity. The unimpeded rule of the above conditions is a fact of observation concerning the world as it is or has been, and not a necessary principle which cannot be changed.
>
> (Keynes, 2007, p. 254)

This of course implies that it is possible to use public policy measures to change a volume of employment that is felt to be socially unacceptable. This is an issue that is taken up again in the next chapter.

e) A causal map of the General Theory model

The causal map outlined in Chapter 10 needs only one minor, but important, amendment to incorporate unemployment. The new causal map in real terms starts with the nominal level of aggregate demand (D), the aggregate supply relationship ($\emptyset$) and the wage unit (WU). From this starting point the values of D_w and Z_w can be easily calculated.

When the values of D_w and Z_w are equal the real volume of aggregate effective demand is defined (AED_w). The level of AED_w determines the equilibrium levels of real aggregate income (Y_w), real aggregate saving (S_w) and employment of labour units (N). The equilibrium employment of labour units is associated with a particular volume of total output (Q). The levels of AED_w, WU and Q combined determine the general and wage good price-levels (P_g and P_{wg}, respectively); and WU and P_{wg} combined determine the real wage rate per labour unit (w). Finally, subtracting the equilibrium employment of labour units from the number of labour units consistent with full employment provides the volume of involuntary unemployment (U_{inv}).

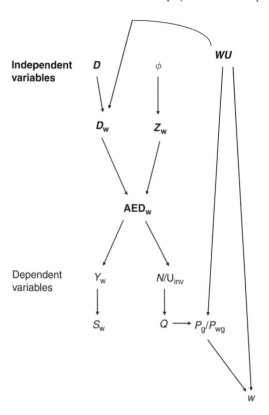

Map 11

f) Summary

The employment function charts how employment responds to changes in real effective demand. It follows that because the real aggregate supply price function is represented by a 45° line, so too will be the employment function. This means that value of the employment function (F) is always equal to unity. The employment function, however, has an upper limit which allows Keynes to define the full employment position free from reliance on the classical postulates. Once full employment is attained, and demand-deficient unemployment is eliminated, further increases in nominal effective demand will prove ineffectual in increasing output or employment.

The elasticity of employment defines the elasticity of all points along the employment function. Assuming that the change in effective demand is foreseen by entrepreneurs some time ahead, the elasticity of employment will tend towards a maximum equilibrium value of unity. But, according to Keynes, there are instances where the elasticity of employment will, for short periods, have a value below its maximum value, especially if a change in effective demand is directed towards the consumption industries. However as time elapses entrepreneurs are able to respond to the change in demand and the elasticities of employment in both consumption and investment sectors will approach their maximum. This helps clarify the time dimension underlying the multiplier process and why the values of the investment and employment multipliers can diverge. From this Keynes suggests an amendment to his earlier simple conclusion that changes in employment depend solely on changes in the level of effective demand. The composition of any change in effective demand must also influence the outcome for employment in the short period.

One of Keynes' most contentious ideas is that a market economy may experience an equilibrium position with demand-deficient unemployment. Keynes argues an economy finds a resting place because of four key psychological propensities that save it from the uncertainty and instability of a completely fluid system. For each state of long-term expectation a long-period volume of employment can be identified. If this employment level is less than full employment an equilibrium volume of involuntary unemployment is specified. Each unemployment equilibrium position is associated with a determinate level of output, a *natural* rate of interest, a specific general level of money wages and prices and a particular real wage rate. In conditions of full employment the equilibrium level of involuntary unemployment is zero and a *neutral* rate of interest applies. An employment function may be used to specify unemployment equilibria free from reliance on the two classical postulates.

Appendix
Analysing Unemployment – A Shifting Equilibrium Concept

The concept of the unemployment equilibrium raises certain methodological problems for macroeconomics. Can an economy be in equilibrium with a permanent excess supply of labour? Precisely what do economists mean when they say a market system is in equilibrium? There are a surprising number of notions of equilibrium that can be gleaned from the literature (Arrow and Debreu, 1954; Minsky, 1982; Chick, 1983; Hansen, 1983; Milgate and Eatwell, 1983; Milgate, 1987, 1988; Amadeo, 1992; Rogers, 1997; Lawlor, 2006). Three of the dominant notions can be summarised in the following way:

1. The *Smithian* notion of permanent and persistent forces working in the long period to establish *natural* levels of activity. In equilibrium conditions there must be a *uniform* rate of profit in different industries which is the way the older classicals, such as Smith and Ricardo, conceive of an equilibrium position.

2. The *Marshallian* notion where permanent forces operate to establish *normal* levels of activity in the long run. Normal profits must be evident in each industry. The Marshallian approach seems to be the source of the oral tradition of explaining equilibrium in terms of a market economy finding a resting place where there are *no forces for change*. The Marshallian concept focuses on what is now called a partial equilibrium. One industry is examined in isolation from all others, *cet. par.*, and the conditions of equilibrium are defined. The Marshallian idea of a partial equilibrium allows for a distinction to be made between the short run and the long run. Firms in a specific industry may for example enjoy super-normal profits in a short-run equilibrium position, which

disappear in the long run. Moreover the Marshallian notion is flexible enough to cope with the existence of market imperfections. In the aggregated labour market, for example, it allows the classical school to define an equilibrium volume of employment, although both frictional and voluntary unemployment persist. Market imperfections do not stop an equilibrium being defined, as long as there are no forces for change.

3. The *Walrasian* notion which has gained ground with the emergence of the general equilibrium model (GEM). This approach is highly mathematical requiring that all markets are in equilibrium simultaneously defined by the criterion that demand equals supply on all markets. As Milgate and Eatwell note, this way of defining an equilibrium position is methodologically different from the older classicals. For although demand equals supply on every market the rate of profit between industries need not be uniform.

The problem with the Walrasian notion is that it denies the existence of an equilibrium position with involuntary unemployment; involuntary idleness can only ever be a *disequilibrium* phenomenon in the Walrasian frame of reference. Moreover in a Walrasian world the economy can only have one true equilibrium position, that being at full employment.

If however it is accepted that a market system can be in equilibrium *below* full employment the traditional notions of equilibrium must be changed. Keynes' analysis suggests the following amendments are necessary.

I. The central notion of equilibrium should be Marshallian in character; that of a resting place, where there are *no permanent and persistent forces for change*. In Keynes' model the persistent forces are the propensity to consume, expectations of prospective yields, the state of liquidity preference, the money supply and the wage unit. Equilibrium need not, however, be a static concept where no variables change at all. As Keynes notes "it is not necessary that the [equilibrium] level of ... employment should be *constant* i.e. long-period conditions are not necessarily static. For example, a steady increase in wealth or population may constitute part of the unchanging expectation" (Keynes, 2007, footnote p. 48, Keynes' emphasis).

II. The state of long-term expectation should have a role in the definition of equilibrium. In this context Keynes distinguishes between *stationary* and *shifting* equilibria. A stationary equilibrium supposes that the character of the economy is predictable and expectations are given and accurate in all respects. A stationary equilibrium according to Keynes allows for an examination of the influence of various economic motives and propensities in either an unchanging economy or one in which changes are predicted at the start of the analysis. This concept of equilibrium is consistent with the special case character of the classical model especially the hypothesis of a calculable future. A stationary equilibrium can also act as a primer for consideration of the more advanced concept of a shifting equilibrium. A shifting equilibrium allows consideration of situations where expectations are not fixed and definite. For example it can be used to analyse a situation where there is the *threat* of a short-period change in the state of long-term expectation raising the possibility that entrepreneurs will vary their investment spending intentions. For Keynes shifting equilibria can consider "the problems of the real world in which our previous expectations are liable to disappointment and expectations of the future affect what we do today" (Keynes, 2007, pp. 293–294). Obviously the concept of a shifting equilibrium is more generally applicable, and given the analysis in the preceding chapters it is reasonable to suggest that the unemployment equilibrium should be seen as a shifting equilibrium.

III. Macroeconomic models should have a *range* of shifting equilibria where a capitalist economy can find rest. One possibility is a full employment or neutral position; but there can be many other resting places, with various levels of involuntary unemployment and "sub normal" levels of economic activity.

12
Public Policy Implications

a) Introduction

Keynes constructs the General Theory model to consider the condition of capitalism and to address the big policy issues of the day. In the 1930s the condition of capitalism was dire; hence the need to explain how advanced, prosperous nations can experience a long-lasting slump and extremely high levels of unemployment. The number one issue for Keynes is what should be done to cure the economic slump and save capitalism, before it is replaced with something else.[1] What is often insufficiently appreciated by new readers of Keynes is that many of his policy recommendations *preceded* the *General Theory*. Keynes' model provides the analytical diagnosis to underpin his previously specified cure.

Post-publication of the *General Theory* Keynes' policy recommendations are underpinned by a clearer theoretical foundation. He focuses on two big questions – how to manage the macroeconomy in wartime conditions and how to promote post-war prosperity and stability. During the wartime conditions of the early 1940s Keynes turns his attention to the issues of how to avoid an inflationary spiral in conditions of labour scarcity and how to provide war finance without recourse to excessive borrowing. In the post-war world Keynes argues that the priority of policy-makers should be to prevent economic fluctuations and create the conditions for long-term economic prosperity – both within a national economy and globally. Keynes is keenly aware that his policy recommendations will change the character of the capitalist system with respect to the role of the State, the distribution of income and wealth and the viability of the rentier class. But for Keynes better a reformed capitalism than no capitalism at all.

Before considering Keynes' public policy recommendations, it is important to appreciate the role that economic models play in policy debates. An economic theory selects and distinguishes between economic *cause* and economic *effect*. The independent variables are cause, the dependent variables effect. As long as the model is correctly specified, policy-makers can manipulate economic outcomes by influencing the independent variables. The General Theory model provides Keynes with a range of ultimate independent variables to be manipulated. They are the:

- propensity to consume;
- expected prospective yields on newly produced capital assets, and, hence, the marginal efficiency of capital;
- state of liquidity preference;
- money supply;
- general level of money wages that is the wage unit.

In earlier chapters some public policy issues have already been touched upon. Chapter 9 examined the efficacy of wage cutting versus expansionary monetary policy as a way of stimulating employment. Chapter 10 considered the theoretical underpinnings of the debate between Pigou and Keynes about using a public investment programme to increase employment. This chapter provides a far more comprehensive coverage of Keynes' public policy proposals, focusing on how public authorities can operate on the independent variables of the General Theory model to achieve desired economic results.

Section (b) considers the role that both discretionary monetary and fiscal policy can play in an expansionary cure for an economic depression and evaluates their respective attributes. A recurring theme of Keynes' fiscal policy recommendations involves the role of a state-led programme of capital development to cure a slump. But he is also concerned about the financing of any capital development programme, which leads him into the controversial territory of tariffs. Using the General Theory model Keynes concludes that either monetary or fiscal policy, pursued separately, can contribute to a cure for a slump. Keynes however identifies serious limitations with the sole use of either fiscal or monetary policy, so the section examines his arguments for the use of coordinated fiscal and monetary action to cure a depression. Section (c) considers Keynes' demand management proposals designed to constrain the growth of private consumption and free up resources in wartime conditions. In the process Keynes outlines a radical plan to control inflation and provide war finance. Section (d) examines Keynes' policy recommendations for the post-war world with the aim of promoting long-term stability and prosperity with full employment. Once again it involves the active use of fiscal and monetary policy. Domestically this encompasses a stable programme of socialised investment and cheap money; and globally this involves signing up to an International Clearing Union that offers an expansionary cure to trade imbalances. Finally Section (e) reminds the reader that despite Keynes' proposals for state intervention he is a staunch supporter of market capitalism. He wishes to reform capitalism whilst retaining its essential properties. This reformed capitalism will have greater state intervention, less inequality and a depleted rentier class. Keynes is, however, always keen to protect as much of the existing capitalist economic order as possible.

b) Curing a depression

As noted earlier the deterioration in the state of long-term expectation can set an economy on a downward path. The decline in the marginal efficiency of capital can be compounded by a higher rate of interest, causing fixed investment spending to decline and, due to the multiplier effect, a sizeable fall in income and employment. The reader should refer to Chapter 8 for a fuller treatment of this process. The result is the emergence of an economic depression and large-scale unemployment. For society the economic problem becomes how to generate useful employment for the unused or under-utilised resources that are involuntarily idle. Chapter 9 demonstrated that cutting the general level of money wages to alleviate a depression – the contractionist cure – is at best an unreliable solution, and could make matters much worse. For Keynes the best cure for a decline in effective demand that causes a depression is to increase effective demand – the expansionary cure. But what is the best way to stimulate demand; should it be through a relaxation of monetary policy or an expansionary fiscal policy, or a combination of the two?

Expansionary monetary policy

In his early career Keynes has a very traditional attitude to the conduct of monetary policy. In the *Tract* he argues that policy should be aimed at stabilising the price-level. Keynes' attitude changes with the new circumstances created by the United Kingdom's re-entry onto the Gold Standard in 1925 at an overvalued exchange rate. To support the high sterling rate domestic interest rates, especially the long-term rate, were kept at unduly high levels, harming capital development, output and employment. As Tily (2007) notes from that time onwards Keynes becomes an advocate of low interest rates – a *cheap money policy*. The onset of the Great Depression and the demise of the Gold Standard strengthen Keynes' belief in the need for lower rates of interest rate. Keynes especially favours a low long-term interest rate which he thinks most influences the investment decisions of entrepreneurs.

But during his participation in the Macmillan Committee, Keynes becomes increasingly aware that he had not been sufficiently clear about "the fundamental arguments in favour of the dogmas [i.e. cheap money] to which I have rashly given utterance without sufficiently substantiating them" (Keynes; quoted by Tily, 2007, p. 52). The *Treatise* is an effort, not entirely successful, to provide a theoretical foundation for the previously recommended cheap money policy. The *General Theory* is a far more successful effort to substantiate the case for cheap money.

In the *General Theory* Keynes rigorously evaluates the cheap money arguments in the context of a Great Depression-style downturn. He poses the question: will an expansionary monetary policy be able to induce a sufficiently low long-term interest rate in order to cure an economic depression? To begin with Keynes accepts there are two basic limitations on the ability of monetary authorities to manage the *long-term* money interest rate. First, monetary authorities, in practice, tend to manipulate the *short-term* interest rate because it is easier to influence. In practice, however, the long-term rate does not always reflect changes in the short-term rate. For example a reduction in the short-term rate will not always lead to a commensurate fall in long-term rates as the latter is influenced by a range of longer term factors (e.g. expectations regarding the position of wealth-holder ten or twenty years hence) that have little impact on short rates. Secondly, interest rates may have an effective floor below which they will not go due to the existence of what Keynes calls *lenders' risk*. This takes the form of the risk of either a voluntary or involuntary default by a borrower on the repayment of a loan; a lender will always charge some interest on a loan to compensate for this risk. Keynes, however, notes that this second limitation is only likely to apply in an era of very low interest rates.

Putting the two basic limitations to one side, Keynes focuses on some rather more important influences on the efficacy of a cheap money policy. Essentially Keynes argues that the effectiveness of monetary policy depends crucially on the state of long-term expectation which representative opinion holds regarding the *future* conduct of monetary policy. Keynes considers two possibilities. The first occurs when a new monetary stance is implemented whilst the state of expectation about the conduct of future monetary policy is *unchanged*. The second possibility occurs when a changed monetary stance *itself* causes a *change* in expectations about future monetary policy.

In the first case monetary policy has the best chance of succeeding in manipulating long-term interest rates to some desired level. In other words the new policy stance seems to the general public as based upon sound and practicable foundations and implemented by a central bank with a track record of competent monetary management. This is most likely to occur when a small relaxation of monetary policy is required to counter a mild recession or encourage an existing recovery. The danger with monetary policy is that too much will be asked of it. This happens, with a *constant state of long-term expectation*, when a new monetary stance is viewed as being experimental by seeking to reduce the long-term interest rate to some unsafe level.[2] If this outcome emerges, an attempt by monetary authorities to reduce the rate of interest *further* may create such a unanimous opinion that there is a mass shift towards the holding of cash. The speculative demand for money therefore becomes extremely elastic when *r* falls below the safe rate. An expansionary monetary policy in these circumstances will fail to reduce interest rates. This is the problem which mainstream Keynesians highlight as the so-called *liquidity trap*.

One follower of Keynes, J.R. Hicks, in particular, stresses the significance of the liquidity trap with the dubious claim that it is "the most important thing in Mr. Keynes' book" (Hicks, 1983, p. 168). Yet it is clear that Keynes does *not* view the liquidity trap as being that significant. For when Keynes sets out the possibility of the trap he mentions that although it may become important in the future there is no obvious contemporary example. Interestingly Hicks provides no textual evidence to support his assertion.

Moreover, Keynes has a more important concern about a cheap money policy. The problem relates to the second possibility noted above that a changed monetary stance may itself change expectations about future monetary policy. Keynes realises that the interest rate can be changed *both* by changes in the money supply with a steady liquidity function *and* by changes in the state of long-term expectation that affects the liquidity function directly. Keynes immediately notes that:

> [o]pen market operations may, indeed, influence the rate of interest *through both channels;* since they may not only change the volume of money, but also give rise to changed expectations concerning the *future* policy of the central bank or of the government.
>
> (Keynes, 2007, pp. 197–198; my emphasis)

In other words a change in the monetary stance can affect both the *supply* of and the *demand* for money. This is most likely to occur if a large increase in the quantity of money is required to significantly lower the rate of interest. This cheap money policy may strike representative opinion as a very risky strategy and change perceptions about the likely conduct of future monetary policy.[3] This can be illustrated in Diagram 12.1. A previously adverse short-period change in the state of long-term expectation has caused the liquidity schedule to settle at $L1$, a point compatible with equilibrium interest rate r^1.

Say a much lower interest rate r^* is compatible with the pre-depression volume of investment spending. To attain r^* by monetary action, however, requires a very large increase in the money supply (from $Ms1$ to $Ms2$). Such an expansionary cure may seem to representative opinion a risky and unwise course of action causing the liquidity function itself to shift rightwards (from $L1$ to $L2$). In these circumstances the new monetary stance will only bring about a fall in the interest rate to r^2 and will fail to induce the appropriate level of investment. The difficulty is that monetary authorities must pursue policies which strike public opinion as prudent and conservative, even when circumstances – such as the Great Depression – demand more unorthodox expansionary responses.

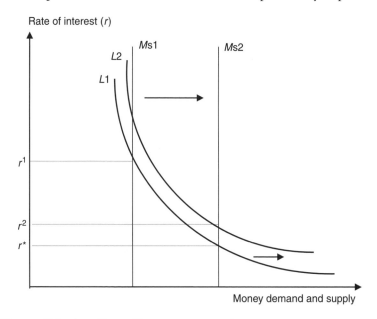

Diagram 12.1   A problem with monetary expansion

Moreover the ultimate problem for monetary action as an expansionary cure is that it does not directly improve either business confidence or expected prospective yields. A lower interest rate cannot by itself revive a deteriorating marginal efficiency of capital. Yet overall Keynes does *not* dismiss monetary policy. There are circumstances where "reasonable and practicable" monetary policy can achieve its objective. But in the midst of an international slump as experienced during the Great Depression Keynes believes that monetary policy alone is insufficiently effective (Keynes, 1981b). As Keynes famously argues:

> If, however, we are tempted to assert that money is the drink which stimulates the system to activity, we must remind ourselves that there may be several slips between the cup and the lip. For whilst an increase in the quantity of money may be expected, *cet. par*, to reduce the rate of interest, this will not happen if the liquidity-preferences of the public are increasing more than the quantity of money; and whilst a decline in the rate of interest may be expected, *cet. par*, to increase the volume of investment, this will not happen if the schedule of the marginal efficiency of capital is falling more rapidly than the rate of interest; and whilst an increase in the volume of investment may be expected, *cet. par*, to increase employment, this may not happen if the propensity to consume is falling off. Finally, if employment increases, prices will rise in a degree partly governed by the shapes of the physical supply functions, and partly by the liability of the wage unit to rise in money terms. And when output has increased and prices have risen, the effect of this on liquidity-preference will be to increase the quantity of money necessary to maintain a given rate of interest.
>
> (Keynes, 2007, p. 173; Keynes' emphasis)

One further aspect of Keynes' approach to monetary policy which has received insufficient attention is his call for a change in the institutional framework for the monetary authority. It must be remembered that up until the mid-1940s the Bank of England was actually a *privately* owned bank, with a high degree of *independence* from government. It is this institutional position which Keynes thinks is sensible to change, by bringing the Bank of England into the public sector and *under political control*. The Government can then ensure that the monetary stance is consistent with other macroeconomic goals, especially the attainment of full employment.

This idea of a central bank under political control is alien to neo-classical economic thinking, and at variance with modern policy-making.[4] What then is the efficacy of a politically independent central bank when the General Theory model is accepted? The volume of aggregate effective demand determines the equilibrium volume of employment and there is no aggregated labour market. In conditions below full employment increases in effective demand generate both inflation and higher output and employment – semi-inflation – and this is not due to money illusion. Demand management policies influence the volume of effective demand – hence employment and output – in each short period, whilst the same is true of the long run, which is simply many short periods added together. In these circumstances an independent central bank targeting low inflation has a strong incentive to overestimate the dangers of inflation and underestimate the potential for higher output and employment. Moreover, a central bank, independent from democratic influences and disciplines, can pursue narrow policy targets inimical to the interests of society, but which democratic representatives are unable to change. The best illustration of this being the actions of the independent Bank of England in the 1930s, but many more examples exist. Given his experiences during the 1930s it is no surprise that Keynes comes down firmly on the side of democratic control of monetary policy-making.

Expansionary fiscal policy

The alternative to using monetary policy to cure a depression is the active use of expansionary fiscal policy. Although in the interwar period the classical school has no great objections to using monetary policy in pursuit of price stability, there are strong reservations about using fiscal policy and most especially government borrowing to stimulate employment. *Theoretically* there are two classical objections. First is Say's law which suggests that, with a given volume of loanable funds, any additional government borrowing must crowd out private investment leaving employment unchanged – the crude "Treasury view" of the interwar period.

Secondly, there is the aggregated labour market analysis that predicts that any additional government spending can only increase employment if it causes an unexpected inflation of prices and a lower real wage rate. If employment is to be increased the proper policy should cut high money wages, rather than deceive workers into the labour market. To appreciate Keynes' attitude to the scope for effective fiscal action it is important to realise that he rejects both Say's law and the classical aggregated labour market and replaces both with his General Theory model. Yet a further objection, *political in nature*, remains to active fiscal policy. This is the Gladstonian liberal view of sound public finance, whereby government has a moral duty to balance its budget, which dominated British economic policy thinking from the last quarter of the nineteenth century. This political judgement sees an unbalanced budget as not only ineffectual in stimulating employment (for the reasons noted above), but, even if it works, morally repugnant as it increases the burden of debt on tax payers. In the context of the exceptional circumstances of the Great Depression, Keynes, the leading liberal economist of his day, reaches a rather different political viewpoint: that it is better to have unbalanced budgets in order to *cure* a massive slump than to balance the budget, allow mass unemployment to persist and have the capitalist system overthrown by totalitarian regimes of extreme right or left.

If a severe international slump, like that experienced during the Great Depression, cannot be properly alleviated by monetary policy then the State will have to step in to directly boost effective demand. What then should be the composition of the expanded effective demand? Keynes advocates an expansionary cure led by extra investment spending rather than greater consumption expenditure. This is a recurrent theme throughout Keynes' policy recommendations from the late 1920s onwards (Keynes and Henderson, 1972; Keynes 1972b, 1972c, 1981a; Liberal Industrial Inquiry, 1977).

Under Keynes' strong influence the Liberal Industrial Inquiry of the late 1920s calls on the Government to embark on a *programme of capital development* specifically to alleviate the United Kingdom's relatively high unemployment at the time. The aim of the programme being to deal with the arrears in national development in areas such as road construction and house-building; telephone and electricity development; railway, docks and harbour improvements; and schemes of afforestation and land drainage. Importantly the programme includes proposals for Government subsidies for private sector investment of national importance, for example assistance to private railway companies to modernise their rolling stock.

As the Great Depression unfolds Keynes argues in the *Macmillan Report* that a major capital programme must involve State *planning* with schemes organised two to three years ahead. By 1933 when the scale of the international slump is more evident Keynes calls not only for a capital development programme at *home*, but for stronger nations to coordinate fiscal efforts to *simultaneously* increase effective demand internationally. In other words an international slump requires a globally coordinated expansionary cure.

The financing of an expansionary capital development programme is an issue to which Keynes constantly returns. Keynes believes that the multiplier effect strongly reinforces the affordability of a capital programme. In the *Means to Prosperity* Keynes uses a multiplier estimate of 1.5 to claim that every extra £100 of State capital spending financed by borrowing – what Keynes calls *loan expenditure* – adds £20 to tax revenues and reduces unemployment spending by £33. Therefore the net cost of the capital projects and the associated employment is roughly half the initial outlay, though the extra tax revenue and lower social security payments only emerge after the elapse of some time.

That said the net cost of such a capital programme might be affordable if Government finances start from a healthy position. But in the midst of the Great Depression this is not so. The UK Government budget in the early 1930s for example was heavily in deficit with falling tax revenues and inflated social security spending. Moreover the Depression had badly harmed business confidence and the United Kingdom's export trade and greatly increased international economic instability. In these circumstances Keynes is keenly aware that to further increase the deficit to finance a capital programme might further undermine business confidence. In addition any extra domestic spending associated with a fiscal expansion must suck in more imports and harm the balance of trade. In Keynes' mind an investment-led fiscal expansion might be put in jeopardy unless an extra source of tax revenue can be found to put the Government budget on a sounder basis, improve the nation's net export position and improve business confidence.

It is in this context that Keynes reluctantly calls for a *revenue tariff* on imports. According to Keynes a revenue tariff is thrice blessed: it provides much-needed tax revenue to balance the Government budget after which a capital development programme can begin; it reduces import penetration and encourages business confidence in the import substitution industries; finally it improves the net export position and provides room for an increase in imports associated with an expansionary capital development programme. Hence for Keynes an effective expansionist cure in the midst of the Great Depression requires the *double harness* of a capital development programme combined with a revenue tariff. Recommending the imposition of tariffs is indeed a radical departure for the leading liberal economist of the day. Keynes, however, argues that the free trade case had always accepted that tariffs may be necessary in an emergency; the Great Depression is that emergency. Whatever the problems of financing an expansionary cure Keynes believes it is much preferable to borrowing money to pay people to remain idle. He berates those who argue against borrowing to finance capital development whilst being content to borrow to pay out unemployment benefits. Moreover none of this denies that Keynes accepts the case for some extra consumption expenditure as part of the expansionist cure. In the *General Theory* Keynes makes a number of references to different schemes of taxation and varying the amount of current public expenditure financed by loans in order to increase the propensity to consume. Yet Keynes is not an advocate of a consumption-led cure to the Great Depression, unlike the propagandists of under-consumptionism.

Keynes' proposal for an expansionary programme of capital development to cure the depression can be illustrated as an outward shift in the marginal efficiency of capital schedule. If the traditional marginal efficiency schedule shows *private* investment demand, a new programme of public investment will mean a higher rate of total fixed investment at every level of marginal efficiency. In Diagram 12.2 the schedule mec0 represents the private demand for new investment and mec1 shows private and public investment demand combined. This means that

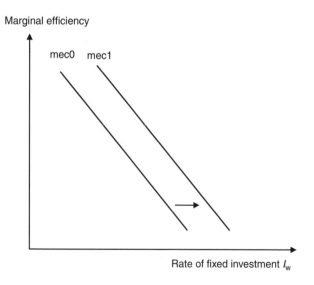

Diagram 12.2 State investment and the marginal efficiency

at any rate of interest total investment demand will be significantly stronger. An increase in aggregate fixed investment spending, and its multiplier effect, stimulates effective demand and increases output and employment and pulls the economy out of depression.

The "double harness" of fiscal and monetary policy

But fiscal policy is no panacea for Keynes. He is acutely aware of the difficulties with using fiscal policy *alone* to cure an economic depression. In the *General Theory* Keynes examines this subject while estimating the value of a multiplier associated with an increase in public investment spending. The conclusions he reaches are applicable to other categories of discretionary fiscal action. Keynes refers to the difficulties with fiscal policy as *offsetting factors* which reduce the value of any investment multiplier effect. He lists the following factors that result from an expansionary fiscal policy.

1. *An increase in the demand for money.* An expansionary fiscal policy that stimulates economic activity will inevitably increase the transactionary demand for money. Moreover as output and employment expand entrepreneurs will purchase more working capital which is likely to further strengthen money demand. Finally, as output rises, so too will the general price-level resulting in additional increases in money demand. All these factors tend to raise the rate of interest causing private sector investment to be crowded out.
2. *An increase in the volume of imports.* A part of any increase in effective demand will leak out of an open economy. This will stimulate the demand for foreign goods and services and increase foreign employment; but the leakage will reduce the size of the multiplier mitigating the effect on the domestic economy.
3. *An increase in the supply price of capital goods.* As output and prices generally increase this must raise the cost of producing capital goods. The marginal efficiency of capital will deteriorate creating another retardation of private investment spending.
4. *A deterioration in the state of business confidence.* If the business community is ill-disposed to government intervention per se or if the Government budget deficit is thought to be growing too rapidly, an expansionary fiscal programme may undermine the state of confidence. A decline in confidence may increase liquidity preferences (and, *cet. par.*, interest rates), diminish the marginal efficiency and retard private investment even further.

5. *A declining marginal propensity to consume.* Given the character of the aggregate consumption function Keynes uses, he argues that if employment and real aggregate income rise substantially the community's marginal propensity to consume will tend to decline. This, in turn, will tend to dampen the value of multiplier.

Once the finance motive to hold money is taken into account a further offsetting factor appears. If government *plans* to increase public works it will need to build up a fund of cash *before* the programme begins. The additional demand for money might, *cet. par.*, raise the rate of interest rate and further deter private investment.

Depending on the relative strengths of these offsetting factors, it is possible to argue that expansionary fiscal action may vary from being very effective at one extreme to almost counter-productive. Keynes is, therefore, very much aware of the limitations of expansionary fiscal action. He raises objections to it that not even Milton Friedman identifies. Yet Keynes concludes that, in appropriate circumstances, fiscal policy has a role to play in an expansionary cure.

On closer inspection it is clear Keynes advocates an expansionary cure based upon the "double harness" of coordinated fiscal and monetary action. In the *Means to Prosperity* Keynes argues that a fiscal expansion has the best chance of succeeding in an environment of cheap money, where bank credit is sufficiently 'cheap and abundant' to finance the restoration of working capital by entrepreneurs once a recovery is underway. In the *General Theory* after covering the offsetting factors associated with expansionary fiscal action, Keynes reminds the reader that some of them may be overcome by an accommodating monetary stance. Moreover, Keynes often refers to the need for monetary authorities to counteract the tendency for the market rate of interest to be too high. He is quite clear that a "reasonable and practicable" cheap money policy, which lowers the long-term money rate of interest for sound borrowers, is an achievable goal.

An expansionary cure based upon the double harness of fiscal and monetary policy can be illustrated using Diagram 12.3. In panel 3a suppose that the desired rate of aggregate investment is I_{w^*}, and this will help attain the full employment level of effective demand. The marginal efficiency schedule mec0 shows private sector investment demand. Prior to any fiscal action panel 3b shows that the equilibrium rate of interest is r^0, consistent with liquidity schedule $L0$. This means that the rate of aggregate investment is I_{w0}, well below the desired rate. With an

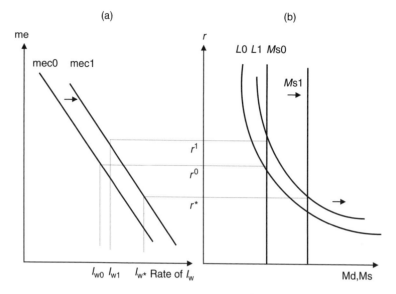

Diagram 12.3   Fiscal and monetary expansion – in double harness

investment-led fiscal expansion (represented by mec1) aggregate economic activity rises, but this then causes the demand for money to strengthen; the liquidity schedule shifts to $L1$. Without monetary action the equilibrium interest rate increases to r^1 and fixed investment only rises to I_{w1}. When however the fiscal expansion is accommodated by a practicable monetary expansion ($Ms0$ to $Ms1$) the equilibrium interest rate can be lowered to r^* and the desirable rate of investment is forthcoming. Hence an expansionary policy involving the double harness of fiscal and monetary action provides the most effective expansionary cure for economic depression.

This diagram only considers the impact of an investment-led fiscal package. It is quite easy to set out an analysis that considers a consumption-led fiscal programme, with its impact primarily on the consumption function. Higher consumption spending also leads to a greater money demand and without a reasonable and practicable monetary expansion it too will find the rate of interest too high to attain the desired level of aggregate effective demand.

In summary Keynes realises that a successful expansionary cure for an economic depression requires policies that influence the propensity to consume, the marginal efficiency of capital *and* the rate of interest to social advantage. As part of an expansionary cure fiscal and monetary action are complements, not substitutes. To paint Keynes as an advocate of fiscal action in preference to monetary action is a serious distortion of the truth. This has not, however, stopped mainstream Keynesians perpetuating the myth.

c) Preventing wartime inflation and financing the war effort

With the onset of hostilities in 1939 Keynes quickly appreciates that economic conditions in the United Kingdom have dramatically changed. The large unused resources of the interwar period – the age of plenty – are to be quickly replaced with the maximum war effort and full resource utilisation – an age of scarcity. The problem facing Government is no longer how to bring into active use the plentiful supply of idle labour and under-utilised capital equipment; it is instead how to allocate scarce resources – especially labour – between competing alternative uses.

By 1941, as Glynn and Booth (1996) note, the lack of labour in the United Kingdom – referred to as a *labour famine* – was the single most important constraint on war production. This was a far cry from the mass unemployment of labour just 10 years earlier. The initial response of the Treasury in 1939 was to announce an expansion of the already sizable rearmaments programme, to be largely financed by increased Government borrowing. Indeed Government borrowing was planned to grow to 25 per cent of GDP in the fiscal year 1939–1940; the Treasury claimed, applying Keynes' ideas of ten years before, that the extra spending would not be inflationary with 9 per cent of the labour-force unemployed (Skidelsky, 2000).

Keynes is immediately aware that Treasury reasoning will quickly become redundant in wartime, as plenty gives way to scarcity. The key problem is how to maximise war production. The constraints are set by how many imports can be afforded, how many exports can be released, the need to operate capital equipment with little scope for new investment and crucially the demands of domestic consumption spending. The latter is the dominant influence, for as previously unemployed workers find employment, and perhaps existing workers enjoy higher money wages, there is strong pressure for domestic consumption spending to rise in real terms. Yet in an age of scarcity the growth of home consumption can only occur if war production is curtailed or imports are increased. If imports are allowed to rise this can only be financed by using up finite foreign assets and exchange reserves, thereby reducing the future capacity to purchase vital hardware from abroad; the imports of consumption goods will also use up vital ship capacity crowding out essential imports from the rest of the world; all of this inevitably harms the war effort. Keynes claims that wartime conditions require there should be no growth of home consumption, if anything it should be lower, in order to free up resources for war production.

Keynes in the influential pamphlet *How to Pay for the War* (Keynes, 1972d) sets out the options facing the United Kingdom by which home consumption may be curtailed.

1. *Inflation.* In this case excessive nominal effective demand, due to Government war spending and increased worker consumption, is allowed to pull up prices. The inflation of prices reduces the purchasing power of money wages, and workers' consumption in real terms is brought down to the available supply. But there is a further advantage to inflation. If workers' wage increases lag behind the rate of increase in prices, businesses enjoy windfall profits. The excess profits can then be commandeered by the Government, by way of higher taxes and greater borrowing, to finance the war effort. This is the "inflation tax" method of financing war, as used by Britain in the First World War. But Keynes notes two problems with this option. First he recognises that workers in the 1940s are far less likely than those in 1914 to allow a significant time lag between price and wage rises. Hence the inflation tax will not be effective as war finance. Second the inflation built into the system during the war has to be expunged after it. The only way to do this is to have a major post-war deflation, as in 1920–1921, with all its undesirable costs in terms of lost output and unemployment.

2. *Universal rationing or generalised price controls.* Another mechanism for curtailing consumption is to ration all relevant goods and services. Although workers have increased incomes they will not be able to spend money on what they desire as government prescribes the limited amounts each individual can consume. Keynes claims this form of crude and arbitrary physical control abolishes consumer choice and treats each individual as if they were identical – bordering he believes on Bolshevism. Another variant of Government control, this time designed to avoid inflation, is generalised price controls. Workers' incomes are allowed to rise without limitation, but the pressure of increased nominal effective demand on prices is legislated away; price rises are made illegal. Keynes explains that with workers' spending power undiminished the inevitable result of price-fixing is long queues, shortages and empty shops – none of which will enhance war morale.

3. *Countering excessive spending – The first Keynes plan*. Using the General Theory model Keynes can see that the cause of inflation or empty shops is the excessive growth of nominal effective demand. The solution is to reduce worker consumption and in the process provide finance for the war effort. One way is for workers to voluntarily save a larger proportion of their increased incomes influenced by wartime propaganda and exhortation. Keynes is a supporter of voluntary schemes to increase saving and sees them as part of the solution. He just does not believe they will suffice. A second possibility is to increase taxation and widen the tax base to include low-paid workers who have never previously been subject to income tax. Keynes certainly advocates higher taxes on the better paid, but is chary about imposing a heavy burden of tax on the poorest paid.

However, to rigorously manage consumption demand Keynes proposes a bold deferred payment scheme – the first so-called *Keynes plan*. As workers' incomes rise Keynes argues some of the increase should be taxed, whilst another portion should be treated as deferred pay – compulsorily held in bank deposits to be paid to workers after the war. The government can manage demand by setting the level of deferred pay at whichever rate is needed to ensure consumption demand is brought into equality with the available output, without inflationary forces building up.

In addition during the war the extra tax revenue plus the compulsory deferred pay (saving) is then available to the Government to finance its war effort. Keynes notes that this way of financing war-related expenditure has the considerable benefit of reducing reliance on traditional, but expensive, forms of government borrowing by issuing debt; mirroring his recommendations for curing a depression Keynes strongly advocates any Government borrowing should be at the lowest possible interest rate – the cheap money policy. The Keynes plan also explains when the optimal time will be for the deferred pay of workers to be released after the war. Keynes argues it should be paid out to coincide with the first post-war depression. Consumption that is curtailed during the war, when it is not needed, is then made effective during a later post-war depression when it helps promote economic recovery.[5] The final part of the Keynes plan concerns the role of the price mechanism in allocating resources to meet the curtailed consumption demand. Once the threat of excessive consumption is alleviated Keynes strongly argues that the market mechanism should be used to decide what the diverse pattern of consumption will be, without recourse to universal rationing or generalised price-fixing. Keynes greatly prefers the price mechanism to allocate resources as it promotes consumer freedom of choice. Indeed Keynes' preference for the market stands out in contrast to other Keynesian-minded economists of the time who advocated more State-led controls. As Skidelsky (2000) notes Keynes actually sees his deferred pay scheme plus the reliance on the market to allocate consumption goods as an alternative to price-fixing, rationing, bureaucratic controls and physical planning proposed by others.[6]

How to Pay for the War was well received in influential circles. It led to a rapprochement between Keynes and both the Bank of England and the Treasury after their disputes during the interwar period. By 1940 Keynes had been invited to return to the Treasury with a roving brief, which included making comments on the 1940 budget preparations. Due to Keynes' influence this budget announced a deferred pay scheme to curtail consumption, though one that was far less ambitious than the Keynes plan. According to Skidelsky in the Keynes plan deferred pay would have paid for about 15 per cent of Government war spending, whilst the 1940 budget scheme of compulsory saving financed only 3 per cent of war expenditure. Despite this domestic consumption in the United Kingdom was curtailed during the Second World War. Glynn and Booth note that private consumption accounted for 73.5 per cent of national income in 1939, with Government military expenditure accounting for only 15 per cent. By 1943 the respective positions had been reversed; the share devoted to private consumption had fallen to 49 per cent but Government war spending had increased to 56 per cent of national income. But if deferred pay had not significantly curtailed consumption, what had? According to Skidelsky the consumption share was reduced by a rising burden of taxation, but also through shortages, universal rationing and some inflation – which *How to Pay for the War* was designed to prevent.

d) Promoting stability and prosperity in the long run

In terms of economic development in the post-war world Keynes is keen to avoid any possible repetition of the Great Depression. When working at the Treasury Keynes addresses the question of how once an economy has reached a prosperous full employment position it can be stabilised at or near that point over the long run. He is convinced that demand management over the long run should seek to keep employment steady by *preventing* major economic fluctuations. Keynes is acutely aware that once a large macroeconomic downturn emerges there may be no effective measures to cure it quickly. Therefore in terms of stabilising an economy at or near the full employment position prevention is better than cure. Of course Keynes' proposals for stabilising an economy inevitably mirror his ideas for curing a depression.

To prevent macroeconomic instability over a longer period Keynes recommends the use of both active fiscal and monetary policy. In terms of monetary policy Keynes remains a firm proponent of cheap money; permanently low interest rates to encourage private investment are an important aspect of Keynes' proposals for preventing economic fluctuations. Yet Keynes argues the main responsibility for preventing domestic fluctuations rests with fiscal policy. Not just any fiscal policy, but one that stresses the role of public investment spending. Hence central to Keynes' ideas for preventing economic fluctuations is that investment in an economy should be *socialised*, that is the State should take control of roughly 65–75 per cent of total investment spending. Second, the State should plan and enact a *stable long-term* programme of public investment over a number of years, allowing items in the programme to be expedited or retarded as appropriate.[7] For example if the economy is slowing down and increasing unemployment is a threat, the rate of socialised investment can be speeded up, and with a multiplier effect, economic activity should recover; conversely when economic conditions are booming this is the time to slow down the rate of socialised investment to ensure inflationary forces do not take hold. Government then determines the overall rate of investment in the economy by amending its own investment intentions, with the rate of interest playing an accommodating role held stable at a very low level. This according to Keynes will provide an overarching framework for a more stable macroeconomic environment. As Keynes explains "if the bulk of investment is in public or semi public control and we go in for a stable long-term programme, serious fluctuations are enormously less likely to occur" (Keynes, 1980e, p. 326).

There is one final reason why Keynes concentrates on public investment spending as a method of stabilising the economy. In the Liberal Industrial Inquiry in the 1920s Keynes identifies considerable arrears of national capital development in the United Kingdom; this issue was not properly addressed in the 1930s and the capital stock was further depleted in the Second World War. By the early 1940s Keynes reasons "that I do not think we have yet reached anything like the point of capital saturation [in the United Kingdom]. It would be in the interests of the standard of life in the long run if we increased our capital quite materially" (Keynes, 1980e, p. 350).

In Keynes' mind the socialisation of investment is not a socialist proposal. For whilst central government should take the lead in planning and organising socialised programmes the actual investment can be conducted by local government, "semi-public bodies" plus partnership schemes of various descriptions between public and private sectors. Moreover private investment will still play an important part in the efficient operation of the economy.

Keynes' proposals follow on logically from the General Theory model. This shows how private investment spending is the inherently unstable component of effective demand and the major cause of economic fluctuations. The most appropriate remedy therefore is for the State to take control of the bulk of investment spending and commit itself to a stable long-term programme of capital development consistent with maintaining full employment. Keynes' preference for public investment is reinforced by the "narrow limitations" he perceives to managing consumption levels to prevent fluctuations. This is particularly true of the use of taxation to influence the propensity to consume to which Keynes raises both practical and political difficulties.

> In the first place, one has not enough experience to say that short-term variations in consumption are in fact practicable. People have established standards of life. Nothing will upset them more than to be subject to pressure constantly to vary them up and down. A remission of taxation of which people could only rely on for an indefinitely short period might have very limited effects in stimulating their consumption. And, if it was successful, it would be extraordinarily difficult from the political angle to reimpose the taxation again when employment improved.
>
> (Keynes, 1980e, p. 319)

These practical difficulties are consistent with Keynes' consumption function theory relating to the limited initial affect on the propensity to consume of a short-period change in income. As noted in Chapter 4 the community's habits with respect to consumption change only slowly. Therefore as aggregate income increases the initial marginal propensity to consume out of this extra income will be quite low until consumer habits adjust to the new circumstances; a lower initial marginal propensity to consume has a dampening influence on the value of the multiplier. Moreover if changes in taxation become too frequent consumers may discount such variations and be unresponsive to different tax regimes. Relying on varying consumption spending to manage demand is, therefore, at best an uncertain science.

Marginal efficiency

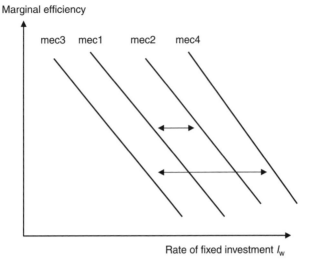

Rate of fixed investment I_w

Diagram 12.4 Socialised investment – dampening fluctuations

Keynes' proposal for a stable long-term programme of socialised investment can be illustrated using a marginal efficiency of capital schedule – Diagram 12.4. The marginal efficiency schedules mec3 and mec4 represent the extent of the fluctuations in the schedule in an economy with investment dominated by the private sector. For all the reasons noted in Chapter 6 through 8 private investment intentions can vary quite considerably. By contrast the marginal efficiency schedules mec1 and mec2 show the much narrower range of fluctuation in an economy with a stable programme of socialised investment. Fluctuations are inevitable given the nature of private investment demand, but because it makes up only 25–35 per cent of aggregate investment its overall impact is much reduced. If total investment spending fluctuates within far smaller limits this means that overall effective demand will be stabilised and major economic fluctuations prevented.

Yet using a stable programme of public investment to prevent fluctuations over the long term has one serious limitation. High levels of sustained public investment will significantly increase the capital stock. Given Keynes' constant concern about capital saturation in a wealthy community, he is acutely aware that a long-term capital development programme has limits beyond which further public investment might be "wasteful and unnecessary" (Keynes, 1980e, p. 321). The longer the period in view, the less viable promoting public investment becomes as a method of preventing economic instability.

Keynes suggests that policy should then shift towards influencing an appropriate long-period trend in the propensity to consume. A long-term taxation policy to promote the desirable levels of consumption expenditure would be important in this respect. In addition government may have to promote a new culture and habits in society to encourage the required propensity to consume; also a permanently low interest rate policy will have a role in promoting the appropriate long-term consumption trend. Therefore Keynes shows himself to be a pragmatist once again. Although he prefers preventing economic fluctuations by increasing the capital stock, he appreciates the limitations of this policy. Hence, the longer the period in view, the greater the emphasis Keynes gives to fiscal policies designed to influence consumption spending. If, however, due to political considerations, the State does not use fiscal policy to guide consumption trends Keynes argues the economy will be forced to rely on:

> millionaires...building mighty mansions to contain their bodies when alive and pyramids to shelter them after death, or, repenting their sins, erect cathedrals and endow monasteries...[to defer] the day when abundance of capital will interfere with abundance of output...
>
> (Keynes, 2007, p. 220)

Keynes thinks a sensible community should be able to devise an alternative to such wasteful forms of private spending to keep effective demand high; but, in the absence of an alternative, better this spending than no spending at all.

Keynes is however keenly aware that the long-run prosperity of a nation cannot be achieved independently of what is happening in the global economy. The interrelations in terms of trade and foreign direct investment mean that nations tend to march together – forward or backward. Nations had marched forward together during the 50 years prior to the First World War, but they had collectively marched backward during the interwar years, and especially during the Great Depression. In the latter period trade in volume and value terms collapsed and foreign direct investment dried up almost completely. The spread of globalised capitalism, and prosperity, which accelerated up until 1914 went into retreat (Keynes, 1971b, 1980a, 1980b, 1980c, 1980d).

In the post-war world Keynes is keen to get the global economy marching forward once again – predominately because this is essential to the long-term maintenance of global full employment. Keynes argues that a necessary complement to a stable programme of public investment and cheap money is a global commercial system that promotes exports and the reliable payment for exports. Moreover this commercial system should encourage nations to recycle export revenues by buying more imports thereby keeping the global level of effective demand rising.

The main obstacle to this expansionary ideal is the existence of trading imbalances. That is some nations, usually the larger and more powerful ones, will run trade surpluses and other nations, usually the smaller and weaker ones, endure trade deficits. In the aftermath of the First World War with its huge economic dislocation, these imbalances were massive. A powerful US economy enjoyed large trade surpluses, whilst others, including the United Kingdom, found their balance of payments position immeasurably weakened. Clearly there must be some process of adjustment to cure trading imbalances. Keynes outlines two possible adjustment processes.

The first is the contractionist cure, where the deficit country pursues a dear money policy and deflation in order to balance off trade at a lower level of economic activity and higher unemployment. The deficit nations take the lead in the adjustment process; however, the surplus countries are not immune from the process. For surplus nations discover that their trade surpluses diminish as weaker nations deflate and economic activity around the globe slows down. Surplus countries therefore also experience higher unemployment, especially in the export sectors. With the contractionary cure the correction of trade imbalances cause all nations to march together *backwards*, although the pain of adjustment in terms of unemployment and social unrest will be most acute for the weaker deficit nations.

This is effectively the way the Gold Standard system worked in the interwar period. Nations sought trade surpluses, and those who succeeded hoarded them – through extra gold holdings – refusing to recycle them by buying more imports. This meant the burden of adjustment fell on the weaker smaller deficit countries, who suffered a disproportionate amount of unemployment and social unrest. And without capital controls, speculative capital movements – hot money – was attracted to the currencies of surplus nations and away from the currencies of those in deficit, thereby amplifying the imbalances and making the pain of adjustment even greater. It is little surprise that the Gold Standard began to break up in this period. In its place a number of dubious "solutions" to the problem of maintaining external balance were tried by different nations – allowing exchanges rates to float freely, competitive exchange rate depreciations, the imposition of tariffs and other barriers to trade. Keynes claims these "solutions" did not resolve global imbalances, and when they reduced the imbalance of one nation this imbalance simply passed on to neighbouring states. But Keynes argues the Gold Standard had not always worked in this way. In the 50 years prior to the First World War trade imbalances had been successfully managed predominantly because the United Kingdom had recycled its trade surpluses through direct foreign investment – capital exports – to the rest of the world. These capital exports stimulated economic expansion and new employment in other nations, who in turn became better customers for the exports of the United Kingdom and other nations. Each national currency was fixed in value in terms of sterling, which in turn had a fixed value with an ounce of gold. This fixed exchange regime encouraged multilateral clearing in which national currencies were convertible and each could be used for trading around the globe. During this period therefore the Gold Standard had provided an expansionary cure for trade imbalances.

Keynes wishes to replicate the expansionist cure for trading imbalances to encourage long-term prosperity in the post-Second World War world, but without a return to the discredited Gold Standard system. Consequently Keynes designs an entirely new global trading and payments system – the second Keynes plan. The starting point for the new system begins by drawing an analogy with the principles of banking in a closed system. For centuries during the middle-ages economic development had been stymied by the hoarding on metallic currency – gold, silver and copper. Banks develop practices to overcome hoarding through the creation of bank money. A depositor with a credit balance only requires a small proportion of these balances to conduct every-day business. The banks recycle the unused balances by lending them out to others who have a demand for money which exceeds their resources. The loans or overdrafts count as deposits for the borrowers, and the volume of bank money is expanded. No harm is done to the person with the credit balance, whilst benefits flow to the borrower and of course the bank (in terms of profits). For the banking system its liabilities and assets balance as the volume of lending expands. The additional loans and overdrafts (assets) are matched by new deposits (liabilities). From the perspective of the overall economy the hoarding of money is eliminated and the elastic volume of bank money expands or contracts with economic activity.

Keynes' genius is to appreciate that the principles of banking for a closed nation can be applied to the global economy. Keynes believes that just as bank money in a closed system can overcome the restrictions of creditors hoarding money, so international bank money can overcome the contractionist tendency of nations with trade surpluses hoarding gold. Of course the creation of international bank money requires the creation of an international bank, which Keynes calls the International Clearing Union (ICU).[8] Keynes proposes that the ICU can accept deposits from countries with trade surpluses and grant overdrafts to nations with trade deficits using an international bank money which he calls *bancor*.[9] Just like bank money in a national system, bancor must be in elastic supply responding to changes in the level of world trade and foreign direct investment and the size of trading imbalances. The fact that a nation is running a trade deficit – being in debit on its account with the ICU – is not a matter for concern. The debit account is treated as an overdraft giving the trade deficit country some leeway to resolve the imbalance by efforts to stimulate exports for example restructuring industries to make them more competitive. For the ICU of course these debit accounts are matched by credit accounts held by countries with trade surpluses – so its liabilities and assets always balance.

To make this international bank money effective, however, requires that the ICU has unchallengeable control over the supply of bancor. Keynes therefore argues that the ICU must only conduct business – open accounts – with the central banks of member states, and that each central bank must monopolise foreign exchange dealing on behalf of its own citizens. This means that the central banks of member states of the ICU will have ICU accounts that reflect the trading position of each state. A nation with a trade surplus will have a central bank with a credit account with the ICU that reflects this surplus; the central bank of a country with a trade deficit will have a debit account with the ICU which reflects this position. Keynes proposes that to make this international bank money widely acceptable a unit of bancor should have a fixed value in terms of an ounce of gold. In turn each member state of the ICU must have its currency fixed in value in terms of bancor. This use of gold – and the subjective emotions it evokes – camouflages the fact that Keynes proposes to create a managed fixed exchange rate system that dethrones gold from its previously privileged position.

Keynes is hopeful that active policies to promote full employment around the world, and the consequent growth of world trade and direct foreign investment, will cause trade imbalances to disappear. But he is wise enough to acknowledge that this might not happen. A nation with a persistent and growing trade deficit might abuse the opportunity to run up an overdraft with the ICU. So just as a national bank will not allow a customer to run up an unlimited overdraft, if the trade deficit of a nation increases beyond some trigger point Keynes proposes that the ICU require it to take action to reduce the bancor debit account.[10] Keynes suggests the ICU have the power to insist a debtor nation devalue its currency – by up to 5 per cent – or restrict capital exports or even deposit some gold reserves with the ICU to reduce its bancor debit.[11]

This is however where the analogy with the practice of a bank in a closed economy ceases. For Keynes argues the ICU must also require a nation with a persistent and growing trade surplus to take remedial action to reduce its bancor credit account. This is perhaps the most imaginative element of Keynes' plan. It means that the adjustment process in this managed fixed exchange rate system is symmetrical – both debtor and creditor must adjust. It is the vital element that ensures the contractionist cure to imbalances is avoided as nations with expanding trade surpluses are not allowed to hoard ever greater credit balances on account with the ICU. Once a trade surplus exceeds a trigger point Keynes argues the ICU should be able to require a creditor nation to enact remedial action to reduce the surplus.[12] This might involve the ICU insisting on the upward revaluation of the currency in terms of bancor, or a more expansionary domestic monetary policy to increase effective demand, or higher money wages, or reduced national tariff levels or even greater foreign direct investment by the nation to less-developed regions of the globe. All of these remedial actions reduce the trade surplus by stimulating global economic activity. Moreover as the trade surplus is lowered so the trade deficits of other nations shrink whilst economic activity rises all around – an expansionist cure to trade imbalances.

The Keynes plan for promoting external balance is a necessary complement for nation states that seek to achieve full employment domestically. It seeks to reinforce the expansionary trend over the long run through a system of multilateral clearing that promotes exports and the payments for exports, whilst encouraging trade surpluses to be recycled into higher import spending. Under his plan all nations once again march together forwards, just as they did in the 50 years prior to the First World War. In the process Keynes hopes for more global prosperity over the long run based upon the freeing up of trade and the lowering of trade barriers, especially tariffs. In this sense Keynes returns to his free trade instincts which he had abandoned when proposing the revenue tariff in the special circumstances of the Great Depression.

There is however one area where Keynes remains a fierce opponent of economic freedom. This relates to the so-called "freedom" to act as a currency speculator on the foreign exchanges. Keynes blames the demise of the Gold Standard in the 1930s in part on the actions of unregulated and uncontrolled currency speculators. Consequently he is not prepared to permit speculator freedom to threaten his plans for a new global trading and payments system. Indeed he claims the unfettered freedom of speculators to move currencies around the globe is really just a "license to promote indiscipline, disorder and bad-neigbourliness" (Keynes, 1980c, p. 131). The Keynes plan is designed to discourage speculative activity. The plan requires that each central bank is able to monopolise currency transactions on behalf of its citizens. The central bank can then provide open licenses for those involved in international trade or foreign direct investment to access foreign currency, whilst speculators will not be granted licenses. The global system will run in the interests of those who engage in trade and invest abroad in order to encourage higher employment. The usual habitat of the currency speculator by contrast will be undermined and such activity will die off – causing the euthanasia of the currency speculator.

Of course the second Keynes plan was never implemented. As Skidelsky (2000) notes it was unacceptable to U.S. interests and instead the Bretton Woods fixed exchange rate system, based around the dollar and an International Monetary Fund (IMF), was established in 1944. Crucially the IMF was not the international bank that Keynes hoped for, nor did it have the credit creation powers which Keynes thought so vital to the long-term achievement of global full employment. However in our present day circumstances beset by global instability the advantages of an international credit-creating bank overseeing a symmetrical fixed exchange rate regime might yet become obvious. That is if global leaders are wise enough to recognise the opportunities Keynes' ideas provide.

e) The implications of Keynes' policy prescriptions

Despite the preceding discussion it is wrong to leave the reader with the impression that Keynes is anti-market and wishes to replace the capitalist system with something entirely different. Indeed Keynes is an elegant advocate of the advantages of the market and the way it promotes private initiative and responsibility. The advantages of capitalism are immensely important. They:

> are...efficiency,...decentralisation and of the play of self interest.
> The advantage to efficiency of the decentralisation of decisions and

of individual responsibility is even greater, perhaps, than the nineteenth century supposed; and the reaction against the appeal to self interest may have gone too far. But, above all, individualism, if it can be purged of its defects and abuses, is the best safeguard of individual liberty in the sense that, compared with any other system, it greatly widens the field for the exercise of personal choice. It is also the best safeguard for the variety of life, which emerges precisely from this extended field of personal choice, and the loss of which is the greatest loss of all the losses of the homogeneous and totalitarian state.

(Keynes, 2007, p. 380)

Keynes' case for intervention to influence effective demand during the Great Depression is actually designed to *defend* the capitalist economic order. As already noted Keynes argues it is better to have unbalanced budgets with capitalism than balanced budgets without it; the lesser of two evils is always preferable. If effective demand is deficient, people are unnecessarily unemployed, resources are wasted and the dice is loaded against the individual entrepreneur. In such circumstances the State needs to act to re-balance the economic system to correct these flaws, but definitely not to replace it with some inferior economic order.

Even during the Second World War Keynes' desire to defend the market mechanism is evident. In wartime, scarcity and inflation are the twin economic problems that face society. Keynes' response in the first Keynes plan is to curtail consumption to avoid inflation through a deferred pay scheme, whilst leaving the market mechanism to allocate diverse patterns of consumption goods to consumers. Moreover in planning for the post-war world Keynes advocates cheap money to encourage private investment spending and – in the second Keynes plan – a new commercial system that encourages freer trade and lower tariff barriers. Therefore the guiding principle of all Keynes' policy recommendations is the desire to preserve as much as possible of the existing capitalist economic order. Keynes accepts that capitalism must be reformed but it must remain essentially capitalist.

Keynes argues that reformed capitalism should not, however, have very great inequalities of income and wealth or indeed a prosperous but functionless *rentier class*. Classical economists always oppose policies to create a less uneven distribution of income and wealth. This started in the early nineteenth century with Ricardo's objections to Malthus' proposals to make the distribution of income more favourable to smaller landlords to the disadvantage of those with very large land-holding.

Ricardo's arguments prevailed and became the foundation for the classical view. Subsequently, socialist proposals for using the tax system to create a distribution more favourable to the working class are also strongly opposed by the classicals.

The classical fear is that high taxation on the rich will make tax evasion too worthwhile and hinder the incentives associated with entrepreneurship and risk taking. Keynes coming from the background he did is susceptible to such naturally conservative concerns. But the classics have a final problem with a less unequal income distribution. This is derived from the belief that the accumulation of capital depends on the strength of individual motives to save. In so far as richer groups save more than poorer sections of society the rich are a vital element in the process of economic growth. Given Keynes' rejection of Say's law this is where Keynes parts company with the classical perspective.

In the General Theory model the volume of *spending* – on consumption and investment – determines the volume of aggregate income, employment and saving. Therefore up to the point of full employment, tax policies to redistribute income to the relatively *poorer* sections of society (who have a high propensity to consume), far from harming the economy, will stimulate the growth of effective demand and total output. Conversely, in an economy operating below the full employment level, a distribution of income and wealth greatly skewed towards the rich (who have a lower propensity to consume) is inimical to policy efforts to promote full employment.

Yet two classical justifications for economic inequality remain, meaning Keynes is unconvinced of the case for a significant and irreversible shift of income and wealth towards the working class. In a typically restrained way Keynes concludes "[f]or my own part, I believe that there is social and psychological justification for *significant inequalities* of incomes and wealth, but not for such large disparities as exist today" (Keynes, 2007, p. 374; my emphasis). Keynes is no armchair revolutionary and is content with inequality, as long as it does not harm the prospects for capitalism's survival.

The rentier class are the privileged, though functionless, wealth-holders of society. The income of this class comes from their ownership of financial assets – namely the interest paid on bonds and the dividend paid on shares. The position of this class is buttressed by the classical loanable funds analysis, which justifies a sufficiently high rate of interest to induce rentiers to abstain from present consumption and provide loanable funds for the purchase of capital equipment. From a classical perspective the unearned income that rentiers glean from interest paid on debts is a vital component of wealth creation.

Keynes, having rejected the loanable funds approach, realises that the rate of interest is simply a reward for rentiers parting with liquid control over their resources. Moreover the key to encouraging full employment is a permanently *low* long-term rate of interest for all sound borrowers. Yet such a monetary policy stance has important implications for the exiistence of the rentier class, as it reduces a prime source of their income. Keynes believes this will lead to the eventual *euthanasia of the rentier*. Armed with his own analytical framework Keynes is not unduly concerned by this possibility. For the only reason why capital goods yield a profit is because they are scarce, and the less scarce they become the lower the rate of profit they yield. In so far as higher interest rate levels mean capital goods are scarcer, the rentier class benefits at the expense of greater wealth accumulation. A cheap money policy, which makes capital goods less scarce, undermines the basis of rentier power but benefits society greatly.

f) Summary

This chapter reviews Keynes' policy proposals for an expansionary cure for an economic depression, for maintaining price stability in wartime conditions and for the promotion of stability and prosperity over the long run. For Keynes the use of a cheap money policy is a worthwhile component of an expansionary cure for a depression. Keynes, however, identifies two main limitations with the sole use of monetary policy. They are the liquidity trap and the possibility that an expansionary monetary policy may fail to achieve a target rate of interest due to a strengthening of liquidity preferences. In terms of the role of fiscal policy even before the *General Theory* Keynes argues for an expansionary cure based around a state-led programme of capital development. Keynes is however acutely aware of two main problems with the sole reliance on an expansionary fiscal cure. First, there are the practical difficulties of financing a capital development programme, which forces Keynes to propose a revenue tariff on imports. Second, there are the offsetting factors which reduce the impact of a fiscal expansion on the domestic economy. Therefore Keynes strongly advocates an expansionary cure based upon the double harness of coordinated fiscal and monetary action. Hence a state-led capital development programme aligned with cheap money is the best way to cure a depression.

With the onset of hostilities in 1939 the economic problem facing the United Kingdom changes – from one of abundance to one of scarcity. Given the requirement to maximise war production Keynes shows that there is a need to curtail domestic consumption spending. He considers a range of options for doing this, but recommends the imposition of a deferred payment scheme for workers plus heavier tax on the better paid, in order to manage consumption demand without inflation. Keynes also argues that the expense of government borrowing should be minimised through a low interest rate policy. Beyond that Keynes argues that wartime consumption should be allocated through the market mechanism to avoid the inefficiencies and injustices associated with universal rationing and generalised price-fixing.

Keynes is keen to promote stability and prosperity in the post-1945 period. He proposes that government policy should focus on attaining full employment and preventing undue domestic fluctuations. To do this Keynes again recommends coordinated fiscal and monetary action; active fiscal policy taking the form of a stable long-term programme of socialised investment that can be increased or reduced as economic events dictate accommodated by a permanently low interest rate policy. This will work for a period up to 20 years, after which further public investment may be wasteful. Beyond 20 years Keynes suggests the management of the propensity to consume, once again involving a low interest rate, may be the best method of preventing economic fluctuations. Finally Keynes is aware that prosperity within a nation cannot be achieved independently of what is happening in the global economy. Keynes therefore designs a new global trading and payments system that replicates the benefits of the Gold Standard whilst avoiding its faults. The new system provides an expansionist cure for trading imbalances. It does this by encouraging the long-term growth of world trade based upon an elastic supply of international bank money provided by an International Clearing Union. Keynes' key innovation is that in response to trade imbalances there should be greater symmetry in the adjustment process which places the onus on both debtor and creditor nations.

Keynes is an elegant advocate of the advantages of the market mechanism. Keynes' main motivation for arguing for State intervention is to preserve as much as possible of the existing capitalist economic order. Yet Keynes is certainly against arbitrary and excessive inequalities if they threaten efforts to promote full employment. Having rejected Say's law, Keynes argues that when an economy is operating below full employment redistributing incomes towards the poor will increase effective demand and economic growth. He does not, however, accept the case for significant reductions in inequality. As a natural conservative he accepts there are good reasons for ensuring rewards significantly diverge between individuals. Finally Keynes' call for permanently low interest rates has implications for the class structure – that is the survival of the rentier class. Given his rejection of the loanable funds theory Keynes does not bemoan the end of the functionless rentier, indeed he believes it will lead to considerable economic advance.

Appendix
Further Comments on Public Policy

This appendix will provide further clarification about Keynes' practical definition of full employment. This is of the utmost importance. For whilst policy-makers might accept a theoretical concept, it is of little use until it is has been operationalised. In terms of full employment to operate effectively policy-makers require either a target percentage of the labour-force employed or, more likely, a target percentage of the labour-force unemployed.

Throughout this book the phrase *full employment* has been used and considerable efforts have been made to define this concept in *theoretical* terms. Chapter 11 probably has the best definition. Namely *full employment is reached when a further increase in nominal effective demand is not accompanied by either an increase in total output or employment*. But no *practical* definition of the concept is forthcoming in the *General Theory*.

Interestingly Keynes only offers practical guidance on the topic when he considers the requirements for a full employment policy in the post-Second World War world. He does so in response to various memoranda written by other Treasury economists about likely employment trends. Some of these economists suggest that given the trends for the 1920s and 1930s, the full employment position might be consistent with a rate of unemployment as high as 7.5–9.4 per cent of the total workforce (Keynes, 1980e). Keynes, by contrast, thinks such predictions are overly pessimistic. If post-war governments have a serious commitment to alleviate demand-deficient unemployment Keynes is more optimistic about the unemployment rate consistent with full employment.

We cannot, on this view, regard the unemployment problem as substantially solved so long as the *average* figure is greater than 800,000, namely 5% of the wage earning population, or rest content without resort to drastic changes of policy so long as it exceeds 1 million [i.e. a rate of 6.25 per cent].

(Keynes, 1980e, p. 355; Keynes' emphasis)

Keynes' practical definition of full employment did not however carry weight with post-war economists and politicians in the United Kingdom. During the Golden Age of economic growth a rate of unemployment of 3 per cent was generally held to be consistent with full employment, though the United Kingdom often had rates as low as 1.5 per cent (Crafts, 1999). The source of the 3 per cent rate as the practical definition of full employment in the United Kingdom is Sir William Beveridge in his work on the post-war social security system. Yet by one of those pleasant quirks of history Keynes reads a draft of Beveridge's *Full Employment in a Free Society*. In a subsequent letter to Beveridge Keynes includes a revealing P.S. which reads "No harm aiming at 3% unemployment. But I shall be surprised if we succeed" (Keynes, 1980e, p. 38).

The irony of Keynes' practical definition is that the 5–6 per cent unemployment rate he thinks feasible is remarkably close to that suggested by Friedman (1968) for his natural rate of unemployment. The circumstances in which these two economists reach their similar conclusions were however markedly different. Keynes' rule of thumb is a guess as to what might be feasible in the future, given the experience of very high unemployment levels during the Great Depression and the very low unemployment rates during the Second World War (lower than 0.5 per cent rate in the United Kingdom). Friedman is writing towards the end of the Golden Age of economic growth when the experience had been of permanently high employment rates for at least a decade in Italy and nearly three decades in the United Kingdom. Friedman suggests policy-makers had kept the economy booming with high employment but at the cost of accelerating inflation.

The reality might be that a practical definition of full employment is inevitably influenced by existing economic circumstance and most importantly the political imperatives of the day. For example the post-war full employment policies must have been partly due to policy-makers wanting to keep the working class content after its wartime efforts, and the fact that the electorate could, in theory, vote to replace capitalism with an alternative economic system. Conversely the much higher unemployment rates thought "natural" from the early 1980s onwards must have been partly due to the strong political forces in favour of lower inflation, and the fact that the only existing alternative to capitalism – the communist system – was slowly imploding.

13

The Classics, Keynes and the Keynesian Mainstream

a) Introduction

This final chapter will assess the contention set out in Chapter 1 that an orthodox counter-revolution has effectively smothered Keynes' more profound, but discomforting, insights. Consequently Keynes' hope of revolutionising the way we think about economic problems and policies has failed. If true, this is a damning indictment of mainstream Keynesianism.

To consider this bold contention this chapter begins by revisiting the Keynes–classics debate. Section (b) reviews the distinctive classical analysis, founded upon on special assumptions, and its macroeconomic policy recommendations. Then Section (c) provides an overview of Keynes' new workable classification which revolutionises macroeconomic theory and policy. Keynes provides a general theory that is applicable in many circumstances, of which the classical theory is a special case. Finally Section (d) sketches out the principal theoretical developments of mainstream Keynesianism and its shifting justifications for "Keynesian" policy responses. It will be demonstrated that the common purpose of mainstream Keynesianism has indeed been to smother Keynes' key ideas and replace them with ones more palatable to economic orthodoxy. Most importantly mainstream Keynesians invert Keynes' claim to have developed a general theory of which the classical analysis is a special case; instead they claim that Keynes' analysis is a special case of the classical approach.

b) The classical macroeconomic analysis

The classical model is made up of three primary theories: the theory of value and distribution, the theory of interest and employment and the theory of money and prices (Keynes, 1971a, 1971b, 1971c, 1973a, 1973b, 2007). These theories can be expressed in terms of a short-period or long-period analysis. The theory of interest and employment and the theory of money and prices together constitute the classical macroeconomic analysis.

The classical theory of interest and employment has a number of key independent variables that determine an equilibrium interest rate and volume of employment on two "markets" – the loanable funds market and the aggregated labour market, respectively. The analysis is conducted using the special case assumptions that the levels of aggregate income and effective demand are constant. Assuming short-term expectations are correct, the levels of aggregate income and effective demand are always equal.

With respect to the treatment of investment the classics apply the hypothesis of a calculable future to deal with long-term expectations. This assumes that decision-makers have sufficient knowledge about the future to be able to accurately estimate prospective yields on capital assets. This calculus of probability guides the investment decisions of entrepreneurs. In this special case the calculus of probability essentially abstracts away from the problem of an uncertain future.

In the classical theory of interest and employment the independent variables are the:

- propensity to save with respect to the rate of interest (assuming a constant level of income);
- demand for aggregate investment with respect to the rate of interest (using the calculus of probability);
- aggregate demand for labour in the economy with respect to money wages (assuming nominal effective demand is given);
- aggregate supply of labour in the economy with respect to money wage rates;
- given price-level for the consumption standard – or the wage good price-level (separately determined by the theory of money and prices).

The main moving forces in this model are the real wage rate and the volume of saving. The classical economists accept *Say's law*. That is the volume of savings determines the volumes of investment and consumption spending. With Say's law the classics suppose that supply creates its own demand and, assuming short-term expectations are correct, effective demand can never be deficient. The loanable funds market ensures that a price – the rate of interest – equilibrates saving and investment. The loanable funds market provides an inter-temporal link between the present and the future; between saving today in order to finance consumption in the future and investment today to provide the capacity to meet this deferred future consumption.

With Say's law and the loanable funds market, the ultimate dependent variable of the model – the volume of employment – must be determined by the real wage rate on an aggregated labour market. Assuming money wages rates are flexible a full employment equilibrium position is always achievable. Unemployment is therefore caused by anything which creates rigidities or imperfections in the aggregated labour market: trade union bargaining, slow adjustment to change, government regulation, imperfect price information and so on.

The classical theory of money and prices covers both the Cambridge and Fisher quantity equations; although these quantity equations take slightly different analytical routes, both come to similar conclusions. Just as with interest and employment, the classical theory of money and prices is founded on special case assumptions. The Cambridge equation assumes the level of "real" income is constant and there is a stable relationship between money demand and real income. The Fisher equation postulates that the volume of transactions is given and the velocity of circulation is steady. The main causal variables in the classical theory of money and prices are:

- a constant level of real income or a given volume of transactions;
- a stable demand for money function or steady velocity of circulation;
- a variable supply of money.

The primary moving force in this theory is the money supply. The demand for money is quite passive, responding only to changes in real income or the volume of transactions. The ultimate dependent variable (or *quaesitum* as Keynes calls it) is the price-level for consumer goods. Inflation of the price-level is caused by an increase in the money supply that is unrelated to the level of real income or transactions; deflation of the price-level is caused by a decrease in the money supply unrelated to the level of real income or transactions. State policy-making, through the issue of notes and coins, influences the money supply and hence the rate of change of prices.

The classical school develops its theories of interest and employment and money and prices quite separately. This is referred to as the *classical dichotomy*. Hence, the volume of employment is determined assuming a given general price-level; conversely, the general price-level is derived assuming the volume of real income and employment are constant. This separate determination of employment and prices is a key characteristic of the classical school's approach.

The overriding classical policy concern is the avoidance of inflation – protecting the value of money. The aim of monetary policy should be to keep a tight rein on the money supply in order to avoid inflation. Fiscal policy, given Say's law, should seek to avoid unnecessary deficits that crowd out private investment. The classics argue the aim of fiscal policy should be to balance the budget.

The classics also appreciate that high levels of unemployment may require a policy response. From this perspective unemployment results from rigidities or imperfections in the labour market that cause wages to be sticky. The solution is to make the supply side of the economy work better by removing government regulation of wages and resisting further strengthening of trade union bargaining. In cases of exceptionally heavy unemployment the classics reluctantly accept the case for Government public works to alleviate the situation in the short run. But this palliative only works by creating inflation which fools workers into the labour market and masks more deep-rooted supply-side failures.

c) Keynes' macroeconomic theory and policy

Keynes departs from the classical school by constructing an innovative new theory – the General Theory model (Keynes, 1973a, 1973b, 1973c, 1973d, 2007). What marks Keynes' approach from that of the classics is the very different causal flow of analysis; Keynes' choice of independent and dependent variables is quite distinct from that of the classical school. In other words Keynes' *ordering* of economic variables diverges from the economic order chosen by the classics: consequently the two approaches generate disparate analytical conclusions and different policy recommendations.

Keynes assumes that some variables in the economic system are given in the short period. These given variables are the existing skill and quantity of available labour; the existing quality and quantity of available equipment; the existing techniques of production; the degree of competition in different sectors of the economy; the tastes and habits of consumers; the disutility of different intensities of labour; the systems of supervision and organisation within firms; and the influence of the social structure on the distribution of income. These are the underlying *cet. par.* assumptions of the model.[1] It is in this sense that that the

General Theory model is a short-period analysis. The advantage of this short-period analysis is first that in the short run we are all alive, and second that economic development over time is simply the aggregation of many short runs.

Keynes discards the main pillars of the classical macroeconomic theory. In its place he proposes a distinctive set of *ultimate independent variables* that are the main moving forces of his analysis. They are the:

- propensity to consume;
- psychological expectations of future yields on capital assets;
- state of liquidity preference;
- money supply;
- aggregate supply relationship.
- money wage rate (or more precisely the wage unit).

These moving forces determine the levels of expected aggregate consumption and expected total investment spending. The propensity to consume in large part determines expected consumption expenditure. The value of the propensity to consume is influenced by a range of factors such as the distribution of income, the rate of interest and windfall changes in capital values.[2] The marginal propensity to consume governs the values of both the investment and employment multipliers. Expected investment spending is determined by the interaction of the marginal efficiency of capital and the rate of interest.[3] The expectation of yields on capital assets largely determines the marginal efficiency of capital, whilst the state of liquidity preferences and the money supply determine the money rate of interest.

Expected prospective yields and liquidity preferences are heavily influenced by the *state of long-term expectation*. Although the General Theory model focuses on the short period, it provides a link to the distant future by examining *short-period* changes in the state of long-term expectations.[4] To explain the formation of long-term expectations, Keynes replaces the calculus of probability with a conventional method of calculation, which decision-makers apply in an uncertain environment. Given uncertain knowledge of the future, short-period changes in the state of long-term expectations are a continual threat.

It is the capricious character of the state of long-term expectation that is the ultimate cause of the instability in investment spending. When the short-period state of long-term expectation deteriorates the marginal efficiency of capital worsens and the rate of interest rises. This causes a cumulative decline in aggregate investment spending. Conversely when the short-period state of long-term expectation improves the marginal efficiency strengthens and the rate of interest falls. This creates a cumulative rise in investment spending. The impact on the economy of changes in investment spending is amplified by the multiplier effect on consumption spending.

The aggregated sum of expected consumption and investment spending determines the aggregate demand price – the actually expected proceeds from the sale of output associated with a volume of employment. The stable aggregate supply relationship determines the value of the aggregate supply price – the expected proceeds which just induce entrepreneurs to offer a volume of employment. Aggregate effective demand is defined when the aggregate demand price and aggregate supply price are equalised. In Keynes' model *aggregate effective demand is the central overarching concept which impacts on all the dependent variables*. Aggregate effective demand can be measured in either nominal values or in wage units (i.e. in real terms). The primary dependent variables are the volume of employment and level of aggregate income. Other dependent variables include the volume of saving (having rejected Say's law), the general price-level and the real wage rate. It is important to emphasise Keynes' claim that (having rejected the aggregated labour market) both aggregate employment and the real wage rate are *dependent variables* in the General Theory model. Moreover note that in Keynes' model the volume of employment *and* the price-level are determined, not separately, but within *one general* theory.

An economy may experience a serious depression with heavy unemployment and a falling price-level due to deficient aggregate effective demand. If effective demand remains depressed the economy can be stuck in an equilibrium position with involuntary unemployment. Faced with large-scale unemployment the classical solution of general money wage cuts – the contractionist cure – can be applied, but with what effect? In the General Theory model a general money wage cut only influences employment if it changes the propensity to consume, the marginal efficiency of capital or the rate of interest; in other words if it changes the value of aggregate effective demand measured in wage units. Keynes concludes that the influence of a money wage cut is ambiguous, either increasing or decreasing employment depending on a variety of circumstances.

An economy can also experience conditions of rapid inflation due to the excessive growth of nominal effective demand. This can happen, for example, in a war economy where all resources are fully utilised and the needs of war production clash with the increasing consumption spending of a fully employed workforce. Without a policy response the result is true inflation as different sectors of the economy compete for scarce resources.

This is the General Theory model, which covers a range of scenarios far wider in scope than the classical special case. It is this new workable classification which Harrod (1982) claims to be a tremendous intellectual feat on a par with the work of Smith and Ricardo, and which Krugman (2007) claims provides an epic journey out of the intellectual darkness.

The General Theory model provides the key intellectual underpinning for Keynes' key policy recommendations, even though many of his proposals pre-date the *General Theory*. In all the contributions Keynes makes to the policy debates in the turbulent 30 years spanning two World Wars (Keynes, 1971b, 1971c; Keynes and Henderson, 1972; Keynes, 1972a, 1972b, 1972c, 1972d, 1980a, 1980b, 1980c, 1980d, 1980e, 1981a, 1981b, 1982; Liberal Industrial Inquiry, 1977), he is concerned with three main issues. First, how can a government cure an economic depression; second, how can a government prevent wartime inflation as the economy is pushed to its absolute capacity limits; and lastly how can state action promote long-term stability and prosperity. Keynes' policy recommendations focus on the management of aggregate effective demand. The continuing policy theme is the need for permanently low interest rates coordinated with active fiscal policy.

To cure a 1930s-style depression Keynes is an eloquent opponent of wage cutting, especially competitive wage cutting on an international scale. Hence Keynes argues the cure can only be found by using expansionary fiscal and monetary policy, operated in double harness. The fiscal expansion should take the form of a state-led capital development programme, perhaps combined with a revenue tariff to counter an excessive budget deficit. Monetary policy should accommodate the fiscal expansion, whilst keeping interest rates low (i.e. cheap money) in order to promote private investment spending. The resulting increase in effective demand will cause output and employment to recover and generate a semi-inflation of the price-level. The semi-inflation is an important part of the recovery as it lowers the real value of debt in an economy.

To prevent true inflation in wartime Keynes recommends a deferred payment scheme for workers, plus heavier tax on the better paid, in order to reduce consumption demand and free resources for the war effort. The extra taxation and deferred pay will finance the war effort without recourse to excessive Government borrowing. The expense of any Government borrowing should be minimised through a low interest rate policy. Beyond that Keynes suggests that wartime consumption should be allocated using markets to avoid the inefficiencies and injustices associated with universal rationing and price-fixing.

In order to promote long-term stability and prosperity Keynes again recommends coordinated fiscal and monetary action; active fiscal policy taking the form of a stable long-term programme of socialised investment accommodated by a permanently low interest rate policy. This will work for a period up to 20 years, after which further public investment may be wasteful. Beyond 20 years Keynes suggests managing the propensity to consume to stabilise the economy, once more involving low interest rates. Moreover to ensure global macroeconomic prosperity with full employment Keynes proposes the creation of an international fixed exchange rate regime. This new regime is to be built around an International Clearing Bank providing a new international form of bank money. The purpose of the ICU is to promote an expansionary cure for trade imbalances, in which both debtor and creditor nations are forced to adjust. The new regime is intended to create the most propitious conditions for greater global trade and prosperity.

Keynes in essence departs from the classical school by asking different theoretical questions, applying a distinctive economic order on a complex reality, and addressing new policy issues. The policy dimensions of Keynes' work, as Krugman notes, continue to have relevance to modern debates.

d) The contribution of the Keynesian mainstream

Mainstream Keynesianism is a broad and elastic classification.[5] A number of writers have sought to classify the various sects within the Keynesian school (Coddington, 1983; Milgate and Eatwell, 1983; Gerrard, 1995). Whilst admitting that the divisions are not clear cut, both Coddington and Gerrard identify two discrete approaches within mainstream Keynesianism – *hydraulicism and reconstituted reductionism*.[6] This section adds a further, more recent, category to the mainstream – namely *hydraulic reductionism* which popularises the abstract ideas of so-called new Keynesians.

Hydraulicism marks the first phase of mainstream Keynesian development. It also marks the original counter-revolutionary attempt to smother the essential ideas of Keynes. The hydraulic approach is encapsulated in Hicks' seminal work on the IS-LM framework (Hicks, 1983) and the textbook treatment of Keynes in the 1950s. Hydraulicism involves the considerable pruning of the contents of the *General Theory* with selective emphasis on three key relationships – the consumption function, the investment demand function and the money demand function. Each of these is assumed to be stable and predictable over time and together provide a partial equilibrium in the goods and money markets determined by the level of aggregate demand. On the supply-side hydraulicism assumes that money wage rates are rigid in a downward direction (Modigliani, 1944) and that prices rise beyond the point of full employment.

From this it is possible to generate either an inflationary gap with rising prices and wages, or a below full employment equilibria – the economics of depression – assuming wage rates are fixed. But if in response to an economic depression wages and prices do fall, the hydraulic analysis suggests this will lower interest rates (the Keynes effect) allowing a recovery of aggregate demand and employment (Patinkin, 1948). Hydraulicism accepts the classical view that involuntary unemployment is ultimately caused by wage rigidity. This is the basis of the so-called neo-classical synthesis, where Keynes' theory is treated as a special, though in practical terms important, case of the more general classical analysis.

Assuming wages are rigid, hydraulic Keynesianism makes a *practical* case for demand management to stabilise the economy at the full employment position. Moreover given "Keynesian" parameters for the elasticities of the investment demand and money demand functions, inelastic and elastic respectively, hydraulic policy is summarised by the vulgar statement "fiscal policy is strong/monetary policy is weak". In order to promote full employment "Keynesian" demand management policies favour active fiscal policy action in preference to discretionary monetary policy.

The other members of the Keynesian mainstream that Coddington identifies are the *reconstituted reductionists*. The proponents of reconstituted reductionism seek to further smother Keynes' revolutionary ideas by squeezing "Keynesianism" into the frame provided by neo-classical microeconomic theory (i.e. reductionism), with its focus on scarcity, individual choice and market forces. The leading proponents of reconstituted reductionism are Patinkin (1965), Clower (1965) and Leijonhufvud (1968).

The problem for the reconstituted reductionists is to find the missing link that reconciles the existence of involuntary unemployment with orthodox microeconomic foundations. The solution they come up with involves amending two assumptions in the Walrasian general equilibrium model (Arrow and Debreu, 1954). In a Walrasian system an auctioneer establishes equilibrium prices on all markets simultaneously in the economy. In addition Walras' law applies in disequilibrium situations – namely that the sum of excess demands and supplies on all markets must equal zero. The auctioneer guarantees that a general equilibrium of exchange emerges without money, with one commodity acting as a numeraire. This justifies the classical dichotomy that money acts as a veil over the operations of the *real* economy. To incorporate Keynesian ideas into the general equilibrium system the reconstituted reductionists first drop the assumption that an auctioneer exists, in which case markets and prices can be in disequilibrium for periods of time, and secondly introduce money into the system.

This is the starting point for Patinkin. Given a reductionist analysis, flexible money wages guarantee the full employment equilibrium. Consequently Patinkin argues that if Keynes has anything new to offer it must be that involuntary unemployment occurs in the dynamic disequilibrium process between equilibria. The focus must be on the speed of adjustment by the market. This is influenced by the imperfections and rigidities (e.g. errors in expectations about the proceeds of employment or slowness of wage adjustment) that occur in the world without an auctioneer. If aggregate demand falls firms may well lower output and employment rather than wages and prices, and workers are forced off their labour supply curves. Workers wish to supply more labour than firms are willing to buy and involuntary unemployment results.

Clower's work complements Patinkin by extending the analysis into the goods market. Clower claims that there is a *dual decision hypothesis* that links labour supply to consumption decisions. Sales of labour by workers generate the income which finances their consumption plans. Households have notional demands for consumption goods assuming they sell all the labour services they intend. If workers sell less labour than they plan, actual income is less than notional income and actual consumption demand is less than the notional intentions. This means that what is important is not notional demand but effective demand – that is demand backed up by money and effected on the market.[7]

From this Clower reaches an important conclusion: in order to generate Keynesian results, in disequilibrium positions Walras' law must be rejected. When there is an excess notional demand for goods, which mirrors an excess supply of labour, this excess demand is not effective as unemployed workers lack purchasing power. Leijonhufvud completes the analysis by identifying various informational imperfections that exist without an auctioneer that explain why firms will, in response to a fall in demand, rationally reduce output and employment rather than wages and prices. For the reconstituted reductionists the classical economists were in one important sense right. If wages and prices are flexible, then full employment does speedily emerge and involuntary unemployment is short-lived. Moreover the longer the period in view the more likely it is that the economy will fully adjust to shocks; market forces will eventually generate full employment. This provides a new frame for the neo-classical synthesis: Keynes is right in the short run, where adjustment is slow, but in the long run the classical analysis applies.

Reconstituted reductionists policy analysis is even more banal than that of the hydraulic Keynesians. The reconstituted reductionists claim demand management policy can be used to alleviate, but not solve, supply-side imperfections and rigidities. In the absence of an auctioneer, government demand management policies are justified to correct market failure and generate more optimal outcomes; the State replaces the auctioneer as overall coordinator of the economy.

In the last quarter of the twentieth century the Keynesian mainstream entered its most recent phase of development and built upon the seminal works of the 1960s. Within a generalised reductionist framework both market imperfections (say due to trade unions or monopoly power) and informational imperfections (e.g. the prisoner's dilemma) are integrated to explain occasional and temporary unemployment based on optimising behaviour (Alchian, 1969; Benassy, 1976; Malinvaud, 1977; Hart, 1982; Snower, 1983; Howitt, 1985). These developments are characterised by the increasing use of obscure mathematical analyses. This third phase is now known as *new Keynesianism* (Mankiw and Romer, 1991a, 1991b; Gerrard, 1995), although its parameters are clearly defined by the two earlier phases of development.

The sophistication of new Keynesianism has, however, led to a pedagogic problem, namely that it is not accessible to a wide student audience. Hence the emergence of a new dominant textbook treatment of Keynes – that can be referred to as *hydraulic reductionism* (Burda and Wyplosz, 1997; Dornbusch, Fischer and Startz, 2004). The hydraulic reductionist analysis provides teachers of economics with an accessible pedagogic tool that introduces students to the essential ideas that new Keynesian researchers are developing.

The hydraulic reductionist analysis is set out in an aggregate demand–supply framework showing the relationship between the price-level and aggregate output. The hydraulic IS-LM model is incorporated to underpin the derivation of an aggregate demand curve as the price-level varies.

To this is added a reductionist framework, with an aggregated labour market and an aggregate production function, that derives the aggregate supply curve. The model determines an equilibrium position where the goods, money and labour markets are in simultaneous equilibrium. However workers in the labour market suffer from imperfect information and labour market institutions create rigidity in wage bargaining. Because the volume of employment is ultimately determined by the real wage rate on a labour market, imperfections can cause the economy to temporarily move away from the natural rate of unemployment when there are changes in aggregate demand.

The pivotal role in this model is played by the aggregate *supply* curve; for its slope depends on how fast wages adjust to price changes. A short run positively sloped "Keynesian" curve holds where money illusion or market imperfections exist, causing changes in wages to lag behind prices. But in the long run a vertical "classical" supply curve emerges; with perfect foresight and information, wage and price adjustments are correctly aligned and the aggregate supply curve mirrors the vertical long run Phillips curve.[8]

In this framework demand management can influence the volume of output and employment in the short run, but only in so far as it causes a change in the real wage rate. "Keynesian" results are limited to periods of adjustment where market imperfections exist. The ultimate remedy for unemployment caused by imperfections is less imperfections; in the absence of efforts to reduce imperfections, demand management is a practical short run necessity to cure macroeconomic instability. In textbooks this is represented as the modern version of the neo-classical synthesis: yet again Keynes' theory is seen as a special case of the more generalised classical analysis.

The sad story of mainstream Keynesianism is essentially one of fear and avoidance. For mainstream Keynesians the ultimate fear is that Keynes' theoretical and policy innovations are just too audacious. Keynes' suggestion that capitalism is systemically weak on the demand side, that it can suffer long-lasting involuntary unemployment and that it requires active State intervention to work effectively is unpalatable to orthodox economics. In order to avoid such uncomfortable ideas the Keynesian mainstream smothers Keynes' key ideas and replaces them with ones more palatable to economic orthodoxy.

The counter-revolution begins with Hicks in 1937. He relegates Keynes' contribution to that of adding a special case – the economics of depression – to existing theory. Modigliani takes it further by arguing that involuntary unemployment only exists because of wage rigidity; if wage rigidity is a fact then the case for state action to manage demand is grudgingly accepted. The reconstituted reductionists continue the process with the attempt to interpret Keynes through the lens provided by Walras. It is only the lack of an auctioneer and the existence of money that causes Keynesian problems. Hence the State should act as a substitute auctioneer to help individuals towards their optimum plans. New Keynesianism completes the counter-revolution, with its explanation of the occasional under-utilisation of labour in terms of market imperfections. Demand management is only accepted as a second best solution for supply-side failures.

The recurrent theme of all mainstream Keynesianism is the desire to neutralise Keynes' more profound yet disturbing conclusions. This means that for mainstream Keynesians the contribution of Keynes only applies in the short run, or the disequilibrium process, or when market imperfections exist. But in the long run, in equilibrium, with perfectly functioning markets, the orthodoxy applies. And when Keynes claims that he provides a generalised theory, of which the orthodoxy is just a special case, he must be wrong.[9] Such is the sad and depressing state into which so-called Keynesian economics has descended.[10]

Luckily a solution is at hand. For a new generation of scholars are beginning to return to Keynes' original writings to re-examine his theory and policy with fresh vigour. Ambrosi (2003) looks afresh at the Keynes–Pigou debates to provide greater appreciation of the Keynes versus the classics debate. Lawlor (2006) seeks to examine the development of Keynes' ideas up to the General Theory in a historical context, especially focusing on the Marshallian influences on Keynes. Hayes (2006) attempts to locate, or position, Keynes' model with respect to both the prior economic theory of the diverse classical school (especially Marshall) and subsequent theoretical developments – in particular "old" Keynesianism, modern general equilibrium analysis, and a variety of Post-Keynesian frameworks. Tily (2007) argues that it is not just Keynes' economic theory that needs to be revisited but also his policy recommendations, especially those relating to the conduct of monetary policy. There are also those who seek to move beyond the General Theory model by building upon its key insights. An exemplar of this is Minsky (1982, 1983) with his financial instability hypothesis which fully recognises Keynes' theoretical contribution to financial issues. As Minsky says he wishes to stand on the shoulder of a giant to move the discipline onwards. All of these scholars might be given the appellation *authentic Keynesians* whose collective efforts, with those of like-minded others, offer fresh hope for Keynesianism in the twenty-first century.

Notes

1 A primer for the General Theory

1. The other text that comes near to offering the uninitiated reader a route into the *General Theory* is the work by Chick. It does provide useful material, but she wishes to go beyond Keynes in order to "rework and extend parts of the theory and point the way to necessary changes" (Chick, 1983, p. vii).
2. This is what Backhouse (1990) refers to as a *historical reconstruction*. It is within the remit of a historical reconstruction for conjectures to be made about how the work of the original author may be made more explicit or developed, as long as two rules are followed. First, that when conjectures of this nature are considered the reader is made aware of them, either in the text or in specific endnotes. Second, any conjecture must be consistent with the spirit of the writer's original theory.

2 Classical macroeconomic theory: the special case

1. This is particularly true of chapters 2 and 14 of the *General Theory*.
2. According to Lawlor (2006) Keynes is always much more of a Marshallian than a Pigouvian.
3. That said Keynes had always been a somewhat semi-detached member of the classical school. Prior to the publication of the *General Theory* he is keenly aware of the inadequacies of the classical approach whilst broadly accepting the confines of its vision, methods and assumptions.
4. In one sense the classical reliance on the calculus of probability is rather puzzling. For the classicals had long since disregarded the "calculus of utility" whereby individuals are supposed to measure cardinally the utility they receive from the consumption of various goods and services. Yet the calculus of probability, which supposes decision-makers have knowledge of all the consequences of actions and can transform this knowledge into cardinal numbers to guide actions, retains some deep-rooted attraction for the classical school.
5. It is also useful to clarify the relationship between Keynes' concepts of cash and saving deposits with the common terms for these deposits used by the banking systems in the United States and the United Kingdom. According to Keynes a cash deposit corresponds to demand deposits in the United States and current accounts in the United Kingdom; and a savings deposit to time deposits in the United States and deposit accounts in the United Kingdom.
6. There is of course no reason why changes in the money supply must instantaneously change the price-level. In the modern re-statement of the Quantity

theory by Friedman in the 1960s he proposes a time lag of between 18 months and 2 years that separates the change in the supply of money from the consequent change in the price-level.

3 Aggregate effective demand

1. It is a matter of debate as to whether Keynes' interpretation of Say's law is entirely fair to Say and the followers of Ricardo (Baumol, 1977). This is however not important for understanding the General Theory model. It is only necessary to appreciate Say's law as Keynes interpreted it.
2. Aggregate effective demand and effective demand are terms used interchangeably in this book just as Keynes does in the *General Theory*. Note Keynes' definition of aggregate effective demand/effective demand is quite distinct from the use of the term effective demand by Clower (1965) and Leijonhufvud (1968) which has wide currency in the new Keynesian literature. Clower and Leijonhufvud distinguish between the level of effective demand which is backed by purchasing power and the volume of notional demand which is not. Ironically this new Keynesian interpretation is closer to Marx than Keynes in seeing the volume of money hoarded as the cause of economic crisis.
3. This assumes that labour is the only factor cost. Keynes does allow other factor costs into his analysis but not in a systematic manner. This limitation is discussed further in Appendix A to this chapter.
4. Equations 1 and 2 are set out in the famous footnote contained on pages 55 and 56 of the *General Theory* which provides much of the justification for what follows. There is one element of the material in the footnote that seems erroneous. It is Keynes' claim that in equation 1 the slope of the nominal aggregate supply function is equal to the reciprocal of the money wage that is $1/WU$. This is not consistent with equation 1. One possibility is that Keynes switched around in his mind the aggregate supply function to solve for $\emptyset N$, in which case the formula becomes $\emptyset N = Z\,(1/WU)$.
5. A discussion of this is included in Chick (1983). The analysis here is not identical to Chick. For Chick does not incorporate in her analysis Keynes' assumption that average and marginal productivity of labour units are equal.
6. See Keynes (2007, p. 281) and Chick (1983, p. 66).
7. This analysis seeks to rectify an omission in Keynes' treatment of the topic which is identified in Patinkin (1982).
8. All this is consistent with the footnote on pages 55 and 56 of the *General Theory*.
9. Keynes of course accepts that each level of real aggregate effective demand can be disaggregated. This means a level of real effective demand can be derived for a specific industry ($\text{AED}_w r$). The latter determines the level of employment in that industry (Nr). The volume of $\text{AED}_w r$ specifies the demand for labour in that industry. This demand is aligned with the supply of labour available to that industry. Demand and supply is balanced at the industry level by bargaining over the money wage rate. For each industry a similar process takes place. This means employment in each specific sector or firm is determined by macroeconomic parameters.

4   The propensity to consume and the multiplier

1. This is a conjecture I have made after careful consideration of Book III of the *General Theory*.
2. Keynes is aware that there are situations in which an increase in Y_w may not be associated with a proportionate rise in employment. This is a subject taken up again in Chapter 11.
3. There can of course be circumstances in which before the equilibrium volume of employment is reached the levels of Y_w and N can diverge – this is discussed again in Chapter 11.
4. For further references, see Keynes (2007), pp. 92, 262, 373.
5. Keynes is aware that this assumption is an oversimplification if decreasing productivity sets in as output rises, in which case prices rise faster than money wages.
6. For an interesting review of this topic, see Thomas (1997).
7. This might imply that a poorer nation with a larger marginal propensity to consume may suffer greater economic fluctuations than a richer nation. But this overlooks the distinction between the marginal and average propensities to consume. Although in a poorer country there might be a large *proportionate* effect from a change in investment spending, the latter will form only a small part of total output (as there is a high average propensity to consume), meaning the absolute effect will be small. Keynes actually provides a numerical example to illustrate this point.
8. The traditional treatment of saving in an inter-temporal setting assumes that there are only two time periods in which an individual must consume all of his income. Taken as a whole over the two periods all savings are spent and all borrowing is repaid. Only in this special case can the choice be said to be between consumption today (this period) or tomorrow (next period). Clearly the traditional approach cleverly sidesteps the crucial issue that Keynes correctly identifies.

6   The practical theory of the future

1. Ice companies operated in major American cities before the generalised introduction of refrigerators and freezers into homes. An ice company would send out trucks to travel the streets which people could stop and they could purchase whatever volume of ice they needed or could afford, much like ice cream vans do today.

7   The inducement to invest – a theory of investment

1. It is important to appreciate that there are different types of fixed investment spending. Using the framework of New (1994) investment in capital equipment may be divided into two categories. First, there is *strategic* fixed investment where there is the application of new plant and machinery involving a major change in technology which significantly expands the capacity to produce; for example, the car industry moving from traditional car assembly techniques towards the use of more robotic machinery. Second, there is

operational fixed investment which is the purchase of new additional machinery or the replacement of an old machine, for example a firm in the steel industry purchasing an additional blast furnace to increase capacity. Operational investment does not involve new technology, and may be described as 'technologically risk free'. Keynes' focus is on the implications of investment spending for effective demand rather than its capacity-creating capabilities. Aggregate fixed investment spending will therefore be made up of both strategic and operational investment spending; the composition of a given level aggregate spending between strategic and operational investments will clearly have implications for the rate of growth of the economy over the long run. But given the short-period character of the General Theory model this is not the focus of Keynes' attention.

2. These figures are effectively a probable forecast of expected profits held with a particular of confidence. Entrepreneurs may make these forecasts, for example, by taking the `average' outcome of the best case and worse case profit forecasts.

3. The notion that capital assets yield profits due to their scarcity dates back to Adam Smith. Keynes' approach also rejects the Marshallian idea that capital is profitable because it is productive.

4. Savings deposits can be thought of as yielding a very small return for a wealth-holder. Whether or not savings deposits offer a yield is however of rather less importance than the fact than that a wealth-holder will obtain a greater return from placing a specific amount of accumulated wealth in a bond than in a saving deposit. For this raises the question of why the wealth-holder will forgo a greater return for a smaller one. The answer of course is that a savings deposit is a far more liquid asset than a bond.

5. Bears are those who wish to sell assets because they anticipate prices will fall; bulls are those who want to buy assets because they anticipate prices will rise.

6. In the *General Theory* itself Keynes only specifies the $Md1$ and $Md2$ demands. In response to criticism in the post-*General Theory* debate Keynes specifies the finance motive. I have incorporated this motive into Keynes' formal model in a way that is, hopefully, consistent with the methodology of historical reconstruction.

7. Note the precautionary motive may also be unstable, especially when the community is fearful of dramatic changes in the future Government policy. This issue is taken up again in Chapter 12.

8. In the analysis of the $L2$ function there is no mention of a short term interest rate on saving deposits – see Note 4.

9. A natural rate of interest compatible with full employment, *cet. par.*, is lower than one consistent with an unemployment equilibrium position. Hence Keynes' agreement with Mercantilist thought that the rate of interest has a tendency to be too high and is not always at the optimal level. This topic is taken up again in Chapter 11.

8   Fluctuations in the inducement to invest

1. Bank lending in this context covers financial arrangements of many varieties, including bank loans repayable over a number of years, leasing and hire purchase deals.

2. It should be noted that finance is not just available for the planned purchase and production of investment goods. For example, an entrepreneur in the consumption goods sector can also obtain finance to fill the gap between the decision to increase production and the actual implementation of this plan. In addition finance is available to allow consumers to purchase significant durable consumer goods (e.g. cars, furniture etc.) and repay the debt from future income flows.

3. Of course in an open economy with an active Government and bank lending available for durable consumption expenditure, the sources of finance available to fund new economic activity are more diverse. For if there is an increase in export spending, or Government loan financed expenditure or consumer loan financed expenditure, *cet. par.*, this will raise aggregate income and saving (especially the profitability of firms). Therefore this higher spending will provide entrepreneurs with more funds to finance additional production of capital and consumer goods.

4. This possibility occurs if banks are unwilling to further expand overdraft facilities to entrepreneurs to satisfy the finance motive. In normal circumstances this is unlikely but it is a circumstance that cannot be entirely discounted.

5. This analysis can also be illustrated on an aggregate demand and supply diagram with real income (Y_w) on the horizontal axis, but the conclusions remain the same.

9   Money wages, employment and effective demand

1. Of course Keynes, being a pragmatist, offers the authorities two other policy options short of leaving the Gold Standard. First, a lowering of domestic interest rates to allow gold to flow out of the United Kingdom thereby increasing the price-level elsewhere. The process of adjustment would then be borne by foreigners rather than the United Kingdom. Second, a form of voluntary incomes policy whereby wages would be lowered by agreement with unions on the proviso that rentiers would be taxed more heavily and prices would fall within a reasonable time period.

2. Kalecki (1982) complains that Keynes' analysis underplays the impact of wage cutting on *current profits*, and hence on expected profitability. For Kalecki the most telling argument in favour of wage cutting is that it raises the current profits of businesses; the higher current profits cause entrepreneurs to infer higher future profitability on capital assets; this increases the marginal efficiency of capital and stimulates a higher rate of investment spending. But if entrepreneurs do not immediately infer that higher current profits will last, then investment spending will not be stimulated, and the increase in current profits proves to be an illusion as wages and prices fall proportionally. Kalecki claims the latter scenario is implicitly assumed by Keynes.

10   Prices and real wages

1. The extent by which the increase in nominal effective demand exceeds the rise in money wages depends on a range of factors – the degree of unionisation, the responsiveness of wage bargaining to a supply of unemployed

labour, the centralisation of wage bargaining – though these things do not detain Keynes in the *General Theory*.

2. Some (neo-classical) interpretations of Keynes have not properly distinguished between the NAC and the classical labour demand curve – most evidently Meltzer in his "restatement" of the *General Theory* (Meltzer, 1981). It leads to the mistaken claim that the marginal product for labour curve, aggregated from microeconomic foundations, is the macroeconomic demand for labour curve in a "Keynesian" system. The errors of such an interpretation are exposed by Davidson (1983) who explains how the equilibrium levels of output and employment are determined by effective demand, whilst the marginal product of labour curve (if actually applicable) shows the resulting real wage rate. Davidson demonstrates how Meltzer, and others, confuse the causation between effective demand, employment and real wages in Keynes' model.

3. Keynes' acceptance of the first classical postulate rests heavily on his use of the short-run law of diminishing productivity. If this short-run law is found to be empirically wanting it can be removed from the analysis, along with the first classical postulate, with little trouble. A more accurate explanation of the short-run relationship between output and employment has been devised by a range of Post-Keynesian economists. After the *General Theory* Keynes – in response to work by Dunlop and Tarshis – suggests such a course of action could simplify the more complicated sections of his theory and direct attention towards the forces which determine output and employment (Keynes, 2007). This may also allow a more realistic and accurate generalised price theory to be developed, while staying true to the spirit of Keynes' analysis.

4. The fact that Keynes' analysis does not rely on money illusion can be checked by reference to the index of the *General Theory*. No item for money illusion is included. Surely it beggars belief that Keynes did not mention money illusion in the whole of the *General Theory* if the key "Keynesian" insight is that workers have imperfect price foresight. A more accurate explanation is that money illusion is not mentioned in the *General Theory* because it does not form part of Keynes' General Theory model.

11 Employment and unemployment

1. There have been occasional bursts of interest in the employment function. Usually the insights that are contained in this literature are constrained by a lack of clarity about the shape of the aggregate supply function (Leijonhufvud, 1974; Wells, 1974).

2. The equations for the industry-based and the economy-wide employment functions are slightly revised from those included in the *General Theory* for ease of exposition. In the *General Theory* they are specified in terms of the real values for the sector demand price ($D_{w}r$) and the aggregate demand price (D_{w}), respectively. But remember that with a constant value for the aggregate supply relationship the real aggregate demand price determines aggregate effective demand (i.e. $D_{w} = \text{AED}_{w}$), and the same is true for each sector of the economy.

3. It should be noted that Keynes supplements the elasticity of employment with three further elasticity concepts. They are the elasticity of expected prices measured in wage units (p_w) in response to a change in effective demand measured in wage units for a given industry; the elasticity of money prices (p) in response to a change in nominal effective demand for a specific sector; and the elasticity of money wages (W) in response to a change in nominal effective demand in a specific sector. Some followers of Keynes who claim that the employment function is derived assuming wages and prices are given (Weintraub, 1983) seem unaware of these three concepts.
4. The term *composition* of effective demand is not used by Keynes. I have applied it to make the treatment more explicit than that found in the General Theory, though hopefully it does no damage to Keynes' essential argument.
5. Minsky (1982) intriguingly refers to such a position as a "virtual" equilibrium.
6. Hopefully it is clear that, starting from employment level N_1 and real wage w^1, a reduction in effective demand will cause employment to decline, money wages to fall and wage good prices to fall by an even greater amount. Consequently associated with a decline in employment below N_1 will be an increase in real wages above w^1.
7. This approach has the additional advantage that the first classical postulate can be disposed of if the empirical evidence for it is dubious. This is clearly what Keynes had in mind when responding to Dunlop and Tarshis, see Appendix 3 to the *General Theory* .

12 Public policy implications

1. At the time three options seemed open for future economic development – Marxist communism, fascism or the middle way of reformed capitalism, with a marriage of market and state (Hobsbawm, 1995). Keynes is always a firm supporter of the middle way.
2. Keynes provides as an example of an unsafe interest rate a country in a fixed exchange rate system operating with a lower interest rate than that in other countries in the system. Agents will lack confidence in the maintenance of such a low interest rate.
3. Keynes is ambiguous about which demand for money strengthens in this case. On page 172 of the *General Theory* he suggests it is due to a strengthening of the precautionary motive, whilst on page 197 he considers the possibility when discussing the speculative motive. It may be a combination of the two.
4. If you accept the neo-classical notion of a natural rate of unemployment, towards which a capitalist economy gravitates, and the long-run independence between the rate of inflation and the rate of output (unemployment) implied by the vertical long run Phillip curve, then a politically independent central bank has obvious advantages. For demand management in the long run can only influence the rate of inflation. Moreover, to ensure politicians are not tempted to manipulate interest rates for political reasons, better to have an independent central bank deciding policy free from the influence of the democracy, interest groups and the electorate.

5. The deferred payments post-war have to be financed by additional Government borrowing, but as Keynes notes the Government would have to borrow anyway to finance additional unemployment benefits during a depression; but better that the borrowing finance consumption by workers rather than benefits paid to idle workers.
6. Keynes took at lot of criticism for his initial plan, printed in the Times newspaper. In *How to Pay for the War* he sought to address some of the concerns raised. He reluctantly agrees that a capital levy on excess post-war profits might be used to finance the release of deferred pay; he recommends family allowances to help the lowest paid who are hit by the deferral of pay, and he even allows that certain essential goods necessary for the physical well-being of workers should be rationed and their prices fixed.
7. By a *stable* programme Keynes does not mean a constant volume of investment; the level of investment may rise or fall but in a planned and predictable manner (Keynes, 1980e).
8. Keynes first addresses the need for the supernational management of the global commercial system in the *Treatise*. There he proposes the creation of a Supernational Bank to manage a Gold Standard system with the purpose of stabilising the international price-level – or what he calls the international standard (Keynes. 1971b).
9. In the *Treatise* Keynes calls the international money Supernational Bank Money (SBM's).
10. The trigger point for a debtor nation is 25 per cent of a quota; the quota is 50 per cent of the combined level of exports and imports of a member state over a three-year period. The ICU actions become more onerous on a member state if the deficit exceeds 50 per cent of the quota (Keynes, 1980c).
11. The ultimate sanction on a non-compliant member state that refuses to follow the instructions of the ICU is that it can be expelled from the ICU meaning it loses its overdraft facility to finance its trade deficit (Keynes, 1980c).
12. The trigger for ICU action in regard to creditor nations begins if the trade surplus exceeds 50 per cent of the quota of the member state (Keynes, 1980c). The reason why the trigger is greater for a trade surplus than a trade deficit nation is as Keynes notes because "we are a little afraid of [the former]" (Keynes, 1980d).

13   The classics, Keynes and the Keynesian mainstream

1. Keynes states that assuming these elements are given does not mean they are unchanging but that they are changing so slowly as not to materially affect the conclusions of the model. To illustrate this point consider Keynes' assumption that the quantity of available capital equipment is given, yet a key component in an economy is net investment spending. The latter must be adding to the stock equipment, and, hence, it is inappropriate to say that the capital stock is "fixed" at a particular level. What Keynes is doing, for the sake of simplicity, is abstracting away from the impact of continual increases in the capital stock on the long-term growth potential of an economy, which allows him to concentrate on the *short-period* impact on the demand-side of

the economy. The same applies to every other "given" element identified by Keynes.

2. The other factors are the subjective motives to save and to spend, the habits of consumers, changes in fiscal policy and changes in the difference between aggregate income and aggregate net income.

3. The propensity to save does influence the marginal efficiency of capital, but in ways quite distinctive from those supposed by the classics – see Chapter 7.

4. The fact that Keynes' model focuses on the short period does not explain the differences with its classical predecessor. For it is possible to relax each of the given elements in the General Theory model to consider the longer term consequences of such changes. This is what Joan Robinson sought to do in the aftermath of the publication of the *General Theory*. Robinson's generalisation of the General Theory model is a much underrated contribution to economics (Robinson, 1979).

5. Indeed the term Keynesianism is used so indiscriminately and so comprehensively it lacks all meaning except as a political appellation.

6. Coddington includes a third category within Keynesianism as a whole which he terms fundamentalism, or what today is better known as the heterodox category that is Post-Keynesianism. That is those who regret that Keynes did not go much further in rejecting the main pillars of orthodox economics – especially the Marshallian micro-foundations. From this perspective Keynes never entirely breaks free from the chains of orthodox economics, allowing orthodoxy scope for its counter-revolution. Certainly some Post-Keynesians would have preferred Kalecki rather than Keynes to have been the first to publish a general theory.

7. Clower's use of the term effective demand has caused considerable pedagogic confusion in Keynesian circles. Clower's definition of effective demand is very different from that of Keynes. For the interested reader, who may well have read Clower prior to the *General Theory*, this creates the problem of distinguishing between different concepts with the same name. In pedagogic terms it is best to put aside Clower's definition as it only clouds the picture. This book – see Chapter 3 – uses the terms aggregate effective demand and effective demand interchangeably (as does Keynes), but always defined in Keynes' terms.

8. In the 1970s this form of analysis caused some hydraulic reductionists to argue that the long run Phillips curve was not vertical, but negatively sloped. But given the theoretical basis of the hydraulic reductionists, especially their acceptance of the natural rate theory, this can best be described as wishful thinking. For more information on this, see Trevithick, Jackman and Mulvey (1981).

9. Patronising anecdotes are wheeled out to confound the interested student; "Keynes was a better philosopher than an economist", or "he learnt his economics in only six weeks from Marshall and can be excused some mistakes" or "yes he was brilliant but enigmatic, intuitive rather than analytical". As Goebbels said the bigger the lie the more people believe it.

10. For Milgate and Eatwell (1983) the dominant contemporary dispute in economics is between a *market mechanism group* – covering monetarists, the rational expectations school and supply-siders – and the *imperfectionists* – which includes mainstream Keynesians. The imperfectionists accept the

power of the market mechanism, but maintain it is inhibited and obstructed by various imperfections. The market mechanism group and the imperfectionist group both believe in the market, but with different degrees of faith, whilst the underlying reductionist theory is common ground. All this is of course anathema to radical Post-Keynesians, but they are on the sidelines of the dispute.

Bibliography

Alchian, A.A. (1969) Information Costs, Pricing and Resource Unemployment. *Western Economic Journal*. Vol. 7, pp. 109–128.

Amadeo, E.J. (1989) *Keynes' Principle of Effective Demand*. Aldershot, Edward Elgar.

——— (1992) Equilibrium Unemployment in Keynes's General Theory: Some Recent Debates. *Contributions to Political Economy*. Vol. II, pp. 1–14.

Ambrosi, G.M. (2003) *Keynes, Pigou and Cambridge Keynesianism*. London, Palgrave-Macmillan.

Arrow, K. and Debreu, G. (1954) Existence of an Equiibrium for a Competitive Economy. *Econometrica*. Vol. 22, No. 3, pp. 265–290.

Asimakopulos, A. (1971) The Determination of Investment in Keynes' Model. *The Canadian Journal of Economics*. Vol. 4, No. 3, August, pp. 382–388.

Backhouse, R.E. (1990) How Should the History of Economic Thought Be Written? An Economist's Response to Rorty's Historiography of Philosophy. Paper Prepared for the *Political Economy Study Group* Meeting 11 May.

Baumol, W.J. (1977) Say's (at Least) Eight Laws, or What Say and Mill May Really Have Meant. *Economica*. Vol. 44, pp. 145–162.

Benassy, J.P. (1976) The Disequilibrium Approach to Monopolistic Price Setting and General Monopolistic Equilibrium. *Review of Economic Studies*. Vol. 43, pp. 69–81.

Brady, M.E. (1990) The Mathematical Development of Keynes' Aggregate Supply Function in the General Theory. *History of Political Economy*. Vol. 17, Spring, pp. 167–172.

Branson, W. (1989) *Macro-Economic Theory and Policy*. 3rd edn. London, Harper Row.

Burda, M. and Wyplosz, C. (1997) *Macro-Economics: A European Text*. Oxford, Oxford University Press.

Cecchetti, S.G. (1992) Prices during the Great Depression: Was the Deflation of 1930–32 Really Anticipated? *The American Economic Review*. Vol. 82, No.1, March, pp. 141–156.

Chick, V. (1983) *Macro-Economics after Keynes: A Reconsideration of the General Theory*. Oxford, Philip Allan.

Clower, R. (1965) The Keynesian Counter-Revolution: A Theoretical Appraisal. Reprinted in R.W. Clower. *Monetary Theory*. London, Penguin, pp. 270–290.

Coddington, A. (1983) *Keynesian Economics: The Search for First Principles*. London, Allen and Unwin.

Crafts, N.F.R. (1999) The Great Boom: 1950–73. In: Schulze, M. (ed.). *Western Europe: Economic and Social Change since 1945*. London, Longman.

Cunningham-Wood, J. (ed.) (1983) *J.M. Keynes – Critical Assessments*. Vols 1–4. Beckenham, Croom Helm.

Davidson, P. (1983) The Marginal Product Curve Is Not the Demand Curve for Labour and Lucas's Labour Supply Function Is Not the Supply Curve for Labour in the Real World. *Journal of Post-Keynesian Economics*. Vol. VI, No. 1, pp. 105–117.

Dillard, D. (1950) *The Economics of John Maynard Keynes: The Theory of a Monetary Economy*. London, Crosby Lockwood.

Dorfman, R. (1989) Thomas Robert Malthus and David Ricardo. *Journal of Political Perspectives*. Vol. 3, No. 3, Summer, pp. 153–164.

Dornbusch, R., Fischer. S., and Startz, R. (2004) *Macro-Economics – International Edition*. 9th edn. New York, McGraw-Hill.

Dow, A. and Dow, S.C. (1988) Idle Balances and Keynesian Theory. *Scottish Journal of Political Economy*. Vol. 35, No. 3, pp. 193–206.

Dow, S.C. (1996) *Methodology of Macro-Economic Thought – A Conceptual Analysis of Schools of Thought in Economics*. Cheltenham, Edward Elgar.

Eatwell, J. and Milgate, M. (eds) (1983) *Keynes's Economics and the Theory of Value and Distribution*. London, Duckworth.

———, and Newman, P. (eds) (1987) *The New Palgrave Dictionary of Economics*. Vols I–IV. London, Macmillan.

Feinstein, C.H., Temin, P., and Toniolo, G. (1997) *The European Economy between the Wars*. Oxford, Oxford University Press.

Friedman, M. (1968) The Role of Monetary Policy. *The American Economic Review*. Vol. 58, No. 1, pp. 1–17.

Fusfeld, D.R. (1985) Keynes and the Keynesian Cross: A Note. *History of Political Economy*. Vol. 17, No. 3, pp. 385–389.

——— (1989) Keynes and the Keynesian Cross: Reply to Don Patinkin. *History of Political Economy*. Vol. 21, No. 3, pp. 545–547.

——— (2002) *The Age of the Economist*. London, Addison-Wesley.

Galbraith, J.K. (1972) *The New Industrial State*. Trowbridge, Andre Deutsch. Revised and Updated Edition.

Garner, C.A. (1983) Uncertainty in Keynes' General Theory: A Comment. *History of Political Economy*. Vol. 15, pp. 83–86.

Gerrard, B. (1988) Keynesian Economics: The Road to Nowhere. In: Hillard, J. (ed.). *J.M. Keynes in Retrospect*. Aldershot, Edward Elgar.

——— (1995) Keynes, the Keynesians and the Classics: A Suggested Interpretation. *The Economic Journal*. Vol. 105, March, pp. 445–458.

Glynn, S. and Booth, A. (1996) *Modern Britain – An Economic and Social History*. London, Routledge.

Hansen, A.H. (1953) *A Guide to Keynes*. New York, McGraw-Hill.

——— (1983) Mr Keynes on Underemployment Equilibrium. In: Cunningham-Wood, J. (ed.). *J.M. Keynes – Critical Assessments*. Vol. 2. Beckenham, Croom Helm.

Harcourt, G.C. and Riach, P.A. (eds) (1997) *A "Second Edition" of the General Theory*. Vols 1 and 2. London, Routledge.

Harrod, R.R. (1982) *The Life of John Maynard Keynes*. London, W.W. Norton Press.

Hart, O. (1982) A Model of Imperfect Competition with Keynesian Features. *Quarterly Journal of Economics*. Vol. 96, pp. 109–138.

Hawtrey, R.G. (1937) *Capital and Employment*. London, Longmans.

Hayes, M. (2006) *The Economics of Keynes: A New Guide to the General Theory*. Cheltenham, Edward Elgar.

Hicks, J. (1983) Mr Keynes and the Classics: A Suggested Interpretation. In: Cunnigham-Wood, J. (ed.).*J.M. Keynes – Critical Assessments*. Vol. 2. Beckenham, Croom Helm.

Hobsbawm, E.J. (1995) *The Age of Extremes – The Short Twentieth Century 1914–1991*. London, Abacus.

Howitt, P. (1985) Transaction Costs and Unemployment. *American Economic Review*. Vol. 75, No. 1, pp. 88–100.

Hume, D. (1938) *An Abstract of a Treatise of Human Nature*. Cambridge, Cambridge University Press.

——— (1962) *A Treatise on Human Nature, Book One*. Cambridge, Fontana.

Kalecki, M. (1966) *Studies in the Theory of Business Cycles*. Warszawa, Basil Blackwell.

——— (1982) Some Remarks on Keynes' Theory. *Australian Economic Papers*. Vol. 21, No. 39, December, pp. 245–253.

Katona, G. (1960) *Powerful Consumers – Psychological Studies of the American Economy*. New York, McGraw-Hill.

Keynes, J.M. (1971a) *Treatise on Money, Collected Writings of J.M. Keynes Volume V*. London, Macmillan.

——— (1971b) *Treatise on Money, Collected Writings of J.M. Keynes Volume VI*. London, Macmillan.

——— (1971c) *Tract on Monetary Reform, Collected Writings of J.M. Keynes Volume IV*. London, Macmillan.

——— (1972a) The Economic Consequences of Mr. Churchill. In *Essays in Persuasion. Collected Writings of J.M. Keynes Vol. IX*. London, Macmillan.

——— (1972b) Mitigation by Tariff. In *Essays in Persuasion. Collected Writings of J.M. Keynes Vol. IX*. London, Macmillan.

——— (1972c) The Means to Prosperity. In *Essays in Persuasion. Collected Writings of J.M. Keynes Vol. IX*. London, Macmillan.

——— (1972d) How to Pay for the War. In *Essays in Persuasion. Collected Writings of J.M. Keynes Vol. IX*. London, Macmillan.

——— (1972e) Inflation. In *Essays in Persuasion. Collected Writings of J.M. Keynes Vol. IX*. London, Macmillan.

——— (1973a) The General Theory of Employment: Fundamental Concepts and Ideas. In *The General Theory and After Part II Defence and Development. Collected Writings of J.M. Keynes Vol. XIV*. London, Macmillan.

——— (1973b) Alternative Theories of the Rate of Interest. In *The General Theory and After Part II Defence and Development. Collected Writings of J.M. Keynes Vol. XIV*. London, Macmillan.

——— (1973c) Ex Post and Ex Ante. In *The General Theory and After Part II Defence and Development.Collected Writings of J.M. Keynes Vol. XIV*. London, Macmillan.

——— (1973d) The Ex Ante Theory of the Rate of Interest. In *The General Theory and After Part II Defence and Development. Collected Writings of J.M. Keynes Vol. XIV*. London, Macmillan.

——— (1973e) *Treatise on Probability. Collected Writings of J.M. Keynes Vol. VIII*. London, Macmillan.

——— (1973f) *The General Theory and After Part I Preparation.Collected Writings of J.M. Keynes Vol. XIII*. London, Macmillan.

——— (1973g) *The General Theory and After Part II Defence and Development. Collected Writings of J.M. Keynes Vol. XIV*. London, Macmillan.

——— (1980a) Post War Currency Policy. In *Activities 1940–44 Shaping the Post War World.Collected Writings of J.M. Keynes Vol. XXV*. London, Macmillan.

—— (1980b) Proposals for an International Currency Union. In *Activities 1940–44 Shaping the Post War World. Collected Writings of J.M. Keynes Vol. XXV.* London, Macmillan.

—— (1980c) Plan for an International Currency (or Clearing) Union. In *Activities 1940–44 Shaping the Post War World. Collected Writings of J.M. Keynes Vol. XXV.* London, Macmillan.

—— (1980d) *Activities 1940–44 Shaping the Post War World.Collected Writings of J.M. Keynes Vol. XXV.* London, Macmillan.

—— (1980e) *Activities 1940–1946 Shaping the Post War World Employment and Commodities. Collected Writings of J.M. Keynes Vol. XXVII.* London, Macmillan.

—— (1981a) Addendum 1 to the Report of the Macmillan Committee on Finance and Industry. In *Rethinking Employment and Unemployment Policies. Collected Writings of J.M. Keynes Vol. XX.* London, Macmillan.

—— (1981b) The Industrial Crisis. In *Rethinking Employment and Unemployment Policies. Collected Writings of J.M. Keynes Vol. XX.* London, Macmillan.

—— (1982) *Social, Political and Literary Writings. Collected Writings of J.M. Keynes Vol. XXVIII.* London, Macmillan.

—— (2007) *General Theory of Employment, Interest and Money.* London, Palgrave-Macmillan.

Keynes, J.M. and Henderson, H. (1972) Can Lloyd George Do It? In *Essays in Persuasion. Collected Writings of J.M. Keynes Vol. IX.* London, Macmillan.

King, J.E. (1997) Under-Consumption. In: Harcourt, G.C. and Riach, P.A. (eds). *A "Second Edition" of the General Theory.* Vol. 1. London, Routledge.

Klein, L. (1947) *The Keynesian Revolution.* New York, Macmillan.

Krugman, P. (2007) Introduction to New Edition. In: Keynes, J.M. *General Theory of Employment, Interest and Money.* London, Palgrave-Macmillan.

Lawlor, M. (2006) *The Economics of Keynes in Historical Context.* London, Palgrave-Macmillan.

Leijonhufvud, A.B. (1968) *Keynesian Economics and the Economics of Keynes.* New York, Oxford University Press.

—— (1974) Keynes' Employment Function. *History of Political Economy.* Vol. 6, pp. 164–170.

Liberal Industrial Inquiry (1977) *Britain's Industrial Future.* London, E. Benn.

Malinvaud, E. (1977) *The Theory of Unemployment Reconsidered.* Oxford, Blackwell.

Malthus, T.R. (1958) *The Principles of Political Economy.* 2nd edn. New York, Kelley.

Mankiw, N.G. and Romer, D. (eds) (1991a) *New Keynesian Economics Volume 1, Imperfect Competition and Sticky Prices.* Cambridge, Mass., MIT.

—— (eds) (1991b) *New Keynesian Economics Volume 2, Coordination Failures and Real Rigidities.* Cambridge, Mass., MIT.

Meeks, J.G. (1978) Keynes on the Rationality of the Investment Decision under Uncertainty. *Mimeo Copy in the Marshall Library Cambridge.*

Meltzer, A.H. (1981) Keynes's General Theory: A Different Perspective. *Journal of Economic Literature.* Vol. 19, No. 1, March, pp. 34–64.

Milgate, M. (1987) Equilibrium: The Development of the Concept. In: Eatwell, J., Milgate, M., and Newman, P. (eds). *The New Palgrave Dictionary of Economics.* Vol. 1. London, Macmillan.

—— (1988) Controversies in the Theory of Employment. *Contributions to Political Economy.* Vol. 7, pp. 65–82.

—— and Eatwell, J. (1983) Unemployment and the Market Mechanism. In: Eatwell, J. and Milgate, M. (eds). *Keynes's Economics and the Theory of Value and Distribution*. London, Duckworth.

Minsky, H. (1982) *Inflation, Recession and Economic Policy*. Brighton, Wheatsheaf.

—— (1983) The Financial Instability Hypothesis: An Interpretation of Keynes and an Alternative to "Standard" Theory. In: Cunnigham-Wood, J. (ed.). *J.M. Keynes – Critical Assessments*. Vol. 4. Beckenham, Croom Helm.

Modigliani, F. (1944) Liquidity Preference and the Theory of the Theory of Interest and Money. *Econometrica*. Vol. 12, pp. 45–77.

Moore, G.E. (1903) *Principia Ethica*. Cambridge, Cambridge University Press.

New, C.C. (1994) The Internal Investment Requirements of UK Manufacturing Businesses: A Survey of Current Practice in 226 Plants. In the Trade and Industry Committee Second Report, *Competitiveness of UK Manufacturing Industry, Volume II*, Memoranda of Evidence. London, HMSO.

Panico, C. (1987) The Evolution of Keynes's Thought on the Rate of Interest. *Contributions to Political Economy*. Vol. 6, pp. 53–71.

Patinkin, D. (1948) Price Flexibility and Full Employment. *The American Economic Review*. Vol. 38, pp. 543–564.

—— (1965)*Money, Interest and Prices*. New York, Harper Row.

—— (1982) *Anticipations of the General Theory*, Oxford, Blackwell.

—— (1987) John Maynard Keynes's. In: Eatwell, J., Milgate, M., and Newman, P. (eds). *The New Palgrave Dictionary of Economics*. Vol. 2. London, Macmillan.

—— (1989) Keynes and the Keynesian Cross: A Further Note, with a Reply to Daniel R. Fusfeld. *History of Political Economy*. Vol. 21, 3, pp. 537–544.

Petrick, K. and Sheehan, B. (2004) The Institution of Marketing – An Economic Perspective. Paper Presented to the *Conference of the Association of Heterodox Economists*, University of Leeds, 16 July.

Potter, D. (1973) *People of Plenty – Economic Abundance and the American Character*. Chicago, University of Chicago Press. First Published 1954.

Robertson, D.H. (1966) *Essays in Money and Interest*. London, Fontana.

—— (1983) Some Notes on Mr Keynes' General Theory of Employment. In: Cunningham-Wood, J. (ed.). *J.M. Keynes – Critical Assessments*. Vol. 2. Beckenham, Croom Helm.

Robinson, J. (1962) *Essays in the Theories of Economic Growth*. London, Macmillan.

—— (1979) *The Generalisation of the General Theory and Other Essays*. London, Macmillan.

Rogers, C. (1997) The General Theory: Existence of a Monetary Long Period Unemployment Equilibrium. In: Harcourt, G.C. and Riach, P.A. (eds). *A Second Edition of the General Theory*. Vol. 1. London, Routledge.

Samuelson, P. (1946) Lord Keynes and the General Theory. *Econometrica*. Vol. 14, pp. 187–200.

Shackle, G.L.S. (1967) *The Years of High Theory: Invention and Tradition in Economic Thought 1926–39*. Cambridge, Cambridge University Press.

Simon, H.A. (1979) From Substantive to Procedural Rationality. In: Hahn, F. and Hollis, M. (eds). *Philosophy and Economic Theory*. Oxford, Oxford University Press.

Skidelsky, R. (1983) *John Maynard Keynes: Hopes Betrayed 1883–1920*. London, Macmillan.

——— (1992) *John Maynard Keynes: The Economist as Saviour 1920–37*. London: Macmillan.

——— (2000) *John Maynard Keynes: Fighting for Britain 1937–1946*. London, Macmillan.

Smith, A. (1976) *An Inquiry into the Nature and Causes of the Wealth of Nations*. Chicago, University of Chicago Press.

Snower, D.J. (1983) Imperfect Competition, Under Employment and Crowding Out. *Oxford Economic Papers*. Vol. 35, pp. 245–270.

Targetti, F. and Kinda-Hass, B. (1982) Kalecki's Review of Keynes' General Theory. *Australian Economic Papers*. Vol. 21, No. 39, December, pp. 244–260.

Thomas, J. (1997) The Propensity to Consume and the Multiplier. In: Harcourt, G.C. and Riach, P.A. (eds). *A "Second Edition" of the General Theory*. Vol. 1. London, Routledge.

Tily, G. (2007) *Keynes' General Theory, the Rate of Interest and Keynesian Economics*. London, Palgrave-Macmillan.

Tobin, J. (1980) *Asset Accumulation and Economic Activity*. Oxford, Blackwell.

Trevithick, J., Jackman, R., and Mulvey, C. (1981) *The Economics of Inflation*. Oxford, Robertson.

Viner, J. (1936) Mr Keynes on the Causes of Unemployment. *Quarterly Journal of Economics*. Vol. 51, pp. 147–167.

Weintraub, E.R. (1974) Keynes' Employment Function. *History of Political Economy*. Vol. 6, pp. 162–164.

Weintraub, S. (1983) Effective Demand and Income Distribution. In: Kregal, J.A. (ed). *Distribution, Effective Demand and International Economic Relations*. London, Macmillan.

Wells, P. (1974) Keynes' Employment Function. *History of Political Economy*. Vol. 6, pp. 158–162.

Index